Success for All

Research and Reform
in Elementary Education

Success for All

Research and Reform
in Elementary Education

Edited by

Robert E. Slavin
Johns Hopkins University

Nancy A. Madden
Success for All Foundation

LAWRENCE ERLBAUM ASSOCIATES, PUBLISHERS
2001   Mahwah, New Jersey   London

Lawrence Erlbaum Associates, Inc., Publishers
10 Industrial Avenue
Mahwah, NJ 07430

Cover design by Kathryn Houghtaling Lacey

Cover photo by Keith Weller, © Success for All Foundation, Inc.

Library of Congress Cataloging-in-Publication Data

Success for All: research and reform in elementary
education / edited by Robert E. Slavin, Nancy A. Madden.
    p. cm.
Includes bibliographical references and index.
ISBN 0-8058-3810-4 (hardcover: alk. paper)
ISBN 0-8058-3811-2 (pbk.: alk. paper)
    1. Success for All (Program) 2. School improvement
programs. 3. Education (Elementary) I. Title: Research
and reform in elementary education. II. Slavin, Robert E.
III. Madden, Nancy A.
    LB2822.8 .S88 2000
    372—dc21   00-044248
                                      CIP

Printed in the United States of America
10 9 8 7 6 5 4 3 2 1

Contents

Preface   vii

Introduction   xi

I   ESSENTIAL RESEARCH ON   1
SUCCESS FOR ALL

1   Success for All: An Overview   3
Robert E. Slavin and Nancy A. Madden

2   Summary of Research on Success for All   17
and Roots & Wings
Robert E. Slavin and Nancy A. Madden

3   Success for All in Memphis: Raising Reading   49
Performance in High-Poverty Schools
Steven M. Ross and Lana J. Smith

II   INTERNATIONAL ADAPTATIONS   79
OF SUCCESS FOR ALL

4   The Implementation and Impact of Success   81
for All in English Schools
Alma Harris, David Hopkins, and Judith Wordsworth

5   Can Success for All Succeed in Canada?   93
Bette Chambers, Philip C. Abrami, and Scott Morrison

6 A Longitudinal Evaluation of the Schoolwide   111
Early Language and Literacy Program (SWELL)
Yola Center, Louella Freeman, and Gregory Robertson

7 Success for All: A Community Model   149
for Advancing Arabs and Jews in Israel
Rachel Hertz-Lazarowitz

8 Success for All in Mexico   179
Margarita Calderón

**III IMPLICATIONS FOR POLICY   195
AND PRACTICE**

9 Disseminating Success for All: Lessons   197
for Policy and Practice
Robert E. Slavin and Nancy A. Madden

Author Index   227

Subject Index   231

Preface

Throughout the developed world, education is in a constant state of both turmoil and reform. Changes in governance, funding, standards, assessments, and other policies are continually being proposed and implemented. However, although changes of this kind may create the possibility of change at the individual school or classroom level, they do not directly affect what teachers do on a day to day basis. Policy makers who are serious about school reform often feel powerless to affect classroom practice, although they are as aware as anyone that fundamental change cannot take place unless schools and teachers are using more effective programs and materials. Demonstrations that only a few schools can produce remarkable improvements in the achievement of children who are placed at risk due to poverty or other factors are important, but they are not useful to policy makers who do not have a means of causing good practices to be disseminated on a scale large enough to matter. Furthermore, the research base for effective and replicable programs has been too limited and too weak to be useful as a guide to policy.

This situation is now undergoing a major change. Since the mid-1980s, a number of networks have sprung up across the United States to create, evaluate, and disseminate comprehensive reform models. When these models are shown to be effective in rigorous evaluations, and are shown to be broadly replicable, educators and policymakers finally have tools available that can be used to introduce effective practices in hundreds or thousands of schools.

Although there are many comprehensive reform models that have been developed in recent years, the one that has been most widely disseminated in the United States and elsewhere is Success for All. As of this writing, Success for All is used in more than 1,800 schools in 49 states and has been adapted for use in five other countries. Success for All is also one of the most extensively evaluated programs ever to exist, having been compared to control schools in dozens of studies done by diverse groups of researchers in five countries.

The purpose of this book is to present in one place the key research on Success for All and to describe the dissemination and policy impact of the program. It contains reviews of the entire body of research done to evaluate the model, a summary of a remarkable series of studies done over a 9-year period in Memphis, and descriptions and evaluations of program adaptations in Canada, England, Australia, Israel, and Mexico. The sheer volume and quality of the research, the number of locations and investigators involved, and the variety of methodologies employed in these studies should put to rest the criticism heard so often about educational programs that they are only evaluated by their developers. Research on Success for All, and its broad impact on practice, provide a serious challenge to traditional practices and policies. It is impossible to argue that schools cannot be changed with externally developed programs when time after time, in location after location, schools have successfully transformed themselves by making intelligent use of the tools provided by Success for All and other research-based reform models.

ACKNOWLEDGMENTS

The development, dissemination, and evaluation of Success for All and Roots & Wings are the product of the dedicated efforts of hundreds of educators, developers, trainers, and researchers throughout the United States and other countries. Research and development of Success for All has been funded by the Office of Educational Research and Improvement, U.S. Department of Education (Grants No. OERI-R-117-R90002 and OERI-R-117-D40005), and by the Carnegie Corporation of New York, the Pew Charitable Trusts, the Abell Foundation, and the France and Merrick Foundations. Roots & Wings has been funded by the New American Schools Development Corporation, the Dana Foundation, and the Knight Foundation.

The not-for-profit Success for All Foundation, established in 1998 to take on the development and dissemination of Success for All and Roots & Wings, has been supported by grants and loans from the Sandler Family Foundation, the Stupski Family Foundation, the MacArthur Foundation, the Ford Foundation, and the New Schools Fund. Development, research, and dissemination in Britain is being funded by the Fischer Family Trust.

In addition to the authors of this volume, many other researchers have been involved in development, evaluation, and dissemination of Success for All. These include Margarita Calderón, Barbara Wasik, Robert Cooper, Amanda Datnow, and Nancy Karweit of Johns Hopkins University; Barbara Livermon of Notre Dame College; Robert Stevens of Penn State University; Steve Ross, Lana Smith, and Jason Casey of the University of Memphis;

John Nunnery of the Memphis City Schools; Marcie Dianda of the National Education Association; Philip Abrami of Concordia University in Montreal; Yola Center of Macquarie University in Sydney, Australia; David Hopkins and Alma Harris of Nottingham University (England); Rachel Hertz-Lazarowitz and Bruria Schaedel of Haifa University (Israel); and Bette Chambers, Barbara Haxby, Kathy Simons, Cecelia Daniels, Eric Hurley, and Anne Chamberlain of the Success for All Foundation.

The development of Success for All and Roots & Wings has also involved too many talented and dedicated individuals to name here, but the current leaders of the development teams, all of whom work at the Success for All Foundation under the overall direction of Nancy Madden, are as follows. For reading, writing, and language arts, development leaders are Holly Coleman, Laura Burton Rice, and Martha French. Kathy Simons leads mathematics development, and Cecelia Daniels, Susan Magri, and Coleen Bennett lead both WorldLab and middle school development. Bette Chambers is the director of Early Learning development. Barbara Haxby and Susan Milleman direct family support development.

As of this writing, the Success for All Foundation employs more than 200 trainers, without whom the program could not exist. All training is directed by Barbara Haxby, with unit leaders John Batchelor, Susan Boyer, Jane Harbert, Liz Judice, Mark Rolewski, Argelia Carreon, Patrice Case-McFadin, Diane Chapman, Jane Dunham, Jill Ferguson, Connie Fuller, Judy Gill, Norma Godina-Silva, Anna Grehan, Tracy Heitmeier, Irene Kann, Margaret Masten, Wanda Maldonado, Carla Musci, Amanda Nappier, Elma Noyola, Wendy Paule, Vicki Pellicano, Saundra Pool, Judith Ramsey, Dorothy Sauer, Carmen Stearns, and Randi Suppe.

Introduction

A Brief History of Success for All

Success for All (SFA) began in its first school in 1987, but its history really began much earlier. It grew out of a program of research and development going back to the mid-1970s, starting with basic research on cooperative learning strategies. By 1980, our group at Johns Hopkins had learned how to harness the power of kids working with kids by structuring methods in which groups could succeed only if all of their members had mastered the academic material they were studying.

Up to that point, our methods only dealt with instructional processes, not curriculum. They were popular and effective, but we felt that well-structured cooperative learning would never be a fundamental part of daily instruction until it was embedded in curriculum. Beginning in 1980, we developed a complete math program, Team Accelerated Instruction (TAI), which combined cooperative learning with individualized instruction. In 1983, we developed Cooperative Integrated Reading and Composition (CIRC). Research on both TAI and CIRC found strong positive effects on achievement, but even more, our experience with these programs taught us how integrating process and curriculum could make cooperative learning and other effective practices the basis for reform in these basic subjects. However, we were still working classroom by classroom and began to see the need to involve entire schools in the reform process in order to deal with issues that individual teachers could not confront alone.

In 1985 we began work on the cooperative elementary school, a model that combined TAI and CIRC with school organization changes, assertive efforts to integrate special education students, and family support programs. Again, the results were very positive, and the experience taught us how working with whole schools could enhance professional development, implementation quality, and outcomes for all children. At about the same time, we wrote a book (with Nancy Karweit), *Effective Programs for Students at Risk* (1989), that reviewed research on a wide variety of approaches that had been effective with disadvantaged, minority, and academically handicapped students.

In 1986 we had a visit from Kalman "Buzzy" Hettleman, a former Maryland Secretary of Human Resources, who engaged us in a series of discussions on the question of what we would do if we had total freedom to restructure an inner-city elementary school, if our objective was to make certain that every child would be successful. In the early spring of 1987, Hettleman announced to us that he'd gotten enthusiastic approval from the then-superintendent and school board president in Baltimore to actually do what we had been talking about. We set to work right away. Karweit, with Barbara Livermon of Notre Dame College, designed the first version of what has become Reading Roots, and a tutoring component to go along with it. Karweit designed preschool and kindergarten programs. By September 1987, we had finished the prototype, selected a pilot school (Abbottston Elementary), trained the teachers, and started implementation.

From the start, it was clear that we had a winner. Children at Abbottston surged forward in their reading and writing, and early evaluations confirmed what everyone involved could see. In 1988 we added four more schools in Baltimore and one in Philadelphia, and these started off with great success as well.

Then disaster struck. A new mayor brought in a new superintendent. This led to a long series of political problems. Funding for our pilot schools was withdrawn, supportive principals were replaced by principals with new agendas, and one by one, schools dropped out. However, our difficulties in Baltimore might have been a blessing in disguise. We had established a strong research base in those early pilots and then moved quickly to establish and evaluate pilots in other places.

By the early 1990s, we were developing our research base and roughly doubling the number of schools we served each year. In 1992, another crucial event took place. We received funding from the New American Schools Development Corporation (now New American Schools, or NAS) to develop Roots & Wings. The main purpose of this funding was to add MathWings and WorldLab to SFA, but it also enabled us to greatly improve all of our existing programs and professionalize our dissemination.

Throughout the 1990s, we were adding about 60% more schools each year, which means quadrupling every 3 years. Our growing staff of trainers kept new and old schools growing and developing, and kept adapting to necessary changes as we added schools. Research that we were doing at Johns Hopkins continued to show strong positive effects of SFA on reading and writing achievement, and other researchers elsewhere, especially Steve Ross and Lana Smith at the University of Memphis, began to evaluate SFA and to confirm our own findings.

Also in the mid-1990s we began to work in other countries, first in Canada, later in England and Mexico, and in adapted forms in Israel and Australia. Studies by researchers in Canada, England, Israel, and Australia compared their adaptations of SFA to matched control schools and, once again, found the kinds of effects on student reading achievement that we had found in the United States. Further, we began to get evidence, from our own research and from research at what was then Southwest Regional Laboratory (SWRL) in Los Angeles, that the bilingual and English as a Second Language (ESL) adaptations of SFA were producing positive effects on Spanish- and English-reading measures.

Our business side began to develop in 1996, when it became obvious that university systems were not designed to keep track of the things we were doing with the number of schools we were working with. In 1997, we realized that we were just too big and complex to remain within Johns Hopkins. At one point, one fourth of all hiring at Johns Hopkins, Baltimore's largest private employer, was for us. We negotiated a friendly departure. On July 1, 1998, we left Hopkins and became the SFA Foundation. We moved to our own space in December of 1998. In 1998–1999 we served 1,100 schools, doubled our training staff, and tripled our support staff. We also started a parallel organization in England, SFA-UK, started work on Curiosity Corner for 3- and 4-year-olds, got funding to accelerate work on the Success for All Middle School, and much more. SFA is now in 1,800 schools in 49 states, serving more than 1 million children.

As of spring 2000, our focus is still on developing and disseminating high-quality programs, now for children from prekindergarten to eighth grade, and on dealing with the problems inherent in maintaining quality and effectiveness in a rapidly growing organization. However, new developments are making our work even more visible and influential. In 1997, Congress allocated $150 million to help schools adopt "proven, comprehensive reform models." Comprehensive School Reform Demonstration, or CSRD, has so far funded almost 1,800 schools; about 300 of these used CSRD funds to adopt SFA or Roots & Wings, far more than any other model. More importantly, the concept of tying serious federal money to evidence of effectiveness for externally developed programs is revolutionary. Recently, Congress increased funding for CSRD and is moving similar language into the bill reauthorizing Title I, sending a message that Title I needs to focus its resources on programs known to work. Positive independent evaluations of SFA in a review by the American Institutes of Research and the Fordham Foundation have made SFA the prototype for research-based reform models.

SFA is not magic; our own research and that of others has demonstrated time and again that achievement outcomes are closely related to quality of implementation. SFA does not work for every child in every school. However, the story of SFA is one of relentless efforts by a remarkable group of developers, researchers, trainers, teachers, school leaders, and communities to put proven programs in every school willing to undergo extensive reform. We have not yet achieved success for *all*, but with every passing year we move closer to that goal.

REFERENCE

Slavin, R. E., Karweit, N. L., & Madden, N. A. (1989). *Effective programs for students at risk*. Boston: Allyn & Bacon.

I

Essential Research on Success for All

1

Success for All:
An Overview*

Robert E. Slavin
Johns Hopkins University

Nancy A. Madden
Success for All Foundation

Ms. Martin's kindergarten class has some of the brightest, happiest, and most optimistic kids you will ever meet. Students in her class are glad to be in school, proud of their accomplishments, certain that they will succeed at whatever the school has to offer. Every one of them is a natural scientist, a storyteller, a creative thinker, a curious seeker of knowledge. Ms. Martin's class could be anywhere, in suburb or ghetto, small town or barrio, it does not matter. Kindergartners everywhere are just as bright, enthusiastic, and confident as her kids are.

Only a few years from now, many of these same children will have lost the spark they all started with. Some will have failed a grade. Some will be in special education. Some will be in long-term remediation, such as Title I or other remedial programs. Some will be bored, anxious, or unmotivated. Many will see school as a chore rather than a pleasure and will no longer expect to excel. In a very brief span of time, Ms. Martin's children will have de-

---

*Portions of this chapter are adapted from Slavin, R. E., Madden, N. A., Dolan, L. J., and Wasik, B. A. (1996). *Every Child, Every School: Success for All*. Thousand Oaks, CA: Corwin.

fined themselves as successes or failures in school. All too often, only a few will still have a sense of excitement and positive self-expectations about learning. We cannot predict very well which of Ms. Martin's students will succeed and which will fail, but we can predict based on the past that if nothing changes, far too many will fail. This is especially true if Ms. Martin's kindergarten happens to be located in a high-poverty neighborhood, in which there are typically fewer resources in the school to provide top-quality instruction to every child, fewer forms of rescue if children run into academic difficulties, and fewer supports for learning at home. Preventable failures occur in all schools, but in high-poverty schools failure can be endemic, so widespread that it makes it difficult to treat each child at risk of failure as a person of value in need of emergency assistance to get back on track. Instead, many such schools do their best to provide the greatest benefit to the greatest number of children possible but, unfortunately, have a well-founded expectation that a certain percentage of students will fall by the wayside during the elementary years.

Any discussion of school reform should begin with Ms. Martin's kindergartners. The first goal of reform should be to ensure that every child, regardless of home background, home language, or learning style, achieves the success that he or she so confidently expected in kindergarten, that all children maintain their motivation, enthusiasm, and optimism because they are objectively succeeding at the school's tasks. Any reform that does less than this is hollow and self-defeating.

What does it mean to succeed in the early grades? The elementary school's definition of success, and therefore the parents' and children's definition as well, is overwhelmingly success in reading. Very few children who are reading adequately are retained, assigned to special education, or given long-term remedial services. Other subjects are important, of course, but reading and language arts form the core of what school success means in the early grades.

When a child fails to read well in the early grades, he or she begins a downward progression. In first grade, some children begin to notice that they are not reading adequately. They may fail first grade or be assigned to long-term remediation. As they proceed through the elementary grades, many students begin to see that they are failing at their full-time jobs. When this happens, things begin to unravel. Failing students begin to have poor motivation and poor self-expectations, which lead to continued poor achievement, in a declining spiral that ultimately leads to despair, delinquency, and dropout.

Remediating learning deficits after they are already well established is extremely difficult. Children who have already failed to learn to read, for example, are now anxious about reading, and doubt their ability to learn it.

Their motivation to read may be low. They may ultimately learn to read but it may always be a chore, not a pleasure. Clearly, the time to provide additional help to children who are at risk is early, when children are still motivated and confident and when any learning deficits are relatively small and remediable. The most important goal in educational programming for students at risk of school failure is to try to make certain that we do not squander the greatest resource we have: the enthusiasm and positive self-expectations of young children.

In practical terms, what this perspective implies is that schools, and especially Title I, special education, and other services for at-risk children, must be shifted from an emphasis on remediation to an emphasis on *prevention* and *early intervention*. Prevention means providing developmentally appropriate preschool and kindergarten programs so that students will enter first grade ready to succeed, and it means providing regular classroom teachers with effective instructional programs, curricula, and professional development to enable them to ensure that most students are successful the first time they are taught. Early intervention means that supplementary instructional services are provided early in students' schooling and that they are intensive enough to bring at-risk students quickly to a level at which they can profit from good-quality classroom instruction.

The purpose of this book is to present research on a program built around the idea that every child can and must succeed in the early grades, no matter what this takes. The name of this program is *Success for All* (SFA). The idea behind SFA is to use everything we know about effective instruction for students at risk to direct all aspects of school and classroom organization toward the goal of preventing academic deficits from appearing in the first place, recognizing and intensively intervening with any deficits that do appear, and providing students with a rich and full curriculum to enable them to build on their firm foundation in basic skills. The commitment of SFA is to do whatever it takes to see that every child becomes a skilled, strategic, and enthusiastic reader by the end of the elementary grades. As SFA has developed, it now provides materials in math, science, and social studies that can help children achieve success in these areas as well.

Usual practices in elementary schools do not support the principle of prevention and early intervention. Most provide a pretty good kindergarten, a pretty good first grade, and so on. Starting in first grade, a certain number of students begin to fall behind, and over the course of time these students are assigned to remedial programs (e.g., Title I) or to special education, or are simply retained.

Our society's tacit assumption is that those students who fall by the wayside are defective in some way. Perhaps they have learning disabilities, low IQs, poor motivation, parents who are unsupportive of school learning, or other problems. We assume that because most students do succeed with standard, pretty good instruction in the early grades, there must be something wrong with those who do not.

Success for All is built around a completely different set of assumptions. The most important assumption is that every child can learn. We mean this not as wishful thinking or just a slogan, but as a practical, attainable reality. In particular, every child without organic retardation can learn to read. Some children need more help than others and may need different approaches than those needed by others, but one way or another every child can become a successful reader.

The first requirement for the success of every child is prevention. This means providing excellent preschool and kindergarten programs; improving curriculum, instruction, and classroom management throughout the grades; assessing students frequently to make sure they are making adequate progress; and establishing cooperative relationships with parents so they can support students' learning at home.

Top-quality curriculum and instruction from age 4 on will ensure the success of most students, but not all of them. The next requirement for the success of all students is intensive early intervention. This means one-to-one tutoring for first graders having reading problems. It means being able to work with parents and social-service agencies to be sure that all students attend school, have medical services or eyeglasses if they need them, have help with behavior problems, and so on.

The most important idea in SFA is that the school must relentlessly stick with every child until that child is succeeding. If prevention is not enough the child may need tutoring. If this is not enough he or she may need help with behavior, attendance, or eyeglasses. If this is not enough he or she may need a modified approach to reading or other subjects. The school does not merely provide services to children, it constantly assesses the results of the services it provides and keeps varying or adding services until every child is successful.

ORIGINS OF SUCCESS FOR ALL

The development of the SFA program began in 1986 as a response to a challenge made to our group at Johns Hopkins University by Baltimore's superintendent, Alice Pinderhughes, its school-board president, Robert Embry, and a former Maryland Secretary of Human Resources, Kalman "Buzzy" Hettleman. They asked us what it would take to ensure the success of every child in schools serving large numbers of disadvantaged students.

At the time, we were working on a book called *Effective Programs for Students at Risk* (Slavin, Karweit, & Madden, 1989), so we were very interested in this question. After many discussions, the superintendent asked us to go to the next step, to work with Baltimore's Elementary Division to actually plan a pilot program. We met for months with a planning committee and finally produced a plan and selected a school to serve as a site. We began in September 1987 in a school in which all students were African-American and approximately 83% qualified for free lunch. Initially the additional costs needed to fund the program came from a Chapter 2 grant, but the program was soon supported entirely by the same Chapter 1 funds received by all similar schools.

The first-year results were very positive (see Slavin, Madden, Karweit, Livermon, & Dolan, 1989). In comparison to matched control students, SFA students had much higher reading scores, and retentions and special education placements were substantially reduced.

In 1988–1989, SFA was expanded in Baltimore to five schools. We also began the implementation of SFA at one of the poorest schools in Philadelphia, in which a majority of the students are Cambodian. This school gave us our first experience in adapting SFA to meet the needs of limited English-proficient students. In 1990–1991 we developed a Spanish version of the SFA reading program, called *Lee Conmigo* (*Read With Me*), and began to work in more bilingual schools as well as schools providing English as a Second Language instruction. In 1992, we received a grant from the New American Schools Development Corporation (NASDC) to develop Roots & Wings, which adds constructivist math, science, and social studies to the reading and writing programs of SFA. Roots & Wings is currently beginning to be disseminated widely.

In more recent years, SFA has grown exponentially. Figure 1.1 shows this growth, which has been from 40% to 100% each year since 1989. As of 1999–2000, it was in about 1500 schools in 670 districts in 48 states throughout the United States. The districts range from some of the largest in the country, such as New York, Houston, Memphis, Los Angeles, Cincinnati, and Miami, to such middle-sized districts as Tuscon, Arizona; Hartford, Connecticut; Columbus, Ohio; Rockford, Illinois; and Modesto and Riverside, California, to tiny rural districts, including schools on several Indian reservations. Success for All reading curricula in Spanish have been developed and researched and are used in bilingual programs throughout the United States. Almost all SFA schools are high-poverty Title I schools, and the great majority are schoolwide projects. Otherwise, the schools vary widely.

OVERVIEW OF SUCCESS FOR ALL COMPONENTS

SFA has somewhat different components at different sites, depending on the school's needs and resources available to implement the program. However, there is a common set of elements characteristic of all.

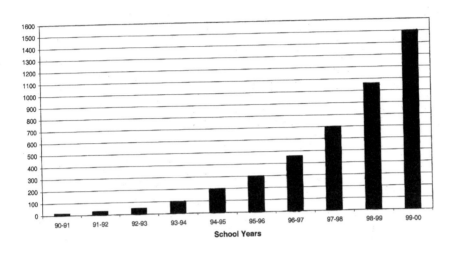

FIG. 1.1   Numbers of Success for All schools, 1990–2000.

Reading Program

SFA uses a reading curriculum based on research and effective practices in beginning reading (e.g., Adams, 1990) and an appropriate use of cooperative learning (Slavin, 1995; Stevens, Madden, Slavin, & Farnish, 1987).

Reading teachers at every grade level begin the reading time by reading children's literature to students and engaging them in a discussion of the story to enhance their understanding of the story, listening and speaking vocabulary, and knowledge of story structure. In kindergarten and first grade, the program emphasizes development of basic language skills with the use of Story Telling and Retelling (STaR), which involves the students in listening to, retelling, and dramatizing children's literature. Big books as well as oral- and written-composing activities allow students to develop concepts of print as they also develop knowledge of story structure. Peabody Language Development Kits are used to further develop receptive and expressive language.

Reading Roots (Madden, 1995) is introduced in the second semester of kindergarten. This K–1 beginning reading program uses as its base a series of phonetically regular but meaningful and interesting minibooks and emphasizes repeated oral reading to partners as well as to the teacher. The minibooks begin with a set of *shared stories*, in which part of a story is written in small type (read by the teacher) and part is written in large type (read by the students). The student portion uses a phonetically controlled vocabulary. Taken together, the teacher and student portions create interesting, worthwhile stories. Over time, the teacher portion diminishes and the student portion lengthens, until students are reading the entire book. This scaffolding allows students to read interesting literature when they only have a few letter sounds.

Letters and letter sounds are introduced in an active, engaging set of activities that begins with oral language and moves to written symbols. Individual sounds are integrated into a context of words, sentences, and stories. Instruction is provided in story structure, specific comprehension skills, metacognitive strategies for self-assessment and self-correction, and integration of reading and writing.

Spanish bilingual programs use an adaptation of *Reading Roots* called *Lee Conmigo*. *Lee Conmigo* uses the same instructional strategies as *Reading Roots*, but is built around shared stories written in Spanish.

When students reach the second-grade reading level, they use a program called *Reading Wings* (Madden et al., 1996) an adaptation of Cooperative Integrated Reading and Composition (CIRC; Stevens et al., 1987). *Reading Wings* uses cooperative-learning activities built around story structure, prediction, summarization, vocabulary building, decoding practice, and story-related writing. Students engage in partner reading and structured discussion of stories or novels and work toward mastery of the vocabulary and content of the story in teams. Story-related writing is also shared within teams. Cooperative learning both increases students' motivation and engages students in cognitive activities known to contribute to reading comprehension, such as elaboration, summarization, and rephrasing (see Slavin, 1995). Research on CIRC has found it to significantly increase students' reading comprehension and language skills (Stevens et al., 1987).

In addition to these story-related activities, teachers provide direct instruction in reading comprehension skills, and students practice these skills in their teams. Classroom libraries of trade books at students' reading levels are provided for each teacher, and students read books of their choice for homework for 20 minutes each night. Home readings are shared via presentations, summaries, puppet shows, and other formats twice a week during book club sessions.

Materials to support *Reading Wings* through the sixth grade (or beyond) exist in English and Spanish. The English materials are build around children's literature and around the most widely used basal series and anthologies. Supportive materials have been developed for more than 100 children's novels and for most current basal series (e.g., Houghton Mifflin, Scott Foresman, Holt, HBJ, Macmillan, McGraw Hill, Silver Burdett-Ginn, Open Court). The upper elementary Spanish program, *Alas para Leer*, is built around Spanish-language novels and basal series.

Beginning in the second semester of program implementation, SFA schools usually implement a writing and language-arts program based primarily on cooperative-learning principles (see Slavin, Madden, & Stevens, 1989, 1990).

Students in Grades 1 to 5 or 6 are regrouped for reading. The students are assigned to heterogeneous, age-grouped classes most of the day, but during a regular 90-minute reading period they are regrouped by reading performance levels into reading classes of students all at the same level. For example, a 2-1 reading class might contain first-, second-, and third-grade students all reading at the same level. The reading classes are smaller than homerooms because tutors and other certificated staff (e.g., librarians or art teachers) teach reading during this common reading period.

Regrouping allows teachers to teach the whole reading class without having to break the class into reading groups. This greatly reduces the time spent in seatwork and increases direct instruction time, eliminating workbooks, dittos, or other follow-up activities that are needed in classes that have multiple reading groups. The regrouping is a form of the Joplin Plan (Slavin, 1987), which has been found to increase reading achievement in the elementary grades.

Eight-Week Reading Assessments

At 8-week intervals, reading teachers assess student progress through the reading program. The results of the assessments are used to determine who is to receive tutoring, to change students' reading groups, to suggest other adaptations in students' programs, and to identify students who need other types of assistance, such as family interventions or screening for vision and hearing problems.

Reading Tutors

One of the most important elements of the SFA model is the use of tutors to promote students' success in reading. One-to-one tutoring is the most effective form of instruction known (see Slavin, Karweit, et al., 1989; Wasik & Slavin, 1993). Most tutors are certified teachers with experience teaching Title I, special education, and/or primary reading. Often, well-qualified paraprofessionals also tutor children with less severe reading problems. Tutors work one-on-one with students who are having difficulties keeping up with their reading groups. The tutoring occurs in 20-minute sessions during times other than reading or math periods.

In general, tutors support students' success in the regular reading curriculum, rather than teaching different objectives. For example, the tutor generally works with a student on the same story and concepts being read and taught in the regular reading class. However, tutors seek to identify learning problems and use different strategies to teach the same skills. They also teach metacognitive skills beyond those taught in the classroom program. Schools may have as many as six or more teachers serving as tutors depending on school size, need for tutoring, and other factors.

During daily 90-minute reading periods, certified teacher-tutors serve as additional reading teachers to reduce class size for reading. Reading teachers and tutors use brief forms to communicate about students' specific problems and needs and meet at regular times to coordinate their approaches with individual children.

Initial decisions about reading-group placement and the need for tutoring are based on informal reading inventories that the tutors give to each child. Subsequent reading-group placements and tutoring assignments are made based on curriculum-based assessments given every 8 weeks, which include teacher judgments as well as more formal assessments. First graders receive priority for tutoring, on the assumption that the primary function of the tutors is to help all students be successful in reading the first time, before they fail and become remedial readers.

Preschool and Kindergarten

Most SFA schools provide a half-day preschool and/or a full-day kindergarten for eligible students. The preschool and kindergarten programs focus on providing a balanced and developmentally appropriate learning experience for young children. The curriculum emphasizes the development and use of language. It provides a balance of academic readiness and nonacademic music, art, and movement activities in a series of thematic units. Readiness activities include use of language development activities and STaR, in which students retell stories read by the teachers (Karweit & Coleman, 1991). Prereading activities begin during the second semester of kindergarten.

Family Support Team

Parents are an essential part of the formula for success in SFA. A Family Support Team (Haxby et al., 1995) works in each school, serving to make families feel comfortable in the school and become active supporters of their child's education as well as providing specific services. The Family Support Team consists of the Title I parent liaison, vice-principal (if any), counselor (if any), facilitator, and any other appropriate staff already present in the school or added to the school staff.

The Family Support Team first works toward good relationships with parents and to increase involvement in the schools. Family Support Team members may complete welcome visits for new families. They organize many attractive programs in the school, such as parenting skills workshops. Most schools use a program called *Raising Readers* in which parents are given strategies to use in reading to their own children. Family support staff also help introduce a social-skills development program called *Getting Along Together*, which gives students peaceful strategies for resolving interpersonal conflicts.

The Family Support Team also intervenes to solve problems. For example, they may contact parents whose children are frequently absent to see what resources can be provided to assist the family in getting their child to school. Family support staff, teachers, and parents work together to solve school behavior problems. Also, family support staff are called on to provide assistance when students seem to be working at less than their full potential because of problems at home. Families of students who are not receiving adequate sleep or nutrition, need glasses, are not attending school regularly, or are exhibiting serious behavior problems, may receive family support assistance.

The Family Support Team is strongly integrated in the academic program of the school. It receives referrals from teachers and tutors regarding children who are not making adequate academic progress, and thereby constitutes an additional stage of intervention for students in need above and beyond that provided by the classroom teacher or tutor. The Family Support Team also encourages and trains parents and other community members to fulfill numerous volunteer roles within the school, ranging from providing a listening ear to emerging readers to helping in the school cafeteria.

Program Facilitator

A program facilitator works at each school to oversee (with the principal) the operation of the SFA model. The facilitator helps plan the SFA program, helps the principal with scheduling, and visits classes and tutoring sessions frequently to help teachers and tutors with individual problems. He or she works directly with the teachers on implementation of the curriculum, classroom management, and other issues, helps teachers and tutors deal with any behavior problems or other special problems, and coordinates the activities of the Family Support Team with those of the instructional staff.

Teachers and Teacher Training

The teachers and tutors are regular certified teachers. They receive detailed teacher's manuals supplemented by 3 days of inservice at the beginning of the school year. For classroom teachers of Grades 1 and above and for read-ing tutors, these training sessions focus on implementation of the reading program (either Reading Roots or Reading Wings), and their detailed teachers' manuals cover general teaching strategies as well as specific les-sons. Preschool and kindergarten teachers and aides are trained in strate-gies appropriate to their students' preschool and kindergarten models. Tutors later receive 2 additional days of training on tutoring strategies and reading assessment.

Throughout the year, additional inservice presentations are made by the facilitators and other project staff on such topics as classroom management, instructional pace, and cooperative learning. Facilitators also organize many informal sessions to allow teachers to share problems and problem solutions, suggest changes, and discuss individual children. The staff development model used in SFA emphasizes relatively brief initial training with extensive classroom follow-up, coaching, and group discussion.

Advisory Committee

An advisory committee composed of the building principal, program facili-tator, teacher representatives, parent representatives, and family support staff meets regularly to review the progress of the program and to identify and solve any problems that arise. In most schools existing site-based man-agement teams are adapted to fulfill this function. In addition, grade level or component teams and the Family Support Team meet regularly to discuss common problems and solutions and to make decisions in their areas of re-sponsibility.

Special Education

Every effort is made to deal with students' learning problems within the context of the regular classroom, as supplemented by tutors. Tutors evalu-ate students' strengths and weaknesses and develop strategies to teach in the most effective way. In some schools, special-education teachers work as tutors and reading teachers with students identified as learning disabled as well as other students experiencing learning problems who are at risk for special-education placement. One major goal of SFA is to keep students with learning problems out of special education if at all possible, and to serve any students who do qualify for special education in a way that does not disrupt their regular classroom experience (see Slavin, 1996).

Roots & Wings

In 1991, we received a grant from NASDC to create a comprehensive ele-mentary school design for the 21st century. We call the program we designed under NASDC funding *Roots & Wings*. Roots & Wings incorporates revisions of all of the elements of SFA—reading, writing, and language-arts programs, prekindergarten and kindergarten programs, tutoring, family support, and so on—but adds to these a program in mathematics, MathWings, and a program that integrates social studies and science, which we call *WorldLab*.

WorldLab

WorldLab is an integrated curriculum for science, social studies, and writing, used in Grades 1 through 5. In it, students take on roles as people in history, in other countries, or in various occupations. For example, fifth graders learn about the American Revolution by participating in the writing of their own "declaration of independence" and by serving as delegates to the Constitutional Convention. Fourth graders learn about physics by creating and testing inventions. Third graders learn about the culture of Africa and about simple machines by serving as a council of elders in an African village trying to design a system for irrigating their fields. First and second graders learn scientific method by becoming scientists collecting and integrating information about trees. WorldLab units incorporate writing, reading, math, fine arts, and music, as well as science and social studies. Children work in small, cooperative groups, and carry out experiments, investigations, and projects.

MathWings

Roots & Wings schools use a constructivist mathematics program called MathWings (Madden, Slavin, & Simons, 1999) in Grades 1 through 5. In this program, based on the standards of the National Council of Teachers of Mathematics, students work in cooperative groups to discover, experiment with, and apply mathematical ideas. The program builds on the practical knowledge base with which all children enter school, helping children build toward formal representations of such familiar ideas as combining and separating, dividing into equal parts and parts of a whole. It incorporates problem solving in real and simulated situations (including WorldLab), skill practice, calculator use, alternative assessments, writing, and connections to literature and other disciplines. Children learn not only to find the right answer but to explain and apply their new understandings.

Relentlessness

Although the particular elements of SFA and Roots & Wings may vary from school to school, there is one feature we try to make consistent in all: A relentless focus on the success of every child. It would be entirely possible to have tutoring, curriculum change, family support, and other services, yet still not ensure the success of at-risk children. Success does not come from piling on additional services but from coordinating human resources around a well-defined goal, constantly assessing progress toward that goal, and never giving up until success is achieved.

None of the elements of SFA or Roots & Wings is completely new or unique. All are based on well-established principles of learning and rigorous instructional research. What is most distinctive about them is their schoolwide, coordinated, and proactive plan for translating positive expectations into concrete success for all children. Every child can complete elementary school a confident, strategic, and joyful learner and can maintain the enthusiasm and positive self-expectations they had when they came to first grade. The purpose of SFA and Roots & Wings is to see that this vision can become a practical reality in every school.

REFERENCES

Adams, M. J. (1990). *Beginning to read: Thinking and learning about print.* Cambridge, MA: MIT Press.

Haxby, B., Lasaga-Flister, M, Madden, N. A., Slavin, R. E., Dolan, L. J. (1995). *Family Support Manual for Success for All/Roots & Wings.* Baltimore: Johns Hopkins University.

Karweit, N. L., & Coleman, M. A. (1991, April). *Early childhood programs in Success for All.* Paper presented at the annual convention of the American Educational Research Association, Chicago.

Madden, N. A. (1995). Reading Roots: Teacher's Manual. Baltimore: Johns Hopkins University.

Madden, N. A., Slavin, R. E., & Simons, K. (1999). *Effects of MathWings on student mathematics performance.* Baltimore: Johns Hopkins University.

Madden, N. A., Slavin, R. E., Farnish, A. M., Livingston, M. A., Calderón, M., & Stevens, R. J. (1996). *Reading Wings: Teacher's manual.* Baltimore: Johns Hopkins University.

Slavin, R. E. (1987). Ability grouping and student achievement in elementary schools: A best-evidence synthesis. *Review of Educational Research, 57,* 347–350.

Slavin, R. E. (1995). *Cooperative learning: Theory, research, and practice* (2nd ed.). Boston: Allyn & Bacon.

Slavin, R. E. (1996). Neverstreaming: Preventing learning disabilities. *Educational Leadership, 53*(5), 4–7.

Slavin, R. E., Karweit, N. L., & Madden, N. A. (Eds.). (1989). *Effective programs for students at risk.* Boston: Allyn & Bacon.

Slavin, R. E., Madden, N. A., Karweit, N. L., Livermon, B. J., & Dolan, L. (1989). Can every child learn? An evaluation of "Success for All" in an urban elementary school. *Journal of Negro Education, 58,* 357–366.

Slavin, R. E., Madden, N. A., & Stevens, R. J. (1989, 1990). Cooperative learning models for the 3 Rs. *Educational Leadership, 47*(4), 22–28.

Stevens, R. J., Madden, N. A., Slavin, R. E., & Farnish, A. M. (1987). Cooperative integrated reading and composition: Two field experiments. *Reading Research Quarterly, 22,* 433–454.

Wasik, B. A., & Slavin, R. E. (1993). Preventing early reading failure with one-to-one tutoring: A review of five programs. *Reading Research Quarterly, 28,* 178–200.

2

Summary of Research on Success for All and Roots and Wings*

Robert E. Slavin
Johns Hopkins University

Nancy A. Madden
Success for All Foundation

From its inception, Success for All (SFA) has been first and foremost a program of research. It was conceived, developed, and evaluated within a federally funded research center, currently called the Center for Research on the Education of Students Placed at Risk, at Johns Hopkins University. SFA is arguably the most extensively evaluated school reform model ever to exist; dozens of studies, done by researchers in many locations within the United States are summarized in this chapter and chapter 3. Based on this research, SFA was cited as one of only two elementary comprehensive designs that meets the highest standards for research in a review of 24 well-known programs done by the American Institutes of Research (Herman, 1999). In addition, studies of SFA adaptations in five other countries appear in chapters 4 through 8.

---

*This chapter is adapted from Slavin, R. E., & Madden, N. A. (2001). *One Million Children: Success for All*. Thousand Oaks, CA: Corwin.

Longitudinal evaluations of SFA began in its earliest sites, six schools in Baltimore and Philadelphia. Later, third-party evaluators at the University of Memphis, Steve Ross, Lana Smith, and their colleagues, added evaluations in Memphis (TN), Houston (TX), Charleston (SC), Montgomery (AL), Ft. Wayne (IN), Caldwell (ID), Tucson (AZ), Clover Park (WA), Little Rock (AR), and Clark County (GA). Studies focusing on English language learners in California have been conducted in Modesto and Riverside by researchers at WestEd, a federally funded, regional educational laboratory. Each of these evaluations has compared SFA schools to matched comparison schools using either traditional methods or alternative reform modes on measures of reading performance, starting with cohorts in kindergarten or in first grade and continuing to follow these students as long as possible (details of the evaluation design appear below). Vaguaries of funding and other local problems have ended some evaluations prematurely, but many have been able to follow SFA schools for many years. As of this writing, we have data comparing matched SFA and traditional control schools from schools in 13 U.S. districts (and their matched control schools), and other studies have compared SFA to a variety of alternative reform models, have compared full and partial implementations of SFA, and have made other comparisons.

STUDIES COMPARING SUCCESS FOR ALL
TO MATCHED CONTROL GROUPS

The largest number of studies has compared the achievement of students in SFA schools to that of children in matched comparison schools using traditional methods, including locally developed Title I reforms. Schools implementing the Reading Recovery tutoring model were included as *traditional controls*, because only a small proportion of students receive tutoring; however, in each case, special analyses compared children tutored in SFA and those tutored in Reading Recovery (those comparisons are discussed in a later section). The only studies excluded are a few studies in which there were pretest differences between SFA and control groups of more than 30% of a standard deviation (e.g., Wang & Ross, 1999a, 1999b; Ross & Casey, 1998a).

Table 2.1 summarizes demographic and other data about the schools involved in the experimental-control evaluations of SFA.

A common evaluation design, with variations due to local circumstances, has been used in most SFA evaluations carried out by researchers at Johns Hopkins University, the University of Memphis, and WestEd. Each SFA school involved in a formal evaluation is matched with a control school that is similar in poverty level (percent of students qualifying for free lunch), historical achievement level, ethnicity, and other factors. Schools are also matched on district-administered standardized test scores given in kinder-

TABLE 2.1

Characteristics of Success for All Schools in Experimental–Control Group Comparisons

District/School	Enrollment	% Free Lunch	Ethnicity	Date Began SFA	Data Collected	Comments
Baltimore						
B1	500	83	B-96% W-4%	1987	88–94	First SFA school; had additional funds first 2 years.
B2	500	96	B-100%	1988	89–94	Had additional funds first 4 years.
B3	400	96	B-100%	1988	89–94	
B4	500	85	B-100%	1988	89–94	
B5	650	96	B-100%	1988	89–94	
Philadelphia						
P1	620	96	A-60% W-20% B-20%	1988	89–94	Large ESL program for Cambodian children.
P2	600	97	B-100%	1991	92–93	
P3	570	96	B-100%	1991	92–93	

(continued on next page)

TABLE 2.1 (*Continued*)

Characteristics of Success for All Schools in Experimental–Control Group Comparisons

District/School	Enrollment	% Free Lunch	Ethnicity	Date Began SFA	Data Collected	Comments
P4	840	98	B-100%	1991	93	
P5	700	98	L-100%	1992	93–94	Study only involved students in Spanish bilingual program.
Charleston, SC						
CS1	500	40	B-60% W-40%	1990	91–92	
Memphis, TN						
MT1	350	90	B-95% W-5%	1990	91–94	Program implemented only in Grades K–2.
MT2	530	90	B-100%	1993	94	
MT3	290	86	B-100%	1993	94	

TABLE 2.1 (Continued)

Characteristics of Success for All Schools in Experimental–Control Group Comparisons

District/School	Enrollment	% Free Lunch	Ethnicity	Date Began SFA	Data Collected	Comments
MT4	370	90	B-100%	1993	94	
Fort Wayne, IN						
F1	396	80	B-45 % W-55%	1991	92–94 97–98	
F2	305	67	B-50% W-50%	1991	92–94 97–98	
F3	588	82	B-66% W-34%	1995	97–98	
Mongomery, AL						
MA1	450	95	B-100%	1991	93–94	
MA2	460	97	B-100%	1991	93–94	
Caldwell, ID						
CI1	400	20	W-80% L-20%	1991	93–94	Study compared two SFA schools to reading recovery school.

(continued on next page)

TABLE 2.1 (*Continued*)

Characteristics of Success for All Schools in Experimental–Control Group Comparisons

District/School	Enrollment	% Free Lunch	Ethnicity	Date Began SFA	Data Collected	Comments
Modesto, CA						
MC1	640	70	W-54% L-25% A-17% B-4%	1992	94	Large ESL program for students speaking 17 languages.
MC2	560	98	L-66% W-24% A-10%	1992	94	Large Spanish bilingual program.
Riverside, CA						
R1	930	73	L-54% W-33% B-10% A-3%	1992	94	Large Spanish Bilingual and ESL programs. Year-round school.
Tucson, AZ						
T1	484	82	L-54% W-34% B-69% A-5%	1995	95–96	Compared to locally developed schoolwide projects.

TABLE 2.1 (Continued)

Characteristics of Success for All Schools in Experimental–Control Group Comparisons

District/School	Enrollment	% Free Lunch	Ethnicity	Date Began SFA	Data Collected	Comments
T2	592	43	W-73% L-23% B-1% A-1%	1995	95–96	Compared to locally developed schoolwide projects and Reading Recovery.
Little Rock, AR						
LR1	302	73	B-80% W-20%	1997	98–99	
LR2	262	79	B-95% L-5%	1997	98–99	
Clark County, GA						
CL1	420	70	B-80% W-20%	1995	97	
CL2	488	72	B-78% W-22%	1995	97	

Note. SFA = Success for All; ESL = English as a Second Language; B = African-American; L = Latino; A = Asian American; W = White.

23

garten or on Peabody Picture Vocabulary Test (PPVT) scores given by the evaluators in the fall of kindergarten or first grade.

The measures used in the evaluations are as follows:

- *Woodcock Reading Mastery Test:* Three Woodcock scales, Word Identification, Word Attack, and Passage Comprehension, were individually administered to students by trained testers. Word Identification assesses recognition of common sight words, Word Attack assesses phonetic synthesis skills, and Passage Comprehension assesses comprehension in context. Students in Spanish bilingual programs were given the Spanish versions of these scales.
- *Durrell Analysis of Reading Difficulty:* The Durrell Oral Reading scale was also individually administered to students in Grades 1 through 3. It presents a series of graded reading passages that students read aloud, followed by comprehension questions.
- *Gray Oral Reading Test:* Comprehension and passage scores from the Gray Oral Reading Test were obtained from students in Grades 4 through 5.

Analyses of covariance with pretests as covariates were used to compare raw scores in all evaluations, and separate analyses were conducted for students in general and, in most studies, for students in the lowest 25% of their grades.

The figures presented in this chapter summarize student performance in grade equivalents (adjusted for covariates) and effect size (proportion of a standard deviation [SD] separating the experimental and control groups), averaging across individual measures. Neither grade equivalents nor averaged scores were used in the analyses, but they are presented here as a useful summary.

Each of the evaluations summarized in this chapter follows children who began in SFA or Roots & Wings in first grade or earlier, in comparison to children who had attended the control school over the same period. Students who start in it after first grade are not considered to have received the full treatment (although they are of course served within the schools).

Results for all experimental–control comparisons in all evaluation years are averaged and summarized in Fig. 2.1 using a method called *multisite replicated experiment* (Slavin, Madden, Dolan, & Wasik, 1996; Slavin, Madden Dolan Wasik, Ross, et al., 1996; Slavin & Madden, 1993).

For more details on methods and findings, see Slavin et al. (Slavin, Madden, Dolan, & Wasik, 1996; Slavin, Madden Dolan Wasik, Ross, et al., 1996) and the full site reports.

READING OUTCOMES

The results of the multisite replicated experiment evaluating SFA are summarized in Fig. 2.1 for each grade level, 1 through 5, and for followup measures

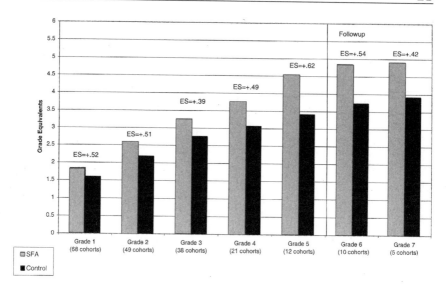

FIG. 2.1 Comparison of Success for All and control schools in mean reading-grade equivalent and effect sizes (1988–1999). *Note*. Effect size(ES) is the proportion of a standard deviation by which Success for All students exceeded controls. Includes approximately 6,000 children in Success for All schools since first grade. Figures 2.1–2.10 are from *One Million Children: Success for All*, by R. E. Slavin and N. A. Madden, 2001, Thousand Oaks, CA: Corwin. Copyright 2001 by Corwin Press. Reprinted with permission.

in Grades 6 and 7. The analyses compare *cohort* means for experimental and control schools. A cohort is all students at a given grade level in a given year. For example, the Grade 1 graph compares 68 experimental to 68 control cohorts, with cohort (50 to 150 students) as the unit of analysis. In other words, each bar is a mean of scores from more than 6,000 students. Grade equivalents are based on the means, and are only presented for their informational value. No analyses were done using grade equivalents.

Statistically significantly ($p = .05$ or better) positive effects of SFA (compared to controls) were found on every measure at every grade level, 1 through 5. For students in general, effect sizes (ES) averaged around a one-half SD at all grade levels. Effects were somewhat higher than this for the Woodcock Word Attack scale in first and second grades, but in Grades 3 through 5 effect sizes were more or less equivalent on all aspects of reading. Consistently, ES for students in the lowest 25% of their grades were particularly positive, ranging from ES = +1.03 in first grade to ES = +1.68 in fourth grade. Again, cohort-level analyses found statistically significant differences favoring low achievers in SFA on every measure at every grade level. A follow-up study of Baltimore schools found that positive program effects continued to Grade 6 (ES = +0.54) and Grade 7 (ES = +0.42), when students were in middle schools.

Quality and Completeness of Implementation

Not surprisingly, effects of SFA are strongly related to the quality and completeness of implementation. In a large study in Houston, Nunnery, Slavin, Ross, Smith, Hunter, and Stubbs (in press) found that schools implementing all program components obtained better results (compared to controls) than did schools implementing the program to a moderate or minimal degree.

In this study, 46 school staffs were allowed to select the level of implementation they wanted to achieve. Some adopted the full model, as ordinarily required elsewhere; some adopted a partial model; and some adopted only the reading program, with few if any tutors, and part-time facilitators or no facilitators. Many of the schools used the Spanish bilingual form of SFA and were assessed in Spanish.

Figures 2.2 and 2.3 summarize the results. The figures show ES comparing SFA to control schools on individually administered measures. On the

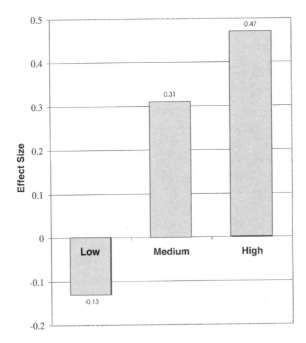

FIG. 2.2   Houston Independent School District (1996). First grade effect
sizes by implementation level: English.

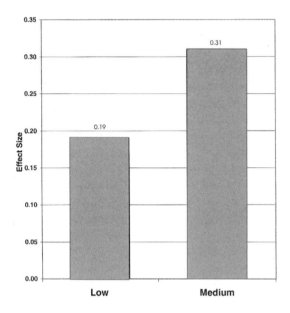

FIG. 2.3   Houston Independent School District (1996). First grade effect sizes by
implementation category: Spanish.

English measure (Fig. 2.2), ES were very positive for the schools using the
full program (ES = +0.47), less positive for those with a medium degree of
implementation (ES = +0.31), but for those implementing the fewest program elements, ES were slightly negative (ES = -0.13), indicating that the
control groups achieved somewhat better scores. Among schools teaching
in Spanish, there were too few certified teacher tutors for any school to qualify as a high implementer (due to a shortage of teachers). However, medium
implementers scored very well (ES = +.31), whereas low implementers
scored less well (ES = +.19; see Fig. 2.3).

A Memphis study (Ross, Smith, Lewis, & Nunnery, 1996; Ross, Smith, &
Nunnery, 1998) compared the achievement of eight SFA schools to that of
four schools using other restructuring designs, matched on socioeconomic
status and PPVT scores. Each pair of SFA schools had one school rated by
observers as a high implementer and one rated as a low implementer. In the

1996 cohort, first-grade results depended entirely on implementation quality. Averaging across the four Woodcock and Durrell scales, every comparison showed high-implementation SFA schools scored higher than their comparison schools, whereas low-implementation SFA schools scored lower (Ross, Smith, Lewis, & Nunnery, 1996). However, by second grade, SFA schools exceeded comparison schools, on average, and there was less of a clear relation with the original implementation ratings, perhaps because implementation quality changed over the 2 year period. Similarly, the 1997 first-grade cohort did not show a clear pattern with respect to quality of implementation.

Cooper, Slavin, and Madden (1998), in an interview study, found that high-quality implementations of SFA depended on many factors, including district and principal support, participation in national and local networks, adequacy of resources, and genuine buy-in at the outset on the part of all teachers.

EFFECTS ON DISTRICT-ADMINISTERED STANDARDIZED TESTS

The formal evaluations of Success for All have relied on individually administered assessments of reading. The Woodcock and Durrell scales used in these assessments are far more accurate than district-administered tests, and are much more sensitive to real reading gains. They allow testers to hear children actually reading the material of increasing difficulty and to respond to questions about what they have read. The Woodcock and Durrell are themselves nationally standardized tests and produce norms (e.g., percentiles, Normal Curve Equivalents (NCE)'s and grade equivalents) just like any other standardized measure.

However, educators often want to know the effects of innovative programs on the kinds of group administered standardized tests they are usually held accountable for. To obtain this information, researchers have often analyzed standardized or state criterion-referenced test data comparing students in experimental and control schools. The following sections briefly summarize findings from these types of evaluations.

Memphis

One of the most important independent evaluations of SFA Root & Wings is a study carried out by researchers at the University of Tennessee–Knoxville for the Tennessee State Department of Education (Ross, Sanders, & Wright, 1998). William Sanders, the architect of the Tennessee Value-Added Assessment System (TVAAS), carried out the analysis. The

TVAAS gives each school an expected gain, based primarily on school poverty levels, and compares it to actual scores on the Tennessee Comprehensive Assessment Program (TCAP). TVAAS scores above 100 indicate gains in excess of expectations; those below 100 indicate the opposite. Sanders compared TVAAS scores in eight Memphis SFA schools to those in matched comparison schools and all Memphis schools.

Figure 2.4 summarizes the results for all subjects assessed. At pretest, the SFA schools were lower than both comparison groups on TVAAS. However, after 2 years, they performed significantly better than comparison schools in reading, language, science, and social studies. Although some schools had implemented aspects of WorldLab, none had implemented MathWings; despite this, even math scores nonsignificantly favored the SFA schools.

A third-year evaluation found that SFA schools averaged the greatest gains and highest levels on the TVAAS of six restructuring designs (Co-nect, Accelerated Schools, Audrey Cohen College, Atlas, and Expedi-

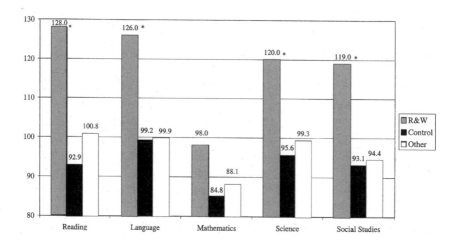

FIG. 2.4   Percent of expected gains on TVAAS for Roots & Wings, Control, and other Memphis schools, Grades 2–5, 1997. *Note.* * = Roots & Wings scores significantly higher than those of control or others (p < .05). Tennessee State Department of Education. See Roth, Sanders, & Wright, 1998.

tionary Learning), as well as exceeding controls, averaging across all sub-jects (Ross, Wang, Sanders, Wright, & Stringfield, 1999).

The importance of the Memphis study lies in several directions. First, it is a completely independent evaluation that involved state assessment scores of the kind used in most state-accountability systems. Second, it shows car-ryover effects of a program focused on reading, writing, and language arts to science and social studies outcomes.

An earlier study of SFA schools in Memphis also showed positive effects on the TCAP. This was a longitudinal study of three SFA and three control schools carried out by Ross, Smith, and Casey (1995). On average, SFA schools exceeded controls on TCAP reading by an effect size of +0.38 in first grade and +0.45 in second grade.

Houston, Texas

Since 1993, Texas has administered the Texas Assessment of Academic Success, or TAAS, assessing reading in Grades 3, 4, and 5 and writing in Grade 4. Recently, Texas put its TAAS scores for every school every year on the Internet, making it possible to compare SFA schools anywhere in the state to gains in the state as a whole. Two analyses of this kind have been carried out, one in Houston and one in San Antonio.

In Houston, SFA began on a large scale in 1995 in two forms. One set of schools ($n = 46$) adopted SFA as part of a study (Nunnery et al., in press) in which they were allowed to implement either the full program, the reading program only, or something in between. As noted earlier, the full-implemen-tation schools obtained excellent outcomes on individually administered tests given to subsamples, in comparison to control schools, whereas moderate-im-plementation schools obtained less positive outcomes and low-implementa-tion schools did not differ from controls (recall Figs. 2.2 and 2.3). After the first 2 years, the Houston district insisted that all SFA schools take on the full model, but because of the incomplete start made by most schools, quality of implementation in these schools never reached the levels typical elsewhere.

In contrast, a set of schools in Houston is implementing SFA as part of a larger program called Project Graduation Really Achieves Dreams (GRAD; Ketelsen, 1994; McAdoo, 1998). Project GRAD, developed and led by a for-mer CEO of Tenneco, works with entire feeder patterns of schools leading into a high school. At the elementary level, Project GRAD uses all Success for All elements but adds a math program called Move-It Math and a school climate program called Consistency Management/Cooperative Discipline (Freiberg, Stein, & Huong, 1995). Most importantly, Project GRAD schools receive the resources, assistance, and monitoring needed to fully implement SFA, and in most cases implementation quality in Project GRAD schools is at or above usual levels for urban SFA schools.

Figure 2.5 shows TAAS gains for Project GRAD schools, other Houston Independent School District (HISD) SFA schools, and the State of Texas. As Fig.2.5 shows, Project GRAD schools ($n = 8$) gained significantly more than HISD Success for All schools ($n = 46$), which in turn gained significantly more than other Texas schools, in reading as well as writing at all grade levels. This result provides one more indication of the importance of high-quality implementation, as well as supporting the broader approach taken by Project GRAD.

Texas

TAAS reading data from all 117 schools that started SFA in Texas in 1993 through 1997 are summarized in Fig. 2.6. TAAS gains from pretest to 1998 were larger for SFA schools than for the state in every group of schools. All of the differences in school mean gains are statistically significant, $p < .05$.

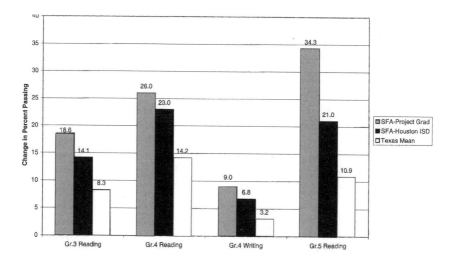

FIG. 2.5   Texas Assessment of Academic Skills gains in percent meeting minimum expectations from spring 1994 to spring 1998: Houston Success for All schools ($N = 46$) versus Project GRAD Success for All schools ($N = 8$), grades 3–5.

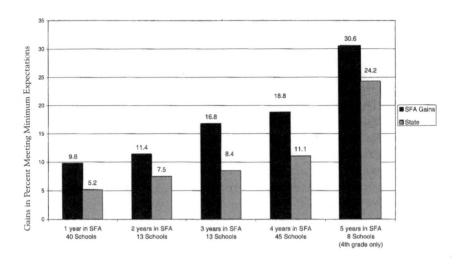

FIG. 2.6   Gains from preimplementation year to 1998: Success for All versus Texas means, Texas Assessment of Academic Success, reading, grades 3, 4, 5.

Baltimore

A longitudinal study in Baltimore from 1987 through 1993 collected Comprehensive Test of Basic Skills (CTBS) scores on the original five SFA and control schools. On average, SFA schools exceeded control schools at every grade level. The differences were statistically and educationally significant. By fifth grade, SFA students were performing 75% of a grade equivalent ahead of controls (ES = +0.45) on CTBS Total Reading scores (see Slavin, Madden, Dolan, Wasik, Ross, & Smith, 1994).

Flint, Michigan

Two schools in Flint, Michigan began implementation of SFA in 1992. The percentage of students passing the Michigan Educational Assessment Program (MEAP) in reading at fourth grade has increased dramatically. Homedale Elementary had a pass rate of 2% in 1992, placing it last among the district's 32 elementary schools. In 1995, 48.6% of students passed, placing it first in the district. Merrill Elementary, 27th in the district in 1992 with only 9.5% of students passing, was twelfth in 1995 with 22% passing.

Over the same period the average for all Flint elementary schools only increased from 18.3% passing to 19.3%.

Ft. Wayne, Indiana

An evaluation in two schools in Ft. Wayne, Indiana (Ross, Smith, & Casey, 1997b) found positive effects of SFA on the reading comprehension scale of the ISTEP, Indiana's norm-referenced achievement test. In first grade, the effect size was +0.49 for students in general and +1.13 for the lowest performing 25%. In second grade, effect sizes were +0.64, and in third grade, ES = +.13.

Roots & Wings

A study of Roots & Wings (Slavin & Madden, 2000) was carried out in four pilot schools in rural southern Maryland and one school in San Antonio, Texas. In both, evaluations compared students' gains on state assessments to those for their respective states as a whole.

In the Maryland evaluation, the Roots & Wings schools served populations that were significantly more disadvantaged than state averages. In the Maryland study, they averaged 48% free and reduced-price lunch eligibility, compared to 30% for the state; 21% of Roots & Wings students were Title I eligible, in comparison to 7% for the state. The assessment tracked growth over time on the Maryland School Performance Assessment Program (MSPAP), compared to growth in the state as a whole. The MSPAP is a performance measure on which students are asked to solve complex problems, set up experiments, write in various genres, and read extended text. It uses *matrix sampling*, which means that different students take different forms of the test.

In both third- and fifth-grade assessments in all subjects tested (reading, language, writing, math, science, and social studies), Roots & Wings students showed substantial growth. As shown in Figs. 2.7 and 2.8, by the third implementation year, when all program components were in operation, the State of Maryland gained in average performance on the MSPAP over the same time period, but the number of Roots & Wings students achieving at satisfactory or excellent increased by more than twice the state's rate on every measure at both grade levels.

After the 1995–1996 school year, when funding for the pilot was significantly reduced, implementation dropped off substantially in the Maryland pilot schools, and MSPAP scores correspondingly failed to increase further, and in some cases slightly declined. Still, 2 years after the end of full implementation, the total gains made by the Roots & Wings schools remained

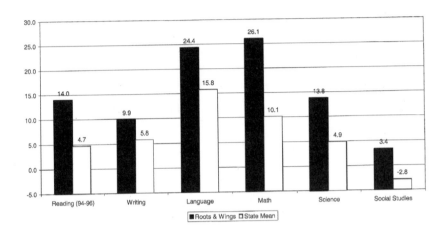

FIG. 2.7 Maryland School Performance Assessment Program gains in percent scoring satisfactory or better: St. Mary's County Roots & Wings schools versus state means, grade 3, 1993–1996 (full implementation).

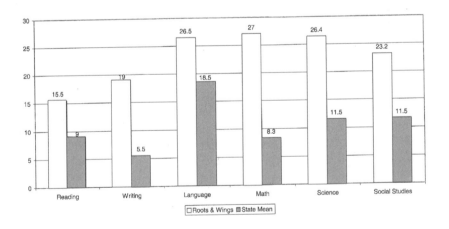

FIG. 2.8 Maryland School Performance Assessment Program gains in percent scoring satisfactory or better: St. Mary's County Roots & Wings schools versus state means, grade 5, 1993–1996. (full implementation).

higher than those for the state as a whole in every subject at both grade levels except for fifth-grade language.

The first evaluation of Roots & Wings outside of Maryland took place at Lackland City Elementary School in San Antonio, Texas (see Slavin & Madden, 2000). This school serves a very impoverished population, with 93% of its students qualifying for free lunch in 1998, up from 88% in 1994. Most of its students (79%) are Hispanic; 16% are White, and 5% African American.

Lackland City adopted SFA in 1994–1995, and then added MathWings for Grades 3 through 5 in 1995–1996 and WorldLab and Primary MathWings in 1996–1997. In contrast to St. Mary's County, implementation of Roots & Wings at Lackland City continues to be strong.

Like Maryland, Texas uses a high-stakes performance measure, the TAAS. Scores on the TAAS for Lackland City were compared to those for the state as a whole for Grades 3 through 5 reading and math and for Grade 4 writing. Scores are the percentages of students scoring above minimum standards.

Figure 2.9 summarizes TAAS gains from 1994 (pretest) to 1998. As in Maryland, the Roots & Wings schools gained substantially more than the state as a whole on each scale, with the largest absolute gains in math, but the largest relative gains in reading and writing.

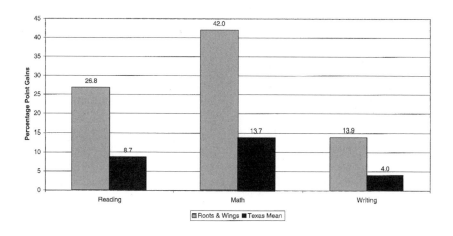

FIG. 2.9   Texas Assessment of Academic Skills gains in percent meeting minimum expectations: Lackland City Elementary School versus State of Texas, grades 3–5, 1995–1998.

Changes in Effect Sizes Over Years of Implementation

One interesting trend in outcomes from comparisons of SFA and control schools relates to changes in effect sizes according to the number of years a school has been implementing the program. Figure 2.10, which summarizes these data, was created by pooling effect sizes for all cohorts in their first year of implementation, all in their second year, and so on, regardless of calendar year.

Figure 2.10 shows that mean reading effect sizes progressively increase with each year of implementation. For example, SFA first graders score substantially better than control first graders at the end of the first year of implementation (ES = + 0.49). The experimental-control difference is even higher for first graders attending schools in the second year of program implementation (ES = + 0.53), increasing to an effect size of + 0.73 for schools in their fourth implementation year. A similar pattern is apparent for second and third grade cohorts.

The data summarized in Fig. 2.10 show that although SFA has an immediate impact on student reading achievement, this impact grows over successive years of implementation. Over time, schools may become

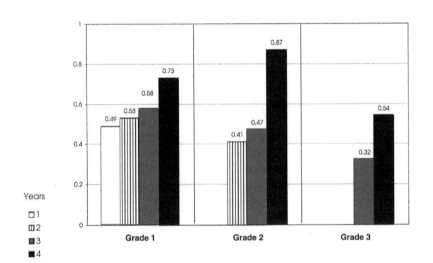

FIG. 2.10   Effect sizes comparing Success for All and control schools according to implementation year.

increasingly able to provide effective instruction to all of their students, to approach the goal of success for all.

SUCCESS FOR ALL AND ENGLISH LANGUAGE LEARNERS

The education of English language learners is at a crossroads. On one hand, research on bilingual education continues to show that children who are initially taught in their home language and then transitioned to English ultimately read as well or better in English than children taught only in English (August & Hakuta, 1997; National Academy of Sciences, 1998). On the other hand, despite these findings, political pressure against bilingual education, most notably in California's Proposition 227, has mounted in recent years based largely on the fact that Latino children perform less well than Anglo children on achievement tests whether or not they were initially taught in Spanish.

Although language of instruction is an essential concern for children who are acquiring English, the quality of instruction (and corresponding achievement outcomes) is at least as important, whatever the initial language of instruction may be. There is a need for better programs for teaching in the home language and then transitioning to English, and for better programs for teaching English language learners in English with support from English as a Second Language (ESL) strategies. Both development and research on Success for All have focused on both of these issues.

Six studies have evaluated adaptations of SFA with language minority children (see Slavin & Madden, 1999). Three of these evaluated *Éxito Para Todos* ("Success for All" in Spanish), the Spanish bilingual adaptation, and three evaluated a program adaptation incorporating ESL strategies.

Bilingual Studies

One study compared students in *Éxito para Todos* to those in a matched comparison school in which most reading instruction was in English. Both schools served extremely impoverished, primarily Puerto Rican student bodies in inner-city Philadelphia. Not surprisingly, *Éxito para Todos* students scored far better than control students on Spanish measures. More important was the fact that after transitioning to all-English instruction by third grade, the *Éxito para Todos* students scored significantly better than controls on measures of English reading. These differences were significant on Word Attack, but not on Word Identification or Passage Comprehension

An evaluation of *Éxito para Todos* in California bilingual schools was reported by Livingston and Flaherty (1997), who studied three successive cohorts of students. On Spanish reading measures, *Éxito para Todos* students scored substantially higher than controls in first grade (ES = +1.03), second grade (ES = +0.44), and third grade (ES = +.23). However, the second and third grade differences almost certainly understate the true effects; the highest-achieving students in the bilingual programs were transitioned early to English-only instruction, and the transition rate was twice as high in the *Éxito para Todos* classes as in the controls.

A large study in Houston compared LEP first graders in 20 schools implementing *Éxito para Todos* to those in 10 control schools (Nunnery et al., in press). As an experiment, schools were allowed to choose SFA/*Éxito para Todos* as it was originally designed, or to implement key components. The analysis compared three levels of implementation: high, medium, and low. None of the *Éxito para Todos* programs were categorized as high in implementation, as a bilingual teacher shortage made it impossible to hire certified teachers as Spanish tutors, a requirement for the high-implementation designation. Medium-implementation schools significantly exceeded their controls on all measures (mean ES = +0.24). Low implementers exceeded controls on the Spanish Woodcock Word Identification and Word Attack scales, but not on Passage Comprehension (mean ES = +0.17).

One additional study evaluated Bilingual Cooperative Integrated Reading and Composition (BCIRC), which is closely related to *Alas para Leer*, the bilingual adaptation of Reading Wings. This study, in El Paso, Texas, found significantly greater reading achievement (compared to controls) for English language learners in Grades 3 through 5 transitioning from Spanish to English reading (Calderón, Hertz-Lazarowitz, & Slavin, 1998).

ESL Studies

Three studies have evaluated the effects of SFA with English language learners being taught in English. In this adaptation, ESL strategies (e.g., total physical response) are integrated into instruction for all children, whether or not they are limited in English proficiency. The activities of ESL teachers are closely coordinated with those of other classroom teachers, so that ESL instruction directly supports the SFA curriculum, and ESL teachers often serve as tutors for Limited English Proficient (LEP) children.

The first study of SFA with English language learners took place in Philadelphia. Students in an Asian (mostly Cambodian) SFA school were compared to those in a matched school that also served many Cambodian-speaking children. Both schools were extremely impoverished, with nearly all children qualifying for free lunches.

At the end of a 6-year longitudinal study, SFA Asian fourth and fifth graders were performing far ahead of matched controls. On average, they were 2.9 years ahead of controls in fourth grade (median ES = +1.49), and 2.8 years ahead in fifth grade (median ES = +1.33). SFA Asian students were reading approximately a full year above grade level in both fourth and fifth grades, whereas controls were almost 2 years below grade level. Non-Asian students also significantly exceeded their controls at all grade levels (see Slavin & Madden, 1999b).

The California study described earlier (Livingston & Flaherty, 1997) also included many English language learners who were taught in English. Combining results across three cohorts, Spanish-dominant English language learners performed far better on English reading measures in SFA than in matched control schools in first grade ($ES = +1.36$) and second grade ($ES = +0.46$), but not in third grade ($ES = +0.09$). As in the bilingual evaluation, the problem with the third grade scores is that many high-achieving children were transitioned out of the ESL designation in the SFA schools, reducing apparent experimental–control differences. Corresponding effect sizes for students who spoke languages other than English or Spanish were $+0.40$ for first graders, $+0.37$ for second graders, and $+0.05$ for third graders.

An Arizona study (Ross, Nunnery, & Smith, 1996) compared Mexican-American English language learners in two urban SFA schools to those in three schools using locally developed Title I reform models and one using Reading Recovery. Two socioeconomic (SES) school strata were compared, one set with 81% of students in poverty and 50% Hispanic students and one with 53% of students in poverty and 27% Hispanic students. SFA first graders scored higher than controls in both strata. Hispanic students in the high-poverty stratum averaged 3 months ahead of the controls (1.75 v. 1.45). Hispanic students in the less impoverished stratum scored slightly above grade level (1.93), approximately 1 month ahead of controls (1.83).

The effects of SFA for language minority students are not statistically significant on every measure in every study, but the overall impact of the program is clearly positive, both for the Spanish bilingual adaptation, *Éxito para Todos*, and for the ESL adaptation. What these findings suggest is that whatever the language of instruction may be, student achievement in that language can be substantially enhanced using improved materials, professional development, and other supports.

COMPARING SUCCESS FOR ALL AND READING RECOVERY

Reading Recovery is one of the most extensively researched and widely used innovations in elementary education. Like SFA, Reading Recovery provides one-to-one tutoring to first graders who are struggling in reading. Research on Reading Recovery has found substantial positive effects of the program as of the end of first grade, and longitudinal studies have found that some portion of these effects maintain at least through fourth grade (DeFord, Pinnell, Lyons & Young, 1988; Lyons, Pinnell, & DeFord, 1993; Pinnell, Lyons, DeFord, Bryk, & Seltzer, 1994).

Schools and districts attracted to SFA are also often attracted to Reading Recovery, as the two programs share an emphasis on early intervention and a strong research base. Increasing numbers of districts have both programs in operation in different schools. One of the districts in the SFA evaluation, Caldwell, Idaho, happened to be one of these. Ross, Smith, Casey, and Slavin (1995) used this opportunity to compare the two programs.

In the Caldwell study, two schools used Success for All and one used Reading Recovery. All three are very similar rural schools with similar ethnic make-ups (10% to 25% Hispanic, with the remainder Anglo), proportions of students qualifying for free lunch (45% to 60%), and sizes (411–451). The SFA schools were somewhat higher than the Reading Recovery school in poverty and percent Hispanic. In 1992–1993, one of the SFA schools was in its second year of implementation and the other was a new school that was in its first year (but had moved a principal and some experienced staff reassigned from the first school). Reading Recovery was in its second year of implementation.

The study compared first graders in the three schools. Students in the SFA schools performed somewhat better than students in Reading Recovery school overall ($ES = +.17$). Differences for special education students were substantial, averaging an ES of $+.77$. Special education students were not tutored in the Reading Recovery school and were primarily taught in a separate resource room. These students scored near the floor on all tests. In contrast, SFA special education students were fully mainstreamed and did receive tutoring, and their reading scores, although still low, showed them to be on the way toward success in reading.

Excluding the special education students, there were no differences in reading performance between tutored students in the SFA and Reading Recovery schools ($ES = .00$). In light of earlier research, these outcomes suggest that both tutoring programs are effective for at-risk first graders.

A second study, by Ross, Nunnery, and Smith (1996), also compared SFA and Reading Recovery. This study, in an urban Arizona school district, compared first graders in three matched schools, in which 53% of students qualified for free lunch, 27% were Hispanic, and 73% were Anglo. One of the schools used SFA, one used Reading Recovery, and one used a locally developed Title I schoolwide project.

Results for the overall sample of first graders strongly favored SFA. Averaging across four individually administered measures, SFA students scored well above grade level ($GE = 2.2$). Those in the Reading Recovery school averaged near grade level ($GE = 1.7$), slightly below the control school ($GE = 1.8$). Effect sizes (adjusted for pretests) comparing the SFA and Reading

Recovery schools averaged +0.68, and effect sizes compared to the locally developed schoolwide project averaged +0.39.

Focusing on the children who actually received one-to-one tutoring, the differences were dramatic. On PPVTs given at pretest, the students tutored in the Reading Recovery school scored 41% of a standard deviation higher than students tutored in the SFA school. Yet at the end of the year, the Reading Recovery students were essentially nonreaders, with an average grade equivalent of 1.2. In contrast, the students tutored in SFA scored at grade level ($GE = 1.85$). The mean effect size for this comparison, $ES = 2.79$, is inflated by a huge difference in Word Attack, but even excluding this scale the effect size mean is +1.65.

The difference between the Idaho and the Arizona findings is probably due in part to the nature of the broader school programs, not just to differences in the tutoring models. The Arizona Reading Recovery school had a program strongly influenced by whole language, and the tutored children performed very poorly on Word Attack measures. In contrast, the Idaho Reading Recovery school used a more balanced approach, so that these children were receiving some phonics instruction in their regular classes.

Reading Recovery can be a powerful means of increasing the reading success of students having reading difficulties, but it needs to be implemented well and supplemented with high-quality instruction that includes a strong phonetic component if it is to produce significant reading gains. Because SFA attends to classroom instruction as well as tutoring, it is able to ensure that the effects of one-to-one tutoring build on high-quality, well-balanced reading instruction, rather than expecting the tutors to teach children to read with little support from classroom instruction.

COMPARISONS WITH OTHER PROGRAMS

A few studies have compared outcomes of SFA to those of other comprehensive reform designs.

As noted earlier, a study of six restructuring designs in Memphis on the TVAAS found that SFA schools had the highest absolute scores and gain scores on the TVAAS, averaging across all subjects (Ross et al., 1999). The TVAAS is a measure that relates performance on the Tennessee Comprehensive Achievement Test to "expected" performance, based primarily on socioeconomic status. The designs, in addition to SFA, were Co-nect, Accelerated Schools, Audrey Cohen College, Atlas, and Expeditionary Learning.

A study in Clover Park, Washington, compared SFA to Accelerated Schools (Hopfenberg & Levin, 1993), an approach that, like SFA, emphasizes prevention and acceleration over remediation, but unlike SFA does not provide specific materials or instructional strategies to achieve its goals.

In the first year of the evaluation, the SFA and Accelerated Schools programs had similar scores on individually administered reading tests and on a writing test (Ross, Alberg, & McNelis, 1997). By second grade, however, SFA schools were scoring slightly ahead of Accelerated Schools in reading, and significantly ahead in writing (Ross, Alberg, McNelis, & Smith, 1998).

SUCCESS FOR ALL AND SPECIAL EDUCATION

Perhaps the most important goal of SFA is to place a floor under the reading achievement of all children, to ensure that every child performs adequately in this critical skill. This goal has major implications for special education. If the program makes a substantial difference in the reading achievement of the lowest achievers then it should reduce special education referrals and placements. Furthermore, students who have IEP's indicating learning disabilities or related problems are typically treated the same as other students in SFA. That is, they receive tutoring if they need it, participate in reading classes appropriate to their reading levels, and spend the rest of the day in age-appropriate, heterogeneous homerooms. Their tutor or reading teacher is likely to be a special education teacher, but otherwise they are not treated differently. One-to-one tutoring in reading, plus high-quality reading instruction in the mainstream at the student's appropriate level, should be more effective than the small-group instruction provided in special education classes. For this reason we expect that students who have been identified as being in need of special education services will perform substantially better than similar students in traditional special education programs.

The philosophy behind the treatment of special education issues in SFA is called *neverstreaming* (Slavin, 1996). That is, rather than waiting until students fall far behind, are assigned to special education, and then may be mainstreamed into regular classes, SFA schools intervene early and intensively with students who are at risk to try to keep them out of the special education system. Once students are far behind special education services are unlikely to catch them up to age-appropriate levels of performance. Students who have already failed in reading are likely to have an overlay of anxiety, poor motivation, poor behavior, low self-esteem, and ineffective learning strategies that are likely to interfere with learning no matter how good special education services may be. Ensuring that all students succeed in the first place is a far better strategy, if it can be accomplished. In SFA, the provision of research-based preschool, kindergarten, and first-grade reading, one-to-one tutoring, and family support services are likely to give the most at-risk students a good chance of developing enough reading skills to remain out of special education, or to perform better in special education than would have otherwise been the case.

The data relating to special education outcomes clearly support these expectations. Several studies have focused on questions related to special education. One of the most important outcomes in this area is the consistent finding of particularly large effects of SFA for students in the lowest 25% of their classes. Although effect sizes for students in general have averaged approximately +0.50 on individually administered reading measures, effect sizes for the lowest achievers have averaged in the range of +1.00 to +1.50 across the grades. In the longitudinal Baltimore study only 2.2% of third graders averaged 2 years behind grade level, a usual criterion for special education placement. In contrast, 8.8% of control third graders scored this poorly. Baltimore data also showed a reduction in special education placements for learning disabilities of approximately half (Slavin, Madden, Karweit, Dolan, & Wasik, 1992). A recent study of two SFA schools in Ft. Wayne, Indiana found that over a 2 year period 3.2% of SFA students in Grades K through 1 and 1 through 2 were referred to special education for learning disabilities or mild mental handicaps. In contrast, 14.3% of control students were referred in these categories (Smith, Ross, & Casey, 1994).

Taken together, these findings support the conclusion that SFA both reduces the need for special education services (by raising the reading achievement of very low achievers) and special education referrals and placements.

Another important question concerns the effects of the program on students who have already been assigned to special education. Here again, there is evidence from different sources. In the study comparing Reading Recovery and SFA described previously, it so happened that first graders in special education in the Reading Recovery group were not tutored, but instead received traditional special education services in resource rooms. In the SFA schools, first graders who had been assigned to special education were tutored one-to-one (by their special education teachers) and otherwise participated in the program in the same way as all other students. As noted earlier, special education students in SFA were reading substantially better ($ES = +.77$) than special education students in the comparison school (Ross, Smith. Casey, & Slavin, 1995). In addition, Smith et al. (1994) combined first-grade reading data from special education students in SFA and control schools in four districts: Memphis, Ft. Wayne (IN), Montgomery (AL), and Caldwell (ID). Success for All special education students scored substantially better than controls (mean $ES = +.59$).

TEACHERS' ATTITUDES TOWARD SUCCESS FOR ALL

Two studies have examined teachers' attitudes toward SFA using questionnaires. Ross, Smith, Nunnery, and Sterbin (1995) surveyed teachers involved in six restructuring designs, including SFA, and found that SFA schools had the most positive attitudes toward the success of the implementation. However, all designs were rated relatively positively, and there was more variation among schools implementing the same designs than between models.

Rakow and Ross (1997) studied teacher attitudes in five SFA schools in Little Rock, Arkansas. Once again, responses varied widely from school to school, but overall effects were very positive. For example, 70% of teachers agreed that SFA was having a positive effect in their schools, and 78% felt positively about using the SFA model.

Perhaps the best indicator of teacher support for SFA is not from a study, but from a vote. In spring 1999, the San Antonio Independent School District, responding to a severe budget shortfall and a change of superintendents, required teachers in all schools using restructuring designs to vote on whether to keep these designs or to return to the district's program. A vote of 80% in favor was required to keep the program. Across 24 SFA schools, the average vote in favor was 81% positive. In contrast, votes for Accelerated Schools (2 schools) averaged 59% positive, Co-nect (11 schools) 32% positive, Expeditionary Learning (9 schools) 43% positive, and Modern Red Schoolhouse (15 schools) 33% positive.

CONCLUSION

The results of evaluations of dozens of SFA schools in districts in all parts of the United States clearly show that the program increases student reading performance. In every district, SFA students learned significantly more than matched control students. Significant effects were not seen on every measure at every grade level, but the consistent direction and magnitude of the effects show unequivocal benefits for SFA students. Effects on district-administered standardized tests reinforce the findings of the studies using individually administered tests. This chapter also adds evidence showing particularly large impacts on the achievement of limited English-proficient students in both bilingual and ESL programs and on both reducing special education referrals and improving the achievement of students who have been assigned to special education. It compares the outcomes of SFA with those of another early intervention program, Reading Recovery. It also summarizes outcomes of Roots & Wings, the next stage in the development of SFA.

The SFA evaluations have used reliable and valid measures, in particular individually administered tests that are sensitive to all aspects of reading: comprehension, fluency, word attack, and word identification. Positive effects on state accountability assessments and on other standardized measures have also been documented many times. Performance of SFA students has been compared to that of matched students in matched control schools, who provide the best indication of what students without the program would have achieved. Replication of high-quality experiments in such a wide variety of schools and districts is extremely unusual. A review of research by the American Institutes of Research (Herman, 1999) found SFA to be one of only two comprehensive elementary reform models to have rigorous, frequently replicated evidence of effectiveness.

An important indicator of the robustness of SFA is the fact that of the more than 1,100 schools that have used the program for periods of 1 to 9 years, only approximately three dozen have dropped out. This usually takes place as a result of a change of principals, major funding cutbacks, or other substantial changes. Hundreds of other SFA schools have survived changes of superintendents, principals, facilitators, and other key staff, major cuts in funding, and other serious threats to program maintenance (see Slavin & Madden, 1998).

The research summarized here demonstrates that comprehensive, systemic school-by-school change can take place on a broad scale in a way that maintains the integrity and effectiveness of the model. The schools we have studied are typical of the larger set of schools currently using SFA and Roots & Wings in terms of quality of implementation, resources, demographic characteristics, and other factors. Program outcomes are not limited to the original home of the program; in fact, outcomes tend to be somewhat better outside of Baltimore. The widely held idea based on the RAND study of innovation (Berman & McLaughlin, 1978; McLaughlin, 1990) that comprehensive school reform must be invented by school staffs themselves is certainly not supported in research on SFA or Roots & Wings. Although the program is adapted to meet the needs of each school and although school staffs must agree to implement the program by a vote of 80% or more, SFA and Roots & Wings are externally developed programs with specific materials, manuals, and structures. The observation that these programs can be implemented and maintained over considerable time periods and can be effective in each of their replication sites certainly supports the idea that every school staff need not reinvent the wheel.

The demonstration that an effective program can be replicated and can be effective in its replication sites removes one more excuse for the continuing low achievement of disadvantaged children. In order to ensure the success of disadvantaged students we must have the political commitment to do so, with the funds and policies to back up this commitment. SFA and Roots & Wings do require a serious commitment to restructure elementary schools and to reconfigure uses of Title I, special education, and other funds to emphasize prevention and early intervention rather than remediation. These and other systemic changes in assessments, accountability, standards, and legislation can facilitate the implementation of SFA, Roots & Wings, and other school reform programs. However, we must also have methods known to be effective. The evaluations presented in this chapter provide a practical demonstration of the effectiveness and replicability of one such program.

REFERENCES

August, D., & Hakuta, K. (1997). *Improving schooling for language-minority children: A research agenda.* Washington, DC: National Research Council.

Berman, P., & McLaughlin, M. (1978). *Federal programs supporting educational change: A model of education change, Vol. VIII: Implementing and sustaining innovations.* Santa Monica, CA: Rand.

Calderón, M., Hertz-Lazarowitz, R., & Slavin, R. E. (1998). Effects of Bilingual Cooperative Integrated Reading and Composition on students making the transition from Spanish to English reading. *Elementary School Journal, 99*(2), 153–165.

Cooper, R., Slavin, R. E., & Madden, N. A. (1998). Success for All: Improving the quality of implementation of whole-school change through the use of a national reform network. *Education and Urban Society, 30*(3), 385–408.

DeFord, D. E., Pinnell, G. S., Lyons, C. A., & Young, P. (1988). *Reading Recovery: Vol. IX, Report of the follow-up studies.* Columbus: Ohio State University.

Freiberg, H. J., Stein, T. A., & Huang, S. (1995). Effects of a classroom management intervention on student achievement in inner-city elementary schools. *Educational Research and Evaluation, 1*(1), 36–66.

Herman, R. (1999). *An educator's guide to schoolwide reform.* Arlington, VA: Educational Research Service.

Hopfenberg, W. S., & Levin, H. M. (1993). *The Accelerated Schools resource guide.* San Francisco: Jossey-Bass.

Ketelsen, J. L. (1994). *Jefferson Davis Feeder School Project.* Houston, TX: Tenneco Corporation.

Livingston, M., & Flaherty, J. (1997). *Effects of Success for All on reading achievement in California schools.* Los Alamitos, CA: WestEd.

Lyons, C. A., Pinnell, G. S., & DeFord, D. E. (1993). *Partners in learning: Teachers and children in Reading Recovery.* New York: Teachers College Press.

McAdoo, M. (1998). Project GRAD's strength is in the sum of its parts. *Ford Foundation Report, 29*(2), 8–11.

McLaughlin, M. W. (1990). The Rand change agent study revisited: Macro perspectives and micro realities. *Educational Researcher, 19*(9), 11–16.

National Academy of Sciences (1998). *The prevention of reading difficulties in young children.* Washington, DC: Author.

Nunnery, J., Slavin, R. E., Ross, S. M., Smith, L. J., Hunter, P., & Stubbs, J. (in press). An assessment of Success for All program component configuration effects on the reading achievement of at-risk first grade students. *American Educational Research Journal.*

Pinnell, G. S., Lyons, C. A., DeFord, D. E., Bryk, A. S., & Seltzer, M. (1994). Comparing instructional models for the literacy education of high risk first graders. *Reading Research Quarterly, 29,* 9–40.

Rakow, J., & Ross, S. M. (1997). *Teacher survey: Success for All, Little Rock City Schools, 1996-97*. Memphis, TN: University of Memphis.

Ross, S. M., Alberg, M., & McNelis, M. (1997). *Evaluation of elementary school school-wide programs: Clover Park School District, Year 1: 1996-97*. Memphis, TN: University of Memphis.

Ross, S. M., Alberg, M., & McNelis, M., & Smith, L. (1998). *Evaluation of elementary school school-wide programs: Clover Park School District, Year 2: 1997-98*. Memphis, TN: University of Memphis.

Ross, S. M., Nunnery, J., & Smith, L. J. (1996). *Evaluation of Title I reading programs: Amphitheater public schools, Year 1: 1995-96*. Memphis, TN: University of Memphis.

Ross, S. M , Sanders, W. L., & Wright, S. P. (1998). *An analysis of Tennessee Value Added Assessment (TVAAS) performance outcomes of Roots & Wings schools from 1995-1997*. Memphis, TN: University of Memphis.

Ross, S. M., Smith, L. J., Casey, J. P. (1995). *1994-1995 Success for All program in Ft. Wayne, IN: Final Report*. Memphis, TN: University of Memphis.

Ross, S. M., Smith, L. J., & Casey, J. P. (1997a). *Final report: 1996-97 Success for All program in Clark County, Georgia*. Memphis, TN: University of Memphis.

Ross, S. M., Smith, L. J., & Casey, J. P. (1997b). Preventing early school failure: *Impacts of Success for all on standardized test outcomes, minority group preference, and school effectiveness. Journal for Education of Students Placed at Risk, 2(1)*, 29– 53.

Ross, S. M., Smith, L. J., Casey, J., & Slavin, R. E. (1995). Increasing the academic success of disadvantaged children: An examination of alternative early intervention programs. *American Educational Research Journal, 32*, 773–800.

Ross, S. M., Smith, L. J., Lewis, T., & Nunnery, J. (1996). *1995-96 evaluation of Roots & Wings in Memphis City Schools*. Memphis, TN: University of Memphis.

Ross, S. M., Smith, L. J., & Nunnery, J. A. (1998, April). *The relationship of program implementation quality and student achievement*. Paper presented at the annual meeting of the American Educational Research Association, San Diego.

Ross, S. M., Smith, L. J., Nunnery, J., & Sterbin, A. (1995). *Fall 1995 teacher survey results for the Memphis City Schools Restructuring designs*. Memphis, TN: University of Memphis.

Ross, S. M., Wang, L. W., Sanders, W. L., Wright, S. P., & Stringfield, S. (1999). *Two- and three-year achievement results on the Tennessee Value-Added Assessment System for restructuring schools in Memphis*. Memphis, TN: University of Memphis.

Slavin, R. E. (1996). Neverstreaming: Preventing learning disabilities. *Educational Leadership, 53*(5), 4–7.

Slavin, R. E., & Madden, N. A. (1993, April). *Multi-site replicated experiments: An application to Success for All*. Paper presented at the annual meeting of the American Educational Research Association, Atlanta.

Slavin, R. E., & Madden, N. A. (1998). *Disseminating Success for All: Lessons for policy and practice*. Baltimore, MD: Johns Hopkins University.

Slavin, R. E., & Madden, N. A. (1999). Effects of bilingual and English as a second language adaptations of Success for All on the reading achievement of students acquiring English. *Journal of Education for Students Placed at Risk, 4*(4), 393–416.

Slavin, R. E., & Madden, N. A. (2000). Roots & Wings: Effects of whole-school reform on student achievement. *Journal of Education for Students Placed at Risk, 5*(1 & 2), 109–136.

Slavin, R. E., Madden, M. A., Dolan, L. J., Wasik, B. A., Ross, S. M., & Smith, L. J. (1994). Whenever and wherever we choose … The replication of Success for All. *Phi Delta Kappan, 75*(8), 639–647.

Slavin, R. E., Madden, N. A., Dolan, L., & Wasik, B. A. (1996). *Every child, every school: Success for All*. Newbury Park, CA: Corwin.

Slavin, R. E., Madden, N. A., Dolan, L., Wasik, B. A., Ross, S. M., Smith, L. J., & Dianda, M. (1996). Success for All: A summary of research. *Journal of Education for Students Placed at Risk, 1*, 41–76.

Slavin, R. E., Madden, N. A., Karweit, N. L., Dolan, L., & Wasik, B. A. (1992). *Success for All: A relentless approach to prevention and early intervention in elementary schools.* Arlington, VA: Educational Research Service.

Smith, L. J., Ross, S. M., & Casey, J. P. (1994). *Special education analyses for Success for All in four cities.* Memphis, TN: University of Memphis.

Wang, W., & Ross, S. M. (1999a). *Evaluation of Success for All program. Little Rock School District, Year 2: 1998-99.* Memphis, TN: University of Memphis.

Wang, W., & Ross, S. M. (1999b). *Comparisons between elementary school programs on reading performance: Albuquerque Public Schools.* Memphis, TN: University of Memphis.

3

Success for All in Memphis: Raising Reading Performance in High-Poverty Schools

Steven M. Ross
Lana J. Smith
The University of Memphis

This chapter tells a story about Success for All (SFA), as it was adopted and expanded in one large inner-city district, Memphis City Schools (MCS). In educational meetings and publications, one hears many stories about "successful" and "innovative" new programs that dramatically improved conditions and achievement at particular schools. Such stories make pleasant reading and buoy the spirits, but they frequently lack two essential qualities that make the Memphis experience unique. One feature is its durability and longevity—a program that has evolved in the school district for 9 years and, most importantly, has continually demonstrated positive impacts on student achievement. The second essential feature is valid research data to confirm that the program is working. The Memphis "story" thus consists of multiple chapters and its genre is nonfiction.

Parts of the Memphis SFA initiative have been reported in previous publications, each focusing on a particular study in a restricted time period (e.g., Ross, Smith, Casey, & Slavin, 1995; Ross, Nunnery, Smith, & Lewis, 1997;

Sanders, Wright, & Ross, 1999). This chapter conveys a more cohesive and global perspective on the past 9 years. We begin with a brief retrospective account of the major events that occurred with SFA in Memphis since its inception at the first Memphis school, Florida Elementary in 1990–1991. Next, we provide summaries and a synthesis of the extensive research on SFA in Memphis performed by the two of us (Ross & Smith) and our associates at The Center for Research in Educational Policy at The University of Memphis. By including in recent years a collaboration with William Sanders, the developer of the Tennessee Value-Added Assessment System (TVAAS; e.g., Sanders & Horn, 1995b), this research has also broken new ground by providing evidence on student year-to-year growth in achievement (using value-added scores) and on teacher effectiveness and mobility in SFA versus control schools. Recent data from these analyses will be presented for the first time in this chapter. Finally, we reflect on the cumulative events and outcomes to draw conclusions about what factors are most critical to make SFA effective and sustainable in a large inner-city school district.

SUCCESS FOR ALL IN MEMPHIS: A BRIEF HISTORY

The School District

MCS is the nation's 21st largest school district, with 117,300 students. Of this population, approximately 70% receive free or reduced-cost lunch, and more than 80% are African American. With more than 15,000 employees, the district is comprised of 104 elementary schools, 21 middle and junior high schools, 30 high schools, 2 special education centers, and 7 vocational or vocational technical centers. Student achievement throughout the district historically has been quite low. These combined factors have produced a large population of students at risk of academic failure.

In fall 1988, MCS were facing the significant challenges of dealing with falling achievement test scores and increasing numbers of disadvantaged students enrolling in its schools each year. An interim superintendent was filling in until a permanent replacement could be found. Despite the existing problems and uncertainties about the future, there was a clear commitment by district leaders to raise student achievement. A special committee consisting of district staff, university faculty, and outside consultants was formed to discuss the problems and possible remedies. Although many ideas were discussed, highest priority was given to improving reading skills in the early grades based on the rationale that reading formed the foundation for achievement in all other subjects in all grades. The two of us (Ross and Smith), as researchers interested in literacy and at-risk learners, were asked to investigate potentially effective programs and strategies for reading instruction.

At that time, the predominant intervention used in the district and nationally to raise the academic achievement of disadvantaged students was pull-out programs—the provision of tutoring and remedial instruction by specially trained teachers working in isolation from other staff (Natriello & McDill, 1999). Such methods have been criticized for a variety of reasons (Leinhart & Pallay, 1982):

- Lack of coordination between instruction in the regular and pull-out classes,
- The pull-out programs supplanting (or replacing) rather than supplementing the regular classes,
- The removal of responsibility from the regular classroom teacher for the academic success of the tutored students, and
- The stigmatizing or labeling of the compensatory students as low achievers.

Instructional practices in regular reading classes in MCS also seemed unlikely to engage poor readers in literacy activities or to remedy their skill deficiencies. Specifically, in a 1990–1991 classroom observation study, involving 80 reading classes in 20 MCS Title I schools, our research team judged reading groups to be used extensively in 75% of the sessions (Ross, Smith, Lohr, & McNelis, 1994; Ross et al., 1991). In a typical classroom, the students were divided into three ability groups based on reading level. The teacher rotated from group to group, spending about 20 minutes at a time with each. The group being taught would sit in a semicircle and engage in choral reading, listening to the teacher read or taking turns reading aloud. The other groups would perform independent practice (or *seatwork*) on workbook or chalkboard exercises at their desks. In the conclusion section of our report, we (Ross et al., 1991) wrote:

> An examination of the data points to possible problem areas in language arts instruction. The lack of independent reading and writing, coupled with a heavy reliance on teacher-led activities, is not likely to have a positive impact on students' verbal abilities or motivation to learn. Restricted resource utilization and frequent usage of worksheets are likely to increase motivation problems while simultaneously subjecting students to a fragmented, uninteresting language experience: worksheets were used as resources 3 to 4 times more frequently than storybooks and 3 times as often as textbooks; reference books, newspapers, or magazines were never used. This pattern of resource utilization suggests that students in observed classrooms are learning verbal skills in isolation from any meaningful contexts. (p. 14)

As indicated, low test scores and high-retention rates in the Title I schools mirrored what appeared to be inappropriate and ineffective strate-

gies for teaching disadvantaged children. Conditions were ripe for the introduction of innovative new methods.

Memphis Success for All Begins

Our search for effective reading programs led us fairly quickly to a new design called Success for All, which had been initiated in one Baltimore elementary school in the 1987–1988 school year. We were familiar with
Slavin's work with cooperative learning and at-risk students and invited
him to speak to the MCS principals on these topics in the fall of 1988. He
overviewed SFA in that talk, and we found the program elements of
one-to-one tutoring, regrouping during reading, a full-time facilitator at
each school, family support, and the 90-minute reading block, to be highly
appealing (see Slavin, Madden, Dolan, & Wasik, 1996) in contrast to the
traditional teacher-centered strategies that predominated reading instruction in the district schools.

Our subsequent trip to Baltimore with two district leaders confirmed
these initial impressions. The reading classes observed were lively and active; both children and teachers appeared to be enjoying their time in the
reading block. Teachers were using new and varied teaching strategies, and
nonacademic problems affecting students' progress were being addressed
through family support services. Most importantly, children in this
high-poverty Baltimore school were learning to read at a higher level and
faster rate than were children at comparable schools.

Our group returned to Memphis and presented its findings to the Title I
director and several principals who were looking for ways of improving their
school-wide programs. Two schools, Florida Elementary and LaRose Elementary, expressed the most interest and explored SFA in more depth
through visits by school representatives to Baltimore and study of the literature. In the spring of 1990, the decision of whether to adopt SFA was put to a
secret ballot vote by the two school staffs. The vote was 100% positive at
Florida, but slightly less than the required minimum of 80% at LaRose. The
Florida staff immediately began planning for implementing SFA the following fall. (LaRose came aboard 5 years later following the staff's dissatisfac-
tion with a traditional basal-oriented program.)

From 1 to 40

Figure 3.1 graphically shows the expansion of SFA in Memphis from
1990–1991 to 1998–1999. The growth rate was slow at first, as the implementation and success of the Florida Elementary program were carefully
monitored (see later section on research results). Specifically, after SFA was

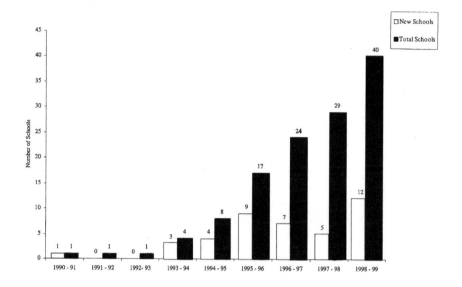

FIG. 3.1 History of Success for All and Roots & Wings startups in Memphis (Two schools consolidated in 1998–1999 to total 40).

in operation at Florida for 3 years, three additional schools (Douglass, Dunn, and Norris) joined in 1993–1994, and all four became part of a longitudinal evaluation of program results in MCS. Four schools followed in 1994–1995, with new expansion every year since. The "boom" years began in 1995–1996 as part of the school district's becoming one of the New American Schools (NAS) jurisdictions, as discussed later.

When schools were selected for the first NAS implementation of Roots & Wings in 1995–1996, eight schools became part of a comprehensive evaluation plan. Of these eight, all were using the SFA reading curriculum and some were using MathWings and World Lab components at various grade levels. The district supported these schools with one design facilitator and contracted support and training from the Johns Hopkins University design team. In 1998–1999, the addition of 12 schools brought the total to 40 implementing various curriculum options of Roots & Wings. These 40 schools are serving more than 17,000 students and are currently supported by four district coordinators, The University of Memphis Regional Success for All office, and the Success for All Foundation in Baltimore.

It is noteworthy that in the almost 10 years that SFA has been in Memphis, only two schools that voted to adopt it did not continue using it. One school implemented it for 1 year but a change in principals led to erosion of support for the program and the decision to abandon it. Another school planned to implement SFA the next fall, but because of an unexpected increase in student enrollment following the vote, it was decided that the regrouping, reduced class size, and tutoring components could not be adequately implemented due to insufficient classroom space.

National and Local Events

Although Memphis SFA originated from the need to improve reading instruction to raise achievement, national and local events since the 1990s have been critical to its success. One of these events was the hiring of Dr. Gerry House in 1992 as the MCS superintendent. House was impressed by the supportive evidence for SFA (Slavin et al., 1996) and by the instructional strategies that she observed in her visits to the early implementations in the local schools. Consequently, she encouraged district elementary schools to adopt a research-based reading program, regardless of their selected school-wide design, and presented SFA as one viable option.

A second event was NAS's development, starting in 1991, of break-the-mold comprehensive reform designs (Stringfield, Ross, & Smith, 1996). Today, eight designs exist and are being used in more than 2,000 schools nationwide. In 1995–1996, MCS became one of 10 national NAS jurisdictions, which involved the district's committing to implementing NAS (or comparable) reform designs in 30% or more of its schools within 5 years. NAS, MCS, and other partners (including The University of Memphis) collaborated in facilitating schools' selection, implementation, and evaluation of the designs. In 1995–1996 an initial group of 34 schools adopted designs; in 1996–1997, 14 more were added; and by 1998–1999, all 161 Memphis schools were implementing a design. Roots &Wings, selected by 40 schools, was the most popular choice.

Most recently, in 1997, the Comprehensive School Reform Demonstration (CSRD) offered funds to states to sponsor competitions to provide individual schools with at least $50,000 per year, for up to 3 years, for implementing research-based whole-school designs. In an independent review of the more popularly known designs, the American Institute for Research (Herman, 1999) identified SFA and Direct Instruction as the only two elementary school designs having strong research support from high-quality studies. The Memphis experience has contributed strongly to those results and to refuting arguments that an externally developed program cannot have significant and sustained positive effects in a school district (Berman & McLaughlin, 1978). We now turn to the findings from the Memphis research.

LONGITUDINAL EVALUATION RESULTS IN MEMPHIS

Tables 3.1 and 3.2 provide a summary of the research findings from the Memphis studies. The results reported show effect sizes that indicate the number of standard deviations by which the SFA group mean was higher or lower than the control group mean on individually administered reading tests (Table 3.1) and state-mandated standardized tests (Table 3.2). The N's refer to the number of SFA schools involved. The individually administered tests consisted of three Woodcock (1987) scales—Word Identification, Word Attack, and Passage Comprehension—and the Durrell Oral Reading scale (Durrell & Catterson, 1980). Word Identification assesses recognition of common sight words, Word Attack assesses phonetic synthesis skills, and Passage Comprehension assesses comprehension in context. The Oral Reading test presents a series of graded passages that students read aloud, followed by comprehension questions.

1990–1991: Grades K–2 With One SFA-Control School

The longitudinal research study was initiated in 1991, the same year Florida Elementary School began implementing SFA (see Ross & Smith, 1991). Students in Grades 1 and 2 at Florida and a comparable control school were matched on the basis of California Achievement Test reading scores obtained the previous year. Analyses were made of reading achievement on both the individually administered reading tests and the reading and language sections of the Tennessee Comprehensive Assessment Program (TCAP), which was a form of the Comprehensive Test of Basic Skills (CTB/McGraw-Hill, 1990). Kindergarten students were compared in the two schools using an independent-samples design.

Although Florida Elementary had been implementing SFA for approximately one half of a year when the achievement data were collected (spring, 1991), the results were generally favorable. SFA kindergarten students had superior reading-readiness skills relative to control students (mean $ES = +1.14$), whereas SFA first-grade students had small advantages overall ($ES = +0.15$), but moderately strong advantages ($ES = +0.41$) in oral reading. No advantages were found in Grade 2. When the scores of students scoring in the lowest 25% on the pretest were examined separately, the SFA advantage increased to $+0.78$ and $+0.49$ in Grades 1 and 2, respectively. TCAP

TABLE 3.1

Summary of Success for All Research: Effect Size Means on Individually Administered Reading Tests

Year	Design	Grades		
		K	1	2
1990–1991	1 SFA 1 Control	+1.14	+0.15	+0.03
1991–1992	1 SFA 1 Control	+0.16	+0.77*	+0.27
1992–1993	1 SFA 1 Control		+0.38	+0.51
1993–1994	1 SFA 1 Control		+1.15*	+0.07
1993–1994	SFA A		+0.50*	
	SFA B		+0.78	
	SFA C 1 Control		+0.57	
1995–1996	4 SFA high-implementer 2 Control		+0.34	
	4 SFA low-implementer 2 Control		-0.17	
1996–1997	8 SFA 4 Controls		-0.03	+0.19*
Overall		+0.65	+0.21	+.20
Number of schools		(n = 2)	(n = 23)	(n = 12)
High-implementers only			+0.29 (n = 19)	

*p < .05

56

TABLE 3.2

Summary of Success for All Research: Effect Size Means
on State-Mandated Standardized Tests

Year	Design	Grades		
		1	2	3–5
1990–1991	1 SFA 1 Control (Total Reading & Language / CTBS-4)	-0.12	0.00	
1991–1992	1 SFA 1 Control (Total Reading & Language / CTBS-4)	+0.14	-0.08	
1992–1993	1 SFA 1 Control (Total Reading / CTBS-4)	+0.02	+0.15	
1993–1994	SFA A	-0.17		
	SFA B	+0.43		
	SFA C / 1 Control	+0.93		
1995–1988	8 Roots & Wings 61 Control schools (Reading, Language, Science, Math, Social Studies on CTBS-4)			+1.10
Overall		+0.21	+0.07	+1.10
Number of schools		(n = 6)	(n = 3)	(n = 8)

results showed no SFA benefits for the overall sample, but small advantages of $ES = +0.24$ and $ES = +0.28$ for Grades 1 and 2 students, respectively.

Qualitative data from questionnaires showed that teachers became increasingly positive about SFA as the year progressed. Components that showed the most positive shifts were: (a) belief in SFA's positive impact on reading achievement and the school, (b) overall acceptance of SFA, (c) the facilitator, and (d) the Story Telling and Retelling (STaR) program. Teachers were skeptical initially about the SFA components but became increasingly favorable as they became more accustomed to the restructuring of the school day and more familiar with the reading curriculum. Classroom obser-

vations further showed that, compared to MCS schools employing traditional reading programs, the SFA classes featured considerably more
student activity through whole-class interactive instruction and cooperative learning.

1991–1992: Grades K Through 2 With One SFA–Control School Pair

In the second year of implementation of SFA at Florida, the same design
from Year 1 was replicated (Ross & Smith, 1992). Sample sizes for analyses
of low-25% performers, however, were not sufficient to provide meaningful
comparisons. In Year 2, kindergarten results on the individually administered tests (see Table 3.1) were comparable for the two schools ($ES =
+0.16$), while Grades 1 and 2 results showed stronger advantages for SFA
($ES = +0.77$ and $+0.27$, respectively) than in the first year. But like the
first year, there were negligible differences on the reading and language
subtests of TCAP ($ES = +0.14$ and -0.08, respectively).

Our interpretation of the TCAP results focused on the high-stakes testing environment in the school district and the pressure on teachers to teach
to the standardized test. Such pressures were seen as putting SFA teachers
at a disadvantage due to the full-time teaching demands of the program curriculum. Furthermore, suspect NCE scores of 99 for one half of the students
in one of the control classes raised questions about the validity of the
SFA–Control comparison. Still, the strong effect on the Grade 1 individual
reading tests offered compelling evidence that program benefits for reading
skills were being realized.

Classroom observations revealed that teachers generally implemented
the program correctly, but there were still many situations in which the prescribed procedures were not followed, especially in the Wings component.
Professional development was limited in Year 2 and needed to be expanded
to achieve a high-quality implementation. Also, teacher morale had diminished somewhat from the first year, especially in the higher grades. TCAP
pressures and the decrease in professional development support were seen
as two likely causes.

1992–1993: Grades 1 Through 2 With One SFA–Control School Pair

In the third year of the evaluation, we (Smith, Ross, Johnson, & Casey, 1993),
attempted to compare the SFA and control schools in Grades 1 through 3 using the longitudinal sample that had been pretested the prior year. However,
due to high-student mobility at both schools, the number of continuing third

graders was too small for making meaningful judgments, as was also the case for the low-25% achievers. Only individual reading test scores were examined in this study. Results showed positive effects of SFA in both Grade 1 (ES = +0.38) and Grade 2 (ES = +0.51). Given that the control school had been highly active in implementing a new reading program (*Writing To Read*) that year, these results remained supportive of SFA's positive impact on reading achievement. Classroom observations and school visits revealed similar conditions as existed in prior years. The Roots component seemed strong, but the Wings implementation and teacher support at the Wings level were relatively weak. The Family Support program was only partially in place and in need of refinement and expansion.

1993–1994: Grades 1 Through 3 With One SFA–Control School Pair

Results for the fourth year of the longitudinal study were inconsistent but generally positive (Smith, Ross, & Casey, 1994). As shown in Table 3.1, the Grade 1 effects were extremely high, with ES = +1.15 averaged across all individual reading tests. In Grade 2 (ES = +0.07), the effects were practically zero. In Grade 3 (not shown on the table), the mean ES = +0.56, but sample sizes were below 10 in each program. Low-25% achievers in SFA outperformed their control counterparts in both Grade 1 (ES = +2.00) and Grade 2 (ES = +0.92), but these results were also based on small sample sizes of from only seven to nine students. Effect sizes on the TCAP were rather small and close to zero, as was the case in all previous years.

Interpretation of the results pointed to the solid Roots program at the school, but continuing weak Wings component (in Grade 2). A highly critical concern was the decision that year by the principal not to employ a full-time facilitator. Despite these barriers, first graders and low achievers in Grades 1 through 3 appeared to be reading at higher proficiency levels than were their control school counterparts.

1993–1994: Grade 1 With Three SFA Schools Matched to One Control

A second study conducted in the fourth year pretested first graders on the Peabody Picture Vocabulary Test (PPVT; Dunn & Dunn, 1981) and compared three SFA schools (A, B, and C) that began implementation in 1993 to a matched control school on the individual reading tests (Casey, Smith, & Ross, 1994). Findings were consistently positive and significant, showing a significant moderate to strong SFA advantage for School A (ES = +0.50), School B (ES = +0.78), and School C (ES = +0.57). Despite small sample n's, effects for the low-25% subsample were also significant in all cases, with $ESs = +0.47, +0.47,$ and $+0.64$ for the three respective schools.

In the Casey, Smith, and Ross (1994) study, we also assessed teacher attitudes toward different SFA components. Teacher responses at all three schools were very positive, especially with regard to "SFA having positive impact on school," "felt prepared to use SFA," "SFA having positive impact on reading interest," and "feel positively about using SFA." Extremely positive responses were also given in reference to the instructional philosophy of SFA, STaR program, reading curriculum, cooperative learning, family support, cross-grade grouping, tutoring, and parental involvement. Components that were viewed relatively less favorably were facilitator support, staff development, and Peabody Language Development Kits.

1993–1994 TCAP Study: Grade 1
With Three SFA Schools Matched to One Control

A third study conducted in 1993–1994 compared the three new SFA schools to the control school on the Total Reading subscale of TCAP (Ross, Smith, & Casey, 1994). As shown in Table 3.2, results showed slightly negative effects for School SFA-A ($ES = -0.17$), moderate positive effects for SFA-B ($ES = +0.43$), and strong positive effects for SFA-C ($ES = +0.93$). The most dramatic advantages for SFA students occurred for the low-25% achievers in SFA-B ($ES = +0.71$) and SFA-C ($ES = +1.60$). This study was the first to reveal significant advantages for the Memphis SFA students on the TCAP. SFA teachers appeared to be developing confidence that teaching the program would develop the reading and language skills necessary for students to perform well on the standardized test.

1994–1995: Teacher Survey Results From
Four New SFA Schools

The 1994–1995 study did not include a testing component but rather examined the reactions of teachers at four new SFA schools to the implementation and effectiveness of various design components (Walsh, Smith, & Ross, 1995). The overall results indicated positive reactions by the majority of teachers, especially to Reading Wings, STaR, and individual tutoring. Least satisfying were the Building Advisory Committee and Family Support Team, but these components had been given relatively little attention the first year compared to the reading curriculum, regrouping, and tutoring. Teachers raised concerns about the late arrival of material (which prompted subsequent improvements in this area). Both principal and district support appeared to be high, and a foundation for a successful long-term implementation was established. In the coming years, this four-school cohort provided considerable leadership in the expansion of the design both in Memphis and in the region.

1995–1996: Grade 1 With Three SFA Schools Matched to One Control

This study, conducted in the 1995–1996 school year, was the first in which the quality of the SFA program implementation at each school was treated as a factor potentially influencing achievement outcomes (Ross, Smith, Lewis, & Nunnery, 1996). The design involved assigning eight Roots & Wings schools to four strata based on four school demographic variables (percentage of students qualifying for free or reduced-price lunch, mobility rate, Peabody Picture Vocabulary Test scores, and percentage of students overage for grade). The Roots & Wings schools at that time were implementing only the SFA reading program, with plans to incorporate other Roots & Wings components in subsequent years.

Within each stratum, one of the Roots & Wings schools was selected based on having high-implementation quality on key SFA program components evaluated by two expert raters familiar with the schools. The other school was selected based on having low-implementation quality on the same components. Each matched SFA high–low implementation pair was then matched to a demographically similar control school, yielding four sets of three schools (SFA-high, SFA-low, and Control). All first graders at the 12 schools were pretested on the Peabody Picture Vocabulary Test and then postested on four individual reading tests and a writing prompt.

Results showed that overall, the four Roots & Wings schools had significantly higher reading and writing scores than the four matched control schools. However, an implementation quality by program interaction also occurred. As shown in Table 3.1, the high-implementation schools surpassed the control schools (mean $ES = +0.34$) whereas the low-implementation schools scored slightly lower than the controls ($ES = -0.17$).

The major conclusion reached was that Roots & Wings program effects were clearly related to implementation quality. Strong program implementations produced significant achievement gains, whereas weaker implementations produced no gains or even small deficits. Similar conclusions were subsequently reached by Nunnery, Slavin, Ross, Smith, Hunter, and Stubbs (in press) in a study of implementation quality in Houston. For MCS and the Johns Hopkins design team, the clear suggestion was making greater effort to ensure that schools were teaching the program and not using variations or adaptations introduced at the school or district level.

1995–1996: Extended-Day Tutoring Using SFA

During the 1995–1996 school year, MCS and the Center for Research in Educational Policy collaborated on the design and evaluation of an extended-day tutoring program in reading for implementation by Title I schools in the district. The program curriculum was modeled on strategies used in the SFA program and other effective reading approaches. Main components included STaR and/or Listening Comprehension, reading and follow-up activities using trade books, Book Club, and test-taking strategies.

A total of 656 students, representing 13 Title I schools, in Grades 2 through 4, participated in the evaluation of the program (Ross, Lewis, Smith, & Sterbin, 1996). At each school, students were individually matched by the principal to a partner on the basis of prior achievement and behavior. One of the students in each pair was selected (sometimes randomly and sometimes not) to participate in the program for 3 days per week, 1 hour per day, for one semester.

Student achievement on the TCAP Total Reading subscale was analyzed to compare tutored and control students. Results directionally favored the tutored group in Grades 2 and 3, with the latter grade showing significance for 80% or higher attenders ($ES = +0.52$), but not for 50% or higher attenders. Fourth-grade differences, however, were close to zero. Given that the program was new, had started later in the year than planned (December rather than early fall), and had weak implementation of several components (Book Club, TCAP review, and writing), the overall five NCE point advantage for tutored students across all grades was considered suggestive of potential long-term benefits. Unfortunately, budgetary restrictions resulted in the discontinuation of the program the following year and subsequently until 1998–1999, when a similar program was implemented by the Memphis Volunteer Center. We are currently evaluating that program in its second year, using a matched-pair design similar to the one just described.

1996–1997: Grades 1 and 2 With Eight
SFA Schools Matched to Four Control Schools

First- and second-grade students from eight Roots & Wings schools and four control schools were tested on the individual reading tests and a writing prompt (Ross, Nunnery, Smith, & Lewis, 1997). The design replicated the prior year's study by classifying two SFA schools and one matched control school into one of four strata based on socioeconomic, mobility, and achievement indicators. Across all tests (see Table 3.1), Roots & Wings second graders performed significantly better than comparison students (mean

$ES = +0.19$), whereas first graders performed about the same as the comparisons ($ES = -0.03$).

In a second part of the study, implementation checks were performed by Johns Hopkins trainers at 24 elementary schools in the district, and the data were analyzed to identify strong and weak areas. Assessment and regrouping, ongoing staff development, Reading Roots lesson content and pacing and management, and tutoring content and instructional processes were the most well-implemented components across sites. Writing instruction generally was rated lower than reading instruction. Tutoring organization was rated extremely low because schools had inadequate staffing levels for tutoring.

The findings suggested that ongoing staff development played a vital role in assuring attainment of implementation benchmarks in organization, curriculum, and instruction. Schools with a full-time facilitator achieved higher standards in ongoing staff development and program implementation than schools with part-time or no facilitators.

1995–1998: TVAAS Studies

The TVAAS was developed by William Sanders and his associates at the University of Tennessee to provide performance scores free of biases normally associated with standardized test outcomes data (Sanders & Horn, 1995a, 1995b). Specifically, it uses scale scores from the norm-referenced components of TCAP as input into a statistical mixed-model process to produce these estimates. From this process, estimates of mean academic gain are provided for each of five subjects. These gains are then compared against the U.S. norm gains for the particular grade and subject. These norms comprise the expected gain for each student, regardless of where his or her score ranks on the percentile scale. For a school or school system, mean scale-score gains by grade and subject can therefore be used to indicate absolute and relative performance compared to the norms.

The index of student achievement used in our Memphis TVAAS studies is the cumulative percent of norm (CPN) mean. This statistic indicates across all grades reported (in this study, Grades 3 through 5) the percent of the national (expected) gain attained. For example, if School A had a CPN gain of 100% in math, it would be achieving at the national or expected level for that subject. If, however, its CPN in social studies was 80%, students' average gain in that subject would be only four-fifths of the expected gain.

Restructuring designs included in the Memphis TVAAS studies (Ross, Wang, Sanders, Wright, & Stringfield, 1999b; Sanders et al., 1999) were those being implemented by at least two elementary schools in a given implementation-year cohort. The designs listed in Figs. 3.2 and 3.3 were those selected. Of the designs that started implementation in 1995, Roots &

Wings had the largest number of schools ($n = 8$). Of the designs selected in 1996, Roots & Wings ($n = 4$) again had the largest number of schools.

Figure 3.2 shows the CPN means for the 1995 design cohorts, nonrestructuring (NR) schools, and the State of Tennessee for all subjects averaged in 1995 (preform year) and 1998, when Roots & Wings, 1995 (R&W-95) had almost completed 3 years of program implementation. Compared to other designs and the NR schools, R&W-95 performed extremely well (mean CPN = 113.5), especially considering that their preform CPN mean of 87.3 was among the lowest of all designs.

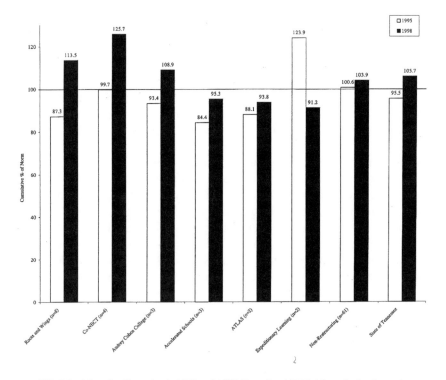

FIG. 3.2 Memphis City schools 1998 and 1995 (Preform) TVAAS results by design for 1995 implementing schools: all subjects averaged.

Figure 3.3 shows the CPN means for the 1996 design cohorts and comparison schools in 1996 (preform year) and 1998. R&W-96 performed slightly lower than the comparison norms in 1998. However, in the preform year (1996), Roots & Wings, 1996 (R&W-96) was the lowest of all cohorts, averaging only 59.9 compared to NR and State means of 81.6 and 93.2, respectively. Its CPN gain of 41.4 points from 1996 to 1998 was the largest of all groups (e.g., State gain = 12.5 points). Both cohorts of schools that later adopted Roots & Wings had been demonstrating very limited success with their existing school-wide programs.

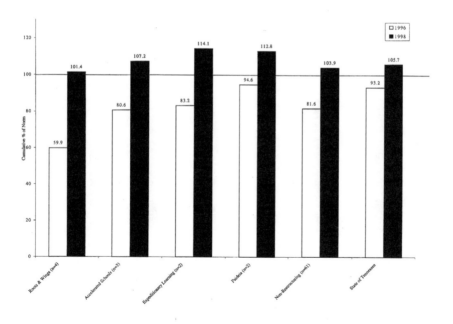

FIG. 3.3 Memphis City schools 1998 and 1996 (Preform) TVAAS results by design for 1996 implementing schools: all subjects averaged.

Due to situational factors that may affect test scores (e.g., district initiatives, the content or difficulty of the state test), what occurs in a given year may not be reflective of actual program effects over time. Figure 3.4 shows the CPN means averaged across all subjects for the preform year (1995) and two years of program implementation (1997 and 1998) for R&W-95, five other designs, and NR schools. As may be seen, despite the R&W-95 cohort's low performance during preform, it had the highest postreform mean (109.2) of all designs and close to a 14-point advantage over the NR schools.

To analyze design effects over time, we conducted for individual designs planned comparisons of the differences between design schools' and NR

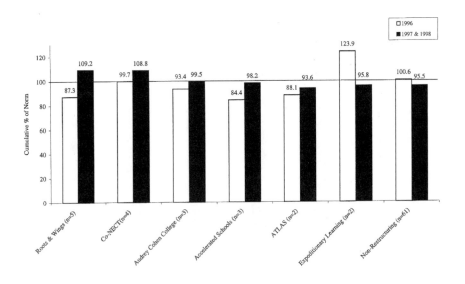

FIG. 3.4   Memphis City schools TVAAS results by design: Year 2 and Year 3 averaged for all subjects.

schools' prereform to postreform CPNs. For the 1995 cohorts, this involved examining the difference from 1995 (prereform) to 1997–1998 averaged (postreform). For the 1996 cohorts, differences were computed from 1995–1996 averaged (prereform) to 1998 (postreform). A positive estimate means that the design schools improved more (or declined less) than the NR schools over time; a negative estimate means the converse. Note, for example, from Fig. 3.4, that Roots &Wings changed from +21.9 CPN points from prereform to postreform, whereas NR schools changed −5.1 points during the same period. The overall advantage for Roots &Wings was therefore 27.0 points.

The only significant design versus NR effect from the analyses of all subjects averaged was for Roots & Wings, 1995 ($p = .003$). The associated effect size of +1.10 indicates that this was also a strong effect. Again, given the way the change analysis was conducted, this effect size would mean that Roots & Wings schools' gain from prereform to postreform was over one standard deviation (SD) higher than the NR gain for the same period.

1997–1998: Implementation Quality as a Factor for TVAAS Results

As a second component of the Memphis TVAAS research (Ross et al., 1999b), we compared the 1998 achievement gains in Reading and Language of 12 Roots &Wings schools rated as high implementers ($n = 6$) or low implementers ($n = 6$) by expert trainers. The results are depicted in Fig. 3.5. As can be seen, in both Reading and Language, the high implementers outperformed both matched Control ($n = 33$) schools and Other ($n = 28$) schools in the district by from 12 to 21 CPN points. Low implementers, however, were comparable or slightly superior to the comparison schools in Reading, but from 6 to 11 points lower in Language.

Inferential analyses compared the two Roots &Wings cohorts to both the Control and Other schools. None of the effects was statistically significant, although power of the analyses was low due to small school n's. However, the high implementers in Language had effect sizes of +0.65 and +0.84 relative to Control and Other schools, respectively. In contrast, the low implementers had parallel Language effect sizes of −0.44 and −0.25.

Analyses of the prereform to postreform changes were significant in three cases. In Reading, the high implementer mean change was 23.0 points greater than that for the Control schools ($p = .030$, $ES = +0.97$). In Language, the high implementer change mean surpassed the mean for the Control schools by 40.0 points ($p = .006$, $ES = +1.22$), and the change mean for Other schools by 36.3 points ($p = 0.14$, $ES = +1.12$).

1995–1998: Teacher Effectiveness and Mobility

In this study (Ross, Wang, Sanders, Wright, & Stringfield, 1999a), we addressed the question of whether teaching in a SFA (Roots & Wings) school influenced teacher effectiveness over time. We used as data the TVAAS Teacher Effect (TTE) score computed by the state for each teacher each year. The TTE measures individual teachers' contributions to their students' academic achievement relative to an average teacher in their school district. Thus, a positive TTE represents an above-average performance,

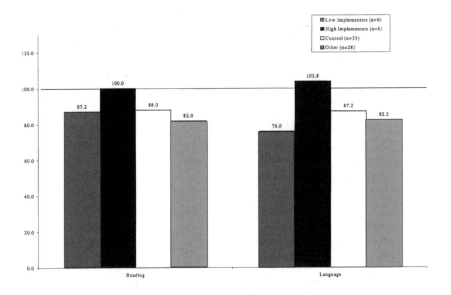

FIG. 3.5   Analysis of implementation influences on 1998 value-added
effects of Roots & Wings.

whereas a negative TTE represents a below-average performance. The TTEs are calculated from a multivariate, longitudinal, mixed-model analysis of TerraNova scores as part of TVAAS (Sanders, Saxon, & Horn, 1997). For the entire school district, the overall mean TTE was essentially zero with a SD of 3.2. There were 59% of the TTEs between –2.00 and +2.00, with 21% below –2.00 and 19% above +2.00.

In this study, we examined teacher effectiveness at restructuring schools using one of eight whole-school models (including Roots & Wings) versus non-restructuring schools for two cohorts—schools that started in 1995 and schools that started in 1996; and three types of teachers—teachers in their first year at the school, teachers having 6 years or more at the school, and all other teachers.

Overall results for all restructuring schools combined were significant for the 1995 schools only. Six-year teachers in restructuring schools showed significantly greater improvement from 1995 (prereform) to 1998 than did 6-year teachers in nonrestructuring schools. First-year teachers in both groupings had negative TTE means, but interestingly, the least effective performances occurred for those at restructuring schools in their third year of implementation. The implication was that once a school has been using a reform model for several years, it may have become more difficult for teachers inexperienced with the model to succeed in their first year.

Analyses were also conducted separately for individual designs. Roots & Wings reflected the only statistically significant pattern, which occurred for 6-year teachers in Roots & Wings, 1995 schools ($p = .0040$). A graphical representation is shown in Fig. 3.6. In 1994–1995, 6-year Roots & Wings teachers ($n = 23$) averaged –0.25 in TTE, whereas they averaged +0.84 ($n = 25$) in 1996–1997 and +2.28 ($n = 19$) in 1997–1998. In other words, these veteran teachers demonstrated substantial improvement in effectiveness over time. A program like SFA may be relatively challenging for teachers to learn, but once they have gained experience and proficiency at using it, they may realize increasing success in raising student performance from year to year.

A contrast with the 6-year teachers is shown in Fig. 3.7, which presents first-year teacher results at the 1995 R&W-95 schools. Although the pattern was not statistically significant, it shows a large deficit in 1995–1996 (Year 1 of implementation) and especially in 1997–1998 (Year 3) relative to first-year teachers at nonrestructuring schools. Although these outcomes need to be replicated to gain credence, the suggestion is that professional development support for new teachers is especially critical for designs like SFA that require learning a new curriculum and methods of teaching. The extremely negative TTE for Roots & Wings first-year teachers in Year 3 (TTE = –2.41) further suggests that professional development support may become less effective or extensive once a school has been implementing SFA for a number of years. Concentrating on better preparing teachers who are newly entering SFA schools, both through preservice and in-service training, is encouraged on the basis of this preliminary evidence.

Teacher mobility data for the R&W-95 and R&W-96 schools generally mirrored the overall tendency in the district for mobility to peak in the first implementation year. Important to the interpretation of results is knowing that MCS intentionally facilitated transfer requests by teachers in the first year of their present schools' design implementation. Consequently, the 1995 restructuring (R&W-95) schools might be expected to have peaked in mobility in 1995–1996, and the 1996 restructuring (R96) schools in 1996–1997.

During 1994–1995 to 1997–1998, nonrestructuring schools in the district had an overall teacher mobility average from 17% to 22%. Designs in the 1995 cohort having the highest mobility levels after one year were

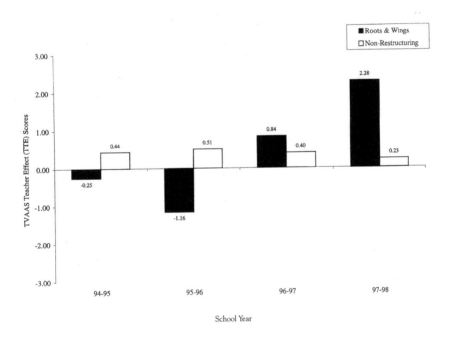

FIG. 3.6   Teacher effectiveness for 1995 Roots & Wings schools: 6-year teachers.

R&W-95 (32%) and Expeditionary Learning—Outward Bound (ELOB)-95 (39%). Statistical comparisons between R95 design schools and NR schools were significant ($p < .05$) in 1995–1996 for R&W-95 ($p = .003$), Co-nect-95 ($p = .025$), and Audrey Cohen College-95 ($p = .047$). In all cases, mobility was higher at the design schools. Comparisons between R&W-96 schools with NR schools showed significantly higher mobility for R&W-96 in 1994–1995 (40.5%, $p = .0005$) and in 1996–1997 (48.6%, $p = .0002$).

These results indicate that, after being selected, Roots & Wings was associated with the highest mobility levels of all designs. Compared to other designs, Roots & Wings involves the most extensive professional development and changes in everyday lesson planning and teaching strategies. However, after the first year, mobility at Roots & Wings schools decreased to the district average, suggesting that staffing became fairly stabilized once the initial changes had been made.

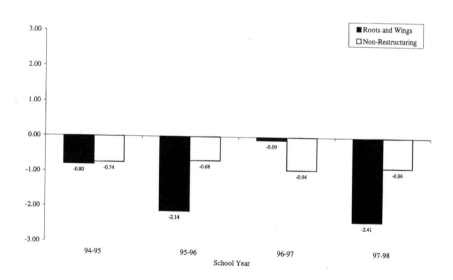

FIG. 3.7 Teacher effectiveness for 1995 Roots & Wings schools: first-year teachers.

CONCLUSIONS

In 10 years, SFA in Memphis has grown from 1 school to 40 schools. During the same time period, only two schools in the district discontinued SFA after adopting it. Evaluation of SFA in the district has been long-term and continuous, has consistently employed a matched control-treatment research design, and has incorporated as dependent measures both individually administered reading tests and state-mandated standardized achievement tests. As will be discussed later, the overall effects of SFA have been positive on both types of assessments of student learning. Experienced teachers at SFA schools have also demonstrated increased effectiveness over time, more so than teachers at schools using other reform designs or traditional programs. These positive-performance outcomes along with special attributes of MCS have contributed to both the growth and stability of SFA in the district.

Student Achievement

As shown in Table 3.1, the Memphis studies have shown positive effects of SFA on student achievement on individually administered reading tests. Mean effect sizes across all studies were +0.65 in kindergarten, +0.21 in first grade, and +0.20 in second grade. The latter two effects would be considered small to moderate in size (Cohen, 1988), but still educationally significant when an average advantage of two tenths of a SD is applied to 35 school comparisons including approximately 2,500 children in the grades tested.

Although suggestive of positive program effects, the Memphis results can hardly be considered conclusive that SFA will raise reading performance in every grade at every school (see, e.g., criticisms of prior research by Pogrow, 1998, 1999). One limitation of the present results is that they are restricted to the primary grades (mainly first grade). However, a true constraining condition for this type of program evaluation is the high student mobility in the school district. In many Memphis schools, only about 25% of third graders and, of course, extremely small percentages of fourth and fifth graders participated in SFA in first grade when their formal reading instruction began. The sample sizes in our longitudinal studies were simply too small to attribute achievement patterns in the upper grades to program influences. Given these natural and irresolvable restrictions, it is noteworthy nonetheless that SFA students first and second graders were averaging close to grade level in this high-poverty school district, whereas students at comparable schools not using SFA were averaging one-third to one-half year below grade level.

In critiquing conventional "experimental" research on effective programs, Pogrow (1999) also raised questions about selectivity in the choice of "control" schools, intimating that "manipulations" of control-group designs may sometimes occur "to benefit the experimental treatment" (p. 26). In the 9 years of the Memphis research, no control school was ever eliminated, and all were selected by the district research office on the basis of providing best matches with the SFA schools, not because that office had any stake in SFA proving effective.

Table 3.2, dealing with results on state-mandated standardized achievement tests, presents evidence that clearly meets stringent criteria for valid scientific assessment of program quality. On the negative side, early studies failed to show any benefits for SFA students compared to matched control students on the state-administered standardized tests. Although a possible argument is that SFA was simply no more effective than other approaches for improving reading performance, a counterpoint is that the very same SFA cohorts surpassed control students on the individual reading tests. The latter tests were not chosen because they were likely to favor SFA (see Pogrow, 1999), but because they provided relative to the state-mandated tests a more authentic assessment of reading skills under highly controlled administration procedures. Specifically, the *Durrell Oral Reading subtest*, which asks students to read and answer comprehension questions about graded passages, contrasts directly from a validity standpoint with standardized multiple-choice tests administered under timed conditions in a group setting with high-stakes consequences for teachers and administrators. More likely, SFA teachers were not incorporating the standardized testing content and objectives in their lessons more effectively than were control teachers. As suggested in some of our qualitative studies (Ross & Smith, 1992), a concern by SFA teachers was that the prescribed reading block activities restricted opportunities relative to other schools to teach to the standardized test and adequately prepare students for the particular skills tested.

Over the years, more emphasis was placed by both the Johns Hopkins trainers and the school district on integrating standardized test objectives into the curriculum at SFA schools. Possibly this effort contributed to the positive outcomes starting in 1993–1994 (see Table 3.2), when one school demonstrated a +0.93 effect size and another a +0.43 effect size on the standardized test (although a third school had a slightly negative effect size of –0.17).

Of all the research conducted on SFA, perhaps the most compelling evidence about its overall effectiveness comes from our Memphis TVAAS analyses (see Figs. 3.2–3.4). Over a 2-year period, Roots & Wings schools were averaging 109% of the national norm gain, whereas control schools and the entire state averaged only about 96% during the same period (Fig.

3.5). These results come from well-known and widely used standardized tests across five subjects in intermediate grades (3 through 5), unbiased external data analysts (Sanders and associates at the University of Tennessee), and testing procedures that in no way could favor any particular program over another. Yet, district wide, the Roots & Wings results were more impressive than those for any other design. Do these results meet Pogrow's (1999) challenge for high-quality programs to bring students to "acceptable" achievement levels? That answer is debatable because Roots & Wings schools still averaged below national norms, with typical median percentiles in the 30s. But, importantly, these extremely high-poverty schools were gaining each year at a significantly faster rate compared to matched control schools as well as other schools in the district and state wide. To offer an analogy to sports, if a runner begins a race two full laps behind her peers, and then finishes only one lap behind, should her performance be considered unsuccessful? In the sense of completely bridging the gap (and winning the race), perhaps so. But surely the performance reflects both high accomplishment in reducing the gap and validation of the associated training regimen.

Teacher Effects

The Memphis results provide unique empirical perspectives on what happens to teachers at SFA schools with regard to their effectiveness in fostering student achievement gains and the likelihood that they will remain at their schools (Ross et al., 1999a). Although these perspectives must be viewed cautiously until results are replicated, they suggest that compared to teachers at nonrestructuring schools and, to a lesser extent, to teachers using other designs, SFA veteran teachers gain more in effectiveness while demonstrating more positive outcomes with increased experience in using the design. On the other hand, first-year teachers at established SFA schools may undergo a difficult adjustment, and realize relatively low student gains. SFA teachers, in general, are more likely than other teachers to transfer schools after the program is selected, but not after it has been implemented at the school for 1 or 2 years.

These results appear at least partially attributable to SFA being highly demanding compared to other reform designs in its requirements for professional development, adaptive instruction, teacher roles and assignments, and learning new curricula and teaching methods. Negative teacher reactions and higher mobility appear likely to occur when school reforms require extensive work and significant changes in the status quo. Preparing first-year teachers to make the adjustments needed and buy into the program is essential to improve their instructional skills, increase their commitment to remain at the school, and allow them to benefit as did the veteran teachers in increasing teaching effectiveness over time.

Implementation Quality and Achievement

The Memphis results (Ross et al., 1996; Sanders et al., 1999) further reinforce the idea that SFA effects are strongly related to the quality of implementation (Nunnery et al., in press). In 1995–1996, using individual reading test results, we found that high-implementing schools had an average effect size of +0.34, whereas lower implementing schools had a slightly negative effect of –0.17. In 1997–1998, high implementers averaged on the Language subtest of TCAP +0.65 and +0.84 (compared to control and other schools, respectively), whereas low implementers averaged –0.44 and –0.25. The weaker the implementation of SFA, probably the greater the frustration for teachers and their reliance on traditional, familiar teaching methods that do not blend well with program strategies. Both logically and empirically, teaching the SFA program raises reading achievement; weak or hybrid implementations yield highly diminished or even negative effects.

Why Success in Memphis?

Having reviewed the history of, and research support for, Memphis SFA, this chapter concludes with our subjective interpretations of why the program has enjoyed a decade of significant achievement and growth in the school district. Like other urban school districts in the nation, MCS faces significant challenges in educating its many socioeconomically disadvantaged students. The school district has its share of highly dedicated principals and teachers who work extremely hard to ensure their students' success. However, we also feel there are several factors that have given Memphis an advantage over other school districts in implementing SFA for so many years in so many of its schools. These interpretations are presented in the following:

Administrative Support. From its inception in the district, SFA enjoyed clear and overt backing from MCS' central administration. That support began under interim leadership but grew substantially when Dr. Gerry House became superintendent in 1992. Her positive views about SFA as an effective reading program increased interest by school leadership teams in exploring it as a design option and their confidence that, if the school adopted SFA, there would be high district assistance in both policies and resources.

Title I Support. Complementary to Dr. House's contributions, the Title I office, directed by Ms. Charlene Parker from 1991 through 1999, served a critical role in promoting SFA as a desirable school-wide program option. In 1994–1995, when eight schools were implementing SFA, the Title I office established an internal training unit that still continues today. Their role, which is now coordinated by the MCS Teaching and Learning Academy, is to supplement external training by providing professional development and administrative assistance to SFA schools throughout the year.

A University Partnership. One of the nine elements of the Comprehensive School Reform Demonstration (CSRD) initiative is collaborating with external partners to increase access to information, critical services, and resources. The value of this element is exemplified, we feel, in the long-term partnership established between The University of Memphis and MCS SFA. In early years, our critical contribution was generating awareness of SFA by Memphis schools, serving as a liaison between the Johns Hopkins design team and school administrators, and helping the schools to use formative evaluation data to increase success. In subsequent years, our role has shifted to conducting and disseminating research and providing training through The University of Memphis Regional Training Center. Presenting research results is especially critical in informing both schools and the public of the outcomes attained. External stakeholders (the school board and the public) must be convinced that the additional money allocated for special programs is well spent. For example, on the very day that this paragraph was drafted, an article appearing in Memphis' daily newspaper, *The Commercial Appeal* (Anderson, 1999) reported our teacher effects results, with specific reference to Roots & Wings veteran teachers demonstrating the most improvement in effectiveness compared to control schools and other design schools.

In countless school districts across the country, implementations of SFA have proven wrong the idea that externally developed programs are unlikely to have sustained positive impacts on reform practices (see Berman & McLaughlin, 1978; McLaughlin, 1990). The Memphis initiative has been exemplary in demonstrating increasing growth, not by district or state mandate, but by individual school choice. We believe that this success is largely attributable to the combination of positive district support; external partnerships for training, evaluation, and research, and, of course, positive achievement outcomes disseminated both nationally and locally.

REFERENCES

Anderson, M. (1999, December 27). Veteran teachers improve with "design models." *Commercial Appeal*, pp. A1, A7.

Berman, P., & McLaughlin, M. W. (1978). *Federal programs supporting educational change (Vol. VIII): Implementing and sustaining innovations.* Santa Monica, CA: RAND.

Casey, J. P., & Smith, L. J., & Ross, S. M. (1994). *Formative evaluation of new SFA schools in Memphis, Tennessee.* Memphis, TN: The University of Memphis.

Cohen, J. (1988). *Statistical power analysis for the behavioral sciences* (2nd ed.). Hillsdale, NJ: Academic.

CTB/McGraw-Hill (1990). *Comprehensive test of basic skills* (4th ed.). Spring Norms Book. Monterey, CA: CTB/MacMillan/McGraw-Hill.

Dunn, L. M. (1981). *Peabody picture vocabulary test* (rev. ed.). Circle Pines, MN: American Guidance Service.

Durrell, D. D., & Catterson, J. H. (1980). *Durrell analysis of reading difficulty* (3rd ed.). New York: The Psychological Corporation.

Herman, R. (1999). *An educators' guide to schoolwide reform.* Arlington, VA: Educational Research Service.

Leinhardt, G., & Pallay, A. (1982). Restrictive educational settings: Exile or haven? *Review of Educational Research, 52,* 557–578.

McLaughlin, M. W. (1990). The Rand change agent study revisited: Macro perspectives and micro realities. *Educational Researcher, 19*(9), 11–16.

Natriello, G., & McDill, E. L. (1999). Title I: From funding mechanism to educational program. In G. Orfield & E. H. DeBray (Eds.), *Hard work for good schools: Facts not fads in Title I reform* (pp. 31–45). Cambridge, MA: The Civil Rights Project, Harvard University.

Nunnery, J., Slavin, R. E., Ross, S. M., Smith, L. J., Hunter, P., & Stubbs, J. (in press). An assessment of Success for All program component configuration effects on the reading achievement of at-risk first-grade students. *American Educational Research Journal.*

Pogrow, S. (1988). What is an exemplary program and why should anyone care? A reaction to Slavin and Klein. *Educational Researcher, 27*(7), 22–28.

Pogrow, S. (1999). Rejoinder: Consistent large gain and high levels of achievement are the best measures of program quality: Pogrow responds to Slavin. *Educational Researcher, 28*(8), 24–26, 31.

Ross, S. M., Lewis, T., Smith, L. J., & Sterbin, A. (1999). *Evaluation of the extended-day tutoring program in Memphis City Schools: Final report to CRESPAR.* Memphis, TN: The University of Memphis.

Ross, S. M., Nunnery, J. A., Smith, L. J., & Lewis, T. (1997). *Evaluation of Success for All programs in Memphis City Schools: 1996–1997.* Memphis, TN: The University of Memphis.

Ross, S. M., & Smith, L. J. (1991). *Final report: 1991 Success for All program in Memphis.* Memphis, TN: The University of Memphis.

Ross, S. M., & Smith, L. J. (1992). *1991–1992 Memphis, Tennessee Success for All results: Final report.* Memphis, TN: The University of Memphis.

Ross, S. M., & Smith, L. J., & Casey, J. P. (1994). *1993–1994 Success for All program in Memphis, Tennessee: Evaluation of SFA TCAP results.* Memphis, TN: The University of Memphis.

Ross, S. M., Smith, L. J., Casey, J., & Slavin, R. E. (1995). Increasing the academic success of disadvantaged children: An examination of early intervention programs. *American Educational Research Journal, 32,* 773–800.

Ross, S. M., Smith, L. J., Lewis, T., & Nunnery, J. A. (1996). *1995–1996 evaluation of Roots & Wings in Memphis City Schools*. Memphis, TN: The University of Memphis.

Ross, S. M., Smith, L. J., Lohr, L. L., McNelis, M., Nunnery, J., & Rich, L. (1991). *Final report: 1991 classroom observation study in Memphis*. Memphis, TN: The University of Memphis.

Ross, S. M., Smith, L. J., Lohr, L. L., & McNelis, M. (1994). Math and reading instruction in tracked first-grade classes. *The Elementary School Journal, 95*(2), 105–120.

Ross, S. M., Wang, W., Sanders, W. L., Wright, S. P., & Stringfield, S. (1999a). *Teacher mobility and effectiveness in restructuring and non-restructuring schools in an inner-city district*. Memphis, TN: The University of Memphis.

Ross, S. M., Wang, W., Sanders, W. L., Wright, S. P., & Stringfield, S. (1999b). *Two- and three-year achievement results on the Tennessee value-added assessment system for restructuring schools in Memphis*. Memphis, TN: The University of Memphis.

Sanders, W. L., & Horn, S. P. (1995a). Educational assessment reassessed: The usefulness of standardized and alternative measures of student achievement as indicators for the assessment of educational outcomes. *Educational Policy Analysis Archives* [Online serial], *3*(6). Available: http://info.asu.edu/asu-cwis/epaa/welcome/html

Sanders, W. L., & Horn, S. P. (1995b). The Tennessee Value-Added Assessment System (TVAAS): Mixed model methodology in educational assessment. In A. J. Shinkfield & D. Stufflebeam (Eds.), *Teacher evaluation: Guide to effective practice* (pp. 337–350). Boston: Kluwer.

Sanders, W. L., Saxon, A. M., & Horn, S. P. (1997). The Tennessee Value-Added Assessment System: A quantitative outcomes-based approach to educational assessment. In J. Millman (Ed.), *Grading teachers, grading schools: Is student achievement a valid education measure?* (Pp. 137–162). Thousand Oaks, CA: Corwin.

Sanders, W. L., Wright, S. P., & Ross, S. M. (1999). *Value-added achievement results for two cohorts of Roots & Wings schools in Memphis: 1995–1998 outcomes*. Memphis, TN: The University of Memphis.

Slavin, R. E., Madden, N. A., Dolan, L. J., & Wasik, B. A. (1996). *Every child, every school: Success for All*. Newbury Park, CA: Corwin.

Slavin, R. E., Madden, N. A., Dolan, L. J., Wasik, B. A., Ross, S. M., Smith, L. J., & Dianda, M. (1996). Success for All: A summary of research. *Journal of Education for Students Placed At Risk, 1*(1), 41–76.

Smith, L. J., Ross, S. M., & Casey, J. P. (1994). *1993–1994 Memphis, Tennessee Success for All results: Final report*. Memphis, TN: The University of Memphis.

Smith, L. J., Ross, S. M., Johnson, B., & Casey, J. P. (1993). *1992–1993 Memphis, Tennessee Success for All results: Final report*. Memphis, TN: The University of Memphis.

Stringfield. S. C., Ross, S. M., & Smith, L. J. (1996). *Bold plans for school restructuring: The New American Schools designs*. Mahwah, NJ: Lawrence Erlbaum Associates.

Walsh, E. J., Smith, L. J., & Ross, S. M. (1995). *1994–1995 first-year implementation of Success for All: Charjean, Kansas, Klondike, and Manor Lake Elementary Schools of Memphis City Schools: Teacher survey results*. Memphis, TN: The University of Memphis.

Woodcock, R. (1987). *Woodcock reading mastery test-revised*. Circle Pines, MN: American Guidance Service.

II

International Adaptations
of Success for All

4

The Implementation and Impact of Success for All in English Schools

Alma Harris
David Hopkins
Judith Wordsworth
University of Nottingham, U.K.

Since the early 1990s, there has been an increasing momentum in the United Kingdom, as in many other educational systems, toward educational reform directed at raising levels of school performance. The emphasis on school improvement has increased as a result of the trend in most Western countries of decentralizing the responsibility for the implementation of educational reform. Alongside this increase in political pressure for institutional renewal, there has been a growing realization that many strategies for educational change have had little impact on schools and classrooms (Fullan, 1999). Consequently, within the United Kingdom a range of government policies have emerged aimed at generating the impetus for school-level and classroom-level change.

In 1997, the U.K. Department for Education and Employment (DfEE) launched its "Improving Schools" program as a direct response to the challenge of raising educational standards. This was accompanied in the same year with the publication of the government's *White Paper:Excellence in*

Schools that outlined a general approach to school improvement. Within this paper a number of themes were identified that provided a policy framework and also reflected some of the key ingredients of a successful contemporary approach to school improvement. At the heart of this policy directive was a focus on raising standards of literacy and numeracy. Particular concern about low levels of literacy nationally prompted the government to set up a Literacy Task Force to advise them on ways of addressing the problem. The final report, produced by the Task Force in summer 1998, proposed a National Literacy Strategy designed to raise standards of literacy in all elementary schools.

Since September 1998, the National Literacy Strategy has been statutory in elementary schools throughout England. The strategy includes a designated literacy hour each day for all pupils in elementary schools and a detailed "Framework for Teaching," which sets out teaching objectives for pupils aged 4 to 11. The Framework has three core components: phonological awareness, grammatical awareness, comprehension, and composition. For each grade the specific content under each of these headings is specified. Teachers are currently using the Framework to guide their lesson planning and teaching during the literacy hour.

Prior to the launch of the National Literacy Strategy and its subsequent development in the United Kingdom, the opportunity arose to pilot the Success for All (SFA) program (see chap. 1., this volume; and Slavin, Madden, Dolan, & Wasik, 1996) in English schools. Since 1997, a research team at the Center for Teacher and School Development, University of Nottingham (SFA-UK), have been working with elementary schools in a high-poverty area of Nottingham, to adapt SFA to the English educational context. Schools in Nottingham were ideally suited to pilot SFA because of their particularly low-literacy levels. When compared with national averages of achievement in literacy, 40% of Nottingham elementary schools are below the 10th percentile and a further 40% lie within the 10- and 40-percentile range. Only 20% of Nottingham schools are in the 40 to 100-percentile range. Consequently, there was much initial support and interest in piloting the SFA program in Nottingham city schools.

In the first phase of the project (1997–1998), one secondary school and five elementary schools in Nottingham were involved in piloting SFA. In 1999, two additional elementary schools joined the program and have been fully involved in the second phase of the development and evaluation work.

In both phases, the schools involved in the program received regular training from the U.S. SFA team and from trainers located in Nottingham. This training focused on the content, approach, and pedagogy of SFA. It is well established that the power of SFA as a curriculum and instructional program comes from the attention that is paid to implementation (Slavin et al., 1996;

Slavin & Madden, in press). The fact that the quality of implementation of the program is regularly monitored has been consistently shown to be a major factor in its positive impact on pupil reading levels (Slavin et al., 1996). Consequently, the schools have been subject to regular implementation checks from the SFA trainers to ensure fidelity in replication of the program and to assist schools in a critical evaluation of their progress.

The implementation of SFA in England has attempted to follow as closely as possible the typical pattern established within the United States. However, the implementation of the program in English schools differs from that in their American counterparts in three important respects. First, English elementary schools are much smaller than those in the United States (in Nottingham school sizes were between 100 and 150 students), and accommodations for grouping and staffing had to be made. Second, although American schools primarily use either certified teachers or paid paraprofessionals as tutors, sometimes supplemented by volunteers, the Nottingham schools have depended entirely on volunteer tutors, as there is no funding analogous to Title I in the United Kingdom to pay for tutors. Third, the family support and integrated service components of SFA have not been reproduced in a consistent way among the SFA schools in England. With these exceptions, variations from the U.S. program have been minor.

THE IMPACT OF SFA IN ENGLISH SCHOOLS

In the academic year 1997–1998, funding was sought from the United Kingdom's Department for Education and Employment (DfEE) to evaluate the initial implementation of the SFA program in Nottingham. The positive response from the DfEE enabled research to be undertaken in the implementation of the SFA program during that year. The purpose of the research was to provide empirical evidence on the process of implementation of SFA and to elicit how SFA might be adopted by other English schools (Hopkins et al., 1998). More recently, in 1999 the SFA-UK program group was fortunate to receive a large grant from the Fischer Family Trust for further evaluation work. This prompted the implementation of a much more extensive evaluation. This evaluation has been under way since July 1999, and incorporates both quantitative and qualitative data collection. It also utilizes a range of program- and school-level data including national test outcomes and implementation information.

Impact of SFA on Reading Levels

In the pilot phase, the impact of SFA on reading levels was assessed by the use of group-reading tests specifically designed for the evaluation. In addition, the formative 8-week assessments formed a prominent feature of the evaluation. Using the data gathered from each year group, a whole-year expected progress value was calculated by subtracting that group's mean initial score from the mean score for the next year group. That value was then taken to be the amount by which the year group might be expected to improve over the current school year. Sampling variability, both within schools (varying abilities in different years) and between schools (different school performance levels) was accommodated by examining all year groups, 1 to 5, and by averaging the calculation across schools.

Extrapolating from that estimate to one term (the length of time for which data were collected), one would expect each group to record a change of approximately one third that level. For every year group, the SFA change exceeded this level. Indeed, for one half of the year groups the actual change was greater than the whole-year expected progress value, which implied that the initiative was achieving reading-score improvements of more than a year in one term (see Hopkins et al., 1998; Hopkins, Youngman, Harris, & Wordsworth, 1999). Four of the remaining year groups recorded improvements equivalent to approximately two terms (twice the expected level), while the other group scored at slightly less than the two-term level. These preliminary findings suggested progress averaging at a level equivalent to approximately 1 school year, or three times what might otherwise be expected. All year groups exceeded normal progress, with the Year 1 pupils showing least relative progress (less than two terms), although they recorded the highest actual improvement in raw-score terms. Mean-progress scores for the gender splits were calculated and the apparent lack of difference between the genders is confirmed by statistical tests. The scheme is seen to be equally effective for boys and girls.

National Test Results

Data from National Tests highlight the impact of SFA in the pilot schools over a 3 year period. The United Kingdom's National Test scores at Key Stage 1 (tested at age 7) and Key Stage 2 (tested at age 11) show that SFA schools have made greater gains in reading performance during the three years of being involved in the SFA program than the United Kingdom as a whole. All schools are coming closer to national averages.

Figure 4.1 shows the national test results for the SFA schools at the end of Key Stage 1 (age 7). The percentage of pupils reaching their chronological reading age in this grade over the 3 years has increased from 39% to 74%. Figures are now just below the national average of 82%.

Figure 4.2 shows the national test results for the SFA schools at the end of Key Stage 2 (age 11). The percentage of pupils reaching their chronological

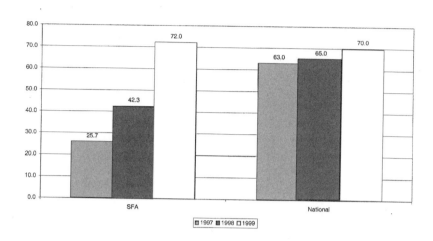

FIG. 4.1   Nottingham Success for All schools overall English-level II or above Key Stage 1.

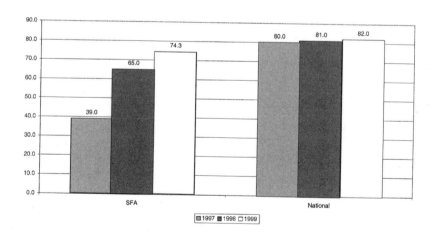

FIG. 4.2   Nottingham Success for All schools overall English-level IV or above Key Stage 2.

reading age in this grade over the three years has increased from 26% to 72%. Put another way, these schools moved from 37 percentage points below national averages to 2 percentage points above. It is evident from these data that the pilot phase schools have continued to make consistent progress over the 3 year period and that their performance has improved by over 200% at Key Stage 2 (Grade 4) and by 100% at Key Stage 1 (Grade 2). This not only represents a remarkable achievement for teachers and pupils within the SFA schools but also confirms the effectiveness of the SFA program within an English school context.

Behavior.   The evaluation evidence shows that the SFA program in English schools continues to have a positive impact on other pupil outcomes, in addition to reading. Schools report that the behavior of pupils has improved over the period that SFA has been operating. The teachers consistently comment that there is a low level of misbehavior during SFA lessons and the incidences of pupils being removed from SFA classes are almost nonexistent. One facilitator commented that "during SFA there are rarely any discipline problems, children with severe behavioral problems are now working well because of the SFA learning strategies." Given the particular context of these schools, poor behavior is an issue that teachers face on a daily basis.

The reason teachers give for the change in pupils' behavior patterns is largely explained in terms of SFA's structure. Teachers feel that the tight structure and quick pace of SFA mean that activities change regularly and consequently pupils are totally engaged in the tasks. Pupils themselves do not tolerate misbehavior because it interrupts the program. The lesson observations conducted and the videotaped lessons both reveal the high level of pupil engagement on task during the 90-minute SFA sessions.

The change in pupil behavior has largely been attributed to the cooperative learning element of the program. The cooperative group work dimension of the program has been shown to engage pupils in listening to others and talking to others during their SFA partnership activities. Teachers feel that this cooperative way of working has encouraged pupils to be more tolerant of each other and to be calmer in their interactions with others. There is also evidence to suggest that this collaborative way of working is operating in other learning contexts within the school and that the social skills pupils are developing are transferable. One teacher commented, "the children in this school lack basic social skills but the SFA partnership activities have allowed them to practice talking and listening. This way of working has meant the children feel more confident working together and this has had major benefits for other lessons that I teach."

Motivation. During the period that SFA has been operating in English schools there has been an upward trend in pupil attendance, and teachers report higher level of motivation among the pupils toward lessons in SFA schools. Teachers explain this increased motivation in terms of pupils' feeling they have achieved through SFA lessons and can achieve generally in their learning. The marked improvement in reading has been a major motivational force with individuals and with whole classes. As one teacher noted,

"there has been an overall improvement in performance, a marked improvement in concentration, cooperation, and behavior. The children bring back their books every day from home. We have happy, reading children who are enthusiastic about learning, and not just in SFA lessons!"

Teachers in the program suggest that the tight structure within SFA means that there is repetition and predictability for pupils within each SFA lesson. As a result, there is less of a need to monitor off-task talk within SFA lessons. As one teacher noted, "children have learned through SFA to talk on task and through this to support each other in learning." There is a high level of pupil engagement within SFA lessons, which contributes to effective learning.

Kindergarten. The SFA program is also considered to be effective teaching kindergarten pupils. The early-learning component of SFA is generally considered by teachers to be working exceptionally well and providing a firm foundation for subsequent reading. The majority of schools report that kindergarten practice is benefitting from SFA and that pupils are being made ready to read. In a number of schools, teachers report such positive outcomes from the Early Learning program that they would continue even if the program stopped in the rest of the school. One teacher commented, "many of the elements of Early Learning have now become a natural part of my teaching approach."

Impact of SFA on Teachers' Professional Development and the Wider Community

Teachers. Despite some early scepticism, the majority of teachers state that they have learned a great deal from SFA particularly about the effective teaching of reading. As a result, many of the teachers commented that the way in which they teach reading is now more effective because of SFA. The positive results from SFA have generated more teacher enthusiasm and commitment to the program. The SFA training events led to collaborative planning and teaching within each school. Such opportunities to work together and to plan together were particularly valued by teachers in the program. One facilitator commented, "we now have a reason to work together, which is a shared desire to improve reading."

Teachers feel the SFA approach they are using is having an impact on raising reading levels across the whole school. The success of the program has now become evident and most teachers feel that they are more effective teachers of reading. One teacher commented, "in the past we all taught reading as best we could, now we know what works and we do not have a child in the school who is not making progress."

The evaluation evidence has shown that SFA has introduced teachers to new and different teaching strategies. Teachers have now developed expertise in cooperative group work by working with the SFA program. One facilitator commented that, "cooperative learning strategies are equally applicable to other areas of the curriculum. Cooperative and collaborative working techniques have become natural to the children through SFA and are now an important dimension of my teaching." Overall, SFA has provided an opportunity for high-quality professional development.

Community.   The involvement of voluntary tutors in the program is centrally important for the one-to-one tutoring component of SFA. A significant feature of the Nottingham SFA pilot has been the involvement of business, in particular the Boots Company, which owns the largest chain of chemist outlets in the United Kingdom. As a result of this collaboration, Boots are providing some 200 volunteers to be involved in tutoring. An independent evaluation of the Boots volunteer scheme has revealed that there is much enthusiasm among the tutors for the program and their role. The majority of volunteers have indicated a wish to remain with SFA and to continue to work with the program. This volunteer program is much larger than any other SFA volunteer tutor program that currently exists in the United States. One facilitator commented, "links with business have been positive—tutors are well organized and effective in their work with children. We have forged links with local businesses, which not only benefits the children with extra learning support, but also establishes our place within the community."

Parents.   There is evidence from all the schools that the SFA program has also had a positive impact on community relations and parental involvement. Principals have reported an increased attendance at parents' meetings and more unsolicited feedback from parents about the program.

Overall, parents are very supportive and positive about the program. The following comment is characteristic: "Before SFA 10% of our parents were regularly involved with their children's reading. This has now increased to around 60% and at least 50% of the children are now visiting the library with their families on a regular basis."

Overall, the evaluation evidence has shown that SFA had a positive impact on pupil-learning gains, teachers' professional development, and on community relations. Clearly, these evaluation findings emanate from 3 years of the program and include a relatively small sample of schools. However, this empirical evidence has provided a basis for eliciting and examining the implementation issues arising from the introduction of SFA in English schools.

THE IMPLEMENTATION OF SUCCESS FOR ALL IN ENGLAND

The introduction and implementation of SFA presented a number of immediate structural difficulties for the schools. First, there was the issue of competition with the National Literacy Strategy (NLS) and the fear that the program would be conflicting with statutory curriculum requirements. For some teachers there were reservations about the fit between SFA and the NLS. However, work carried out by the evaluation team on this issue has reassured both teachers and policy makers of the fit between SFA and the NLS.

Second, a number of the SFA pilot schools faced school inspections during the first two terms of implementation. In the United Kingdom there is a government agency responsible for monitoring and inspecting the quality of educational provision in all schools. The Office for Standards in Education (OFSTED) is charged with inspecting schools approximately every 2 years. Their reports are placed in the public domain and as a consequence, the inspection process is viewed with trepidation by most schools in the United Kingdom. The shadow of school inspections therefore raised initial concerns that SFA would take time away from activities that need to be inspected. In practice, this proved not to be the case, as OFSTED inspectors were generally interested and complimentary about SFA. However, it did cause some initial anxiety and apprehension among teachers.

Third, elementary schools in the United Kingdom are much smaller than their equivalents in the USA. An average U.K. elementary school varies from 80 to 150 pupils whereas in the United States, the average is more than 500 pupils, double the size of the largest primaries in the United Kingdom. As a consequence, the regrouping of pupils following the 8-week assessments proved more difficult in the United Kingdom. With much smaller

groups of pupils to begin with, the regrouping often resulted in dispropor-
tionately sized groups. However, the evaluation evidence has shown that as
the program began to take effect subsequent regroupings were easier and
group sizes reflected a normal pattern of distribution.

As the program has become more established, implementation issues
have tended to move away from the practical to the pedagogical. The issue
of establishing consistency among teaching practices and ensuring that the
program is delivered in the correct sequence still occupies much of the facilitator's time. Indeed, the role of the facilitator has proved to be pivotal in the
effective implementation of SFA.

The training program delivered by the Success for All Foundation trainers proved to be an essential component of successful implementation. Although there were some initial concerns about the highly structured format
of the training, in retrospect teachers have agreed that this was necessary to
familiarize them with the program in the limited time available. Training involving all schools in the pilot phase and subsequently in the second phase
has been wholly positive. A collective approach has proved important particularly within the early phase of implementation of SFA. The mutual support and interdependence of schools has been a powerful motivating force
that has sustained the implementation of SFA. This collaboration among
schools and teachers has undoubtedly been a key factor in the effective implementation of SFA.

The evaluation evidence, however, has revealed some differences between schools despite an adherence to a common approach to SFA and
the collective efforts of the facilitators. It has shown that where schools
are running the program as intended, progress is being made and pupils'
reading scores have increased. Where this was not the case, the results
from the schools were not found to be as positive. In the pilot phase, the
evaluation data showed that the higher the quality of implementation,
the more rapid was the progress being made by pupils. Schools in this
phase were categorized as *low, medium,* or *high* based on their change in
reading scores (see Hopkins et al., 1998, 1999). They were also assessed
as low, medium, or high on the basis of the implementation checks, as
seen in Fig. 4.3.

It is notable that the two pilot schools in the high category for reading
progress were also in the high category for implementation. The two schools
in the middle progress category were rated in the middle implementation
range. In keeping with this trend, the school that scored lowest on the implementation scale also made least progress in terms of raising pupils' reading scores. Overall, this evaluation finding reinforces the importance of
fidelity of implementation and highlights the relation between program implementation and program effect. This relation is being explored in some

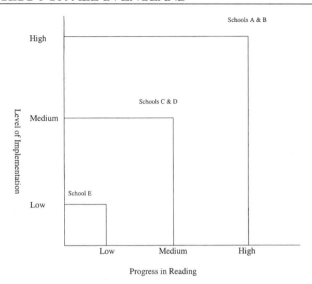

FIG. 4.3   Relation between implementation of SFA and progress in reading
in the pilot SFA schools in England.

depth as part of the current evaluation design and is an important dimension of the extended SFA program in the United Kingdom.

CODA

In policy terms, SFA is one of several comprehensive, school-wide models for school improvement that if well implemented, will significantly enhance pupil achievement. It has been shown to be effective over many years and in different cultural contexts (Slavin et al., 1996; Slavin & Madden, in press). In the United Kingdom, the piloting of SFA has demonstrated the potential of the program to raise literacy levels in areas of high underachievement and relative deprivation. As the SFA research highlights, those children most at risk of failing to read tend to reside in high-poverty families and high-poverty schools. Empirical evidence shows that SFA works exceptionally well in such school contexts (Slavin & Madden, in press).

Schools in the United Kingdom face the task of reaching challenging government literacy targets as they enter the next millennium. For some schools this is both a daunting and gloomy prospect given their socioeconomic contexts and record of poor performance. Although the NLS may be a necessary means of raising literacy levels, for some schools it will not be sufficient. It does seem important, therefore, to consider the potential of SFA to assist certain schools in the United Kingdom to raise their literacy levels. Although SFA may not be a program suited to all elementary schools in the United Kingdom, it does offer those in the most challenging circumstances the possibility of Success for All.

REFERENCES

Fullan, M. (1999). *Change forces: The sequel*. London: Falmer.

Hopkins, D., Harris, A., Youngman, M., Wordsworth, J., Hartas, D., & Slavin, R. (1998). *An evaluation of the initial effects of Success for All in Nottingham*. Nottingham, U.K.: University of Nottingham.

Hopkins, D., Youngman, M., Harris, A., & Wordsworth, J. (1999). Evaluation of the initial effects and implementation of Success for All in England. *Journal of Research in Reading, 22*(3), 257–270.

Slavin, R. (1996). *Education for all*. Lisse, Netherlands: Swets and Zeitlinger.

Slavin, R., & Madden, N. A. (in press). *One million children: Success for All*. Thousand Oaks, CA: Corwin.

Slavin, R., Madden, N. A., Dolan, L. J., & Wasik, B. A. (1996). *Every child, every school: Success for All*. Thousand Oaks, CA: Corwin.

5

Can Success for All
Succeed in Canada?

Bette Chambers
Success for All Foundation

Philip C. Abrami
Scott Morrison
Concordia University, Montreal, Quebec

This chapter describes the financial, procedural, and substantive challenges of implementing a school-restructuring program, Success for All (SFA), in Montreal, Quebec, Canada. The program was implemented in an inner-city school in which more than 50% of the students were coded as having special needs. A quasiexperimental study compared the reading achievement of 543 at-risk elementary students from one experimental and three control schools over 2 years, as measured by standardized reading measures. After 1 year, students participating in the SFA performed significantly better than control students on the Word Attack and Word Identification subtests of the Woodcock, and the Durrell and Gray Oral reading measures. After the first year, the Word Attack and Word Identification subtest scores were also significantly higher for the lower achieving 25% of SFA students than for similar control students. After the second year, the Passage Comprehension subtest was also significantly higher for these students.

CAN SUCCESS FOR ALL SUCCEED IN CANADA?

Substantial evidence now exists that the SFA program improves the reading performance of children in the United States and other countries, as demonstrated by other chapters in this volume. It is now being implemented in 44 states in the United States, and as Canada is the closest neighbor to the United States, one might wonder why Canadian educators have not jumped at the opportunity to implement SFA as well. This chapter describes the practical challenges of implementing SFA in a Canadian school with a high percentage of children with special needs. It also presents the findings of a quasiexperiment comparing the reading achievement of the SFA students with those from control schools, over 2 years of implementation.

The Problem of School Dropout

If children are not reading at grade level by the time they reach Grade 3, the chances of them dropping out of school before graduation are very high (Frymier et al., 1992). The societal implications make school dropout a serious problem for Quebec and Canada, one that threatens to "reduce the national standard of living, heighten demands on social safety nets, and increase the economic burden on individual and corporate taxpayers" (Conference Board of Canada, 1992). Quebec has the lowest literacy rate of the Canadian provinces, leading to problems for the social assistance network of supporting such adults and to a high loss of tax revenue. A report issued by the Montreal Island School Council (Hrimech, Théoret, Hardy, & Gariepy, 1993) indicated that the dropout rate for Quebec was 31%, with some areas of Montreal reaching 50%.

The parents of most school dropouts were also dropouts, which indicates the cycle of low-educational level, illiteracy, and poverty, illustrated by the statistic that 72% of adult welfare recipients have less than a high school education (Statistics Canada, 1996). Educators must seek ways to end this vicious cycle. There is a growing body of research on whole-school restructuring initiatives in the United States that indicates a promising direction.

Research on School Restructuring Programs

After decades of piecemeal educational reform and disillusionment with educational fads, there is a growing movement across the United States to engage in school-wide reorganization and dramatically alter the way in which learning takes place. Increasingly, federal and state funding is being allocated to schools to implement comprehensive school-restructuring models. In 1991, business leaders in the United States founded a nonprofit, nonpartisan organization called *New American Schools* to assist schools in implementing research-based, comprehensive school designs (New American Schools, 1998). After piloting 11 different whole-school designs in the mid-1990s, they eliminated three designs and began a 5-year process of scaling-up, expanding the designs to multiple schools and districts. The RAND Institute on Education and Training is collecting data on the scaling up process and the impact of the various designs on students. After two years, the Roots & Wings design, of which SFA is the main component, appears to be one of the most promising designs (Bodilly, Purnell, Reichhardt, & Schuyler, 1998).

SFA is designed to help children from disadvantaged backgrounds succeed both socially and academically (Slavin et al., 1996). It involves the restructuring of elementary schooling for at-risk students and the provision of tutoring and family support to ensure that these children avoid academic failure. The foundation of the program is the idea that every child can and must succeed in the early grades, and it is based on the principles of prevention and immediate, intensive intervention.

Research on Success for All

Extensive research on SFA indicates that children have demonstrated sustained improvement in reading achievement (Nunnery et al., 1996; Ross, Smith, Casey, & Slavin, 1995; Slavin et al., 1996). However, often when educational innovations are introduced there is much fanfare and high expectations, which can lead to a Hawthorne effect. The results from 5 years of research indicates that the difference between the SFA and control students' reading scores continues to grow with each successive year in the program; thus, novelty does not apparently explain the program's apparent effectiveness (Slavin et al., 1996).

Slavin and his colleagues (Slavin et al., 1994) reported that the program seems to be particularly effective for students who scored in the lowest 25% on the pretest, with effect sizes of +0.82 for first graders, +1.00 for second graders, and +0.98 for third graders. In a comparison of SFA and Reading Recovery, Ross, Smith, Casey, and Slavin (1995) found a mean effect size of +0.77 in favor of the SFA over Reading Recovery students on reading posttest scores. Despite these strong U.S. findings, few Canadian schools have adopted the program. Following are some of the challenges we faced when introducing the program to a Canadian school.

Challenges to the Canadian Implementation.   In attempting to implement SFA in Montreal, we encountered several financial, substantive, and procedural challenges. Some of these issues may prevent schools in

Quebec or in other parts of Canada from adopting SFA (Chambers, Abrami, Massue, & Morrison, 1999). First, in Canada, there is no equivalent to Title I, federal resources provided by formula to schools with many disadvantaged children in the United States. Currently, in the two largest Canadian provinces, Quebec and Ontario, the provincial governments are focusing on issues other than improving the reading level of elementary school children. For example, in Quebec, as of July 1998, the schools were changed from being organized into confessional (Catholic and Protestant) school districts to linguistic (French and English) school boards. School administrators were extremely preoccupied with this school-board restructuring, making the consideration of adopting new programs unlikely. In some cases until spring 1998, school-board officials were not sure which schools would be in which board. In Ontario, the government's focus has been on deficit reduction, which has resulted in the elimination of new initiatives and laying off of teachers and support personnel rather than of contemplating new programs.

Second, whole-language is the Ministry of Education mandated approach to reading instruction in Quebec and in some other provinces. In fact, Quebec was at the forefront of the whole-language movement in the late 1970s. Therefore, some of the experimental teachers were apprehensive about the structured phonics component of SFA, although many had expressed frustration with years of having little success teaching special needs students using the whole-language approach.

Third, because the majority language in Quebec is French, English mother-tongue students spend a significant portion of class time receiving language instruction in French. With the focus on bilingualism across Canada, French immersion is a popular instructional method in other provinces as well. The additional time spent learning another language leaves less time in the school day to schedule the 90-minute block for reading that is the focal point of SFA.

Fourth, teachers in Quebec are not accustomed to being observed by anyone other than their principal. In fact, their collective agreement stipulates that the only individuals who the teachers must permit to observe them at work are their principal and their regional director. Therefore, some teachers were uncomfortable participating in the implementation checks that are an integral part of the SFA program.

In the results section we report how these difficulties were overcome, allowing us to implement the program and proceed with a study that compared the SFA students' reading achievement to that of students in control schools.

Quasiexperimental Study. We predicted that students in the experimental school would demonstrate greater gains in their reading achievement than students in the control schools and that this effect would be most pronounced for the lower achieving 25% of students. We also wanted to determine if there were Hawthorne effects. If there were, then the Year 2 effects would be less than those for the first year; however, if the schools became more adept at implementing the program, the second-year effects would be stronger.

METHOD

Participants

This quasiexperimental study took place in four schools, one experimental school (232 participants) and three control schools (311 participants) in Montreal, Quebec. The schools served multiethnic populations, with the majority of students being bussed from a wide catchment area, mostly disadvantaged areas of the city. As we collected reading achievement data for those students over the age of 7 (Grades 2 through 6), we could only consider a subset of the whole sample for these analyses. Furthermore, owing to participant mobility and other exclusion criteria, the size of that subset varied across each analysis. The first analysis (1995–1996), for example, considered 269 participants (129 experimental and 140 control), whereas the second analysis (1995–1997) used the data from only 175 participants (88 experimental and 87 control).

The participants varied with respect to their age, first language, and special needs. At the start of the study in 1995, there were 135 children at the experimental site who had valid pretest data. These children ranged in age from 6.9 to 12.6 years with a mean of 9.5 years. One hundred-eighteen children spoke English as a first language, whereas 17 spoke a language other than English as a first language. Seventy-two (53%) experimental children were documented by the school system as having special needs. The predominant classification of special needs was *Severe Learning Disability* accounting for 39 of these children. Other special-needs classifications included mild learning and intellectual disabilities, behavioral difficulties (mild to severe), and moderate to severe intellectual disabilities.

At the control schools, there were 149 students who had valid pretest data. These children ranged in age from 7.3 to 12.6 years with a mean of 9.8. Again, English was the predominant first language, with 74 children. Forty-six children spoke a language other than English as a first language; 29

children were missing these data. At the control sites 26 (17%) children were classified as having special needs. Of these children, the largest category of special needs was mild learning disabilities, with 20 children coded as such. Other special-needs students were listed as severely learning disabled, behavioral difficulties, mild, moderate, and severe intellectual disabilities, autism, and physical disabilities.

Group Inequivalencies.   The experimental and control groups were somewhat different at the outset. As a matter of school-district policy, children experiencing learning difficulties were assessed by school psychologists and, if applicable, assigned a special needs code. A chi-square analysis (X^2 (1) = 40.35) supports the observation that the number of learning-disabled children in the experimental condition was proportionally higher than the number in the control condition. Moreover, the weaker students (according to a composite achievement score) in the experimental sample were on average 9 months younger than those in the control sample.

Mortality.   There was a substantial loss of subjects over the 2-year period. For example, of the 284 (135 experimental and 149 control) subjects who had valid data at the time of the initial pretest, only 190 were available for the analysis that compared pretest 1995 scores to posttest 1997 scores. Much of this mortality may be attributed to older participants graduating from the elementary school system. Additionally, there were a small number of subjects who switched between control and experimental groups. These subjects were removed from the study. Overall, the mortality appears to be random. In a multivariate analysis of variance (MANOVA) of pretest differences between experimental and control conditions, using subjects' mortality as a second factor, there was no evidence of differential mortality between the groups with respect to the pretest measures $F(6, 275) = 1.11, p = .358$). As the participants left the study, new participants entered into the control and experimental samples as the study progressed. However, no students introduced after the initial pretest session were included in these analyses.

Exclusion and Missing Data.   Over the course of the three measurement periods, there were 9 subjects (4 experimental and 5 control) who were absent during the first posttest period (spring, 1996). Rather than excluding these participants from analysis, the spring 1996 data of these participants were predicted on the basis of regressing the complete set of fall 1995 and spring 1997 scores on those participants of the appropriate treatment group who were not missing data. Otherwise, participants were removed from the analysis on the basis of listwise deletion on relevant pretest and posttest data.

The difference between the control and experimental students in their students' ability level is evident in a multivariate analysis of their pretest scores. A MANOVA of all relevant pretest reading measures indicate the groups differed significantly in their ability $F(5,273) = 4.39$, $p < .002$. Univariate Fs of the measures support these differences on all measures except the Peabody Picture Vocabulary Test (PPVT). The consideration of these means shows that the control group was substantially higher than the experimental group in initial reading ability and achievement. As a result, pretest scores were used as covariates in all analyses (see following).

Dependent Measures

Three achievement measures were administered to experimental and control subjects during the pretest and posttest sessions. All participants completed the Peabody Picture Vocabulary Test—Revised (PPVT-R; Dunn & Dunn, 1981), which examines a subject's receptive vocabulary utilizing standard American English. The median reliability of this measure is .81.

Three subtests of the Woodcock Reading Mastery Test—Revised (Woodcock, 1987) were administered to the Grade 2 through Grade 6 students: Word Attack, which evaluates subject's phonics knowledge, Passage Comprehension, which taps vocabulary skills and comprehension, and Word Identification, which assesses reading words in isolation. Subtest reliability ranges from +.84 to +.98 (Woodcock, 1987).

Students' ability to read paragraphs and answer comprehension questions was assessed by the Durrell Analysis of Reading Difficulty (Durrell & Catterson, 1983) or the Gray Oral Reading Test (GORT; Wiederholt & Bryant, 1992). A correlation of + .85 was found between the parallel forms of the Durrell Oral Reading subtests (Durrell & Catterson, 1983).

All participants were administered the Durrell Oral Reading Measure or the Gray Oral Reading Test but not both. Initially, the Durrell Oral Reading Inventory was administered to all subjects older than the age of 7 years. In order to compare our findings directly to Slavin's (1996), we began administering the Gray Oral Reading Test (GORT) in fall 1996 to participants over the age of 8 years, as Slavin and his colleagues had done. We continued to administer the Durrell to younger participants. The two measures, which both test oral reading ability, are quite similar and maintain similar variance within the groups over time. In fact, from a correlational analysis of participants who completed the Durrell in the spring and fall 1995 (as a pretest), and spring 1996 (as a posttest) and then administered the GORT in spring 1997, we saw a substantial and significant correlation between scores (r

Durrell 1995 / Durrell 1996 = .76, N = 281, p < .001; r Durrell 1995 / GORT 1997 = .78, N = 185, p < .001). These statistics support the idea that participants who perform well on the Durrell, perform similarly well on the GORT. To facilitate pretest and posttest comparisons of oral-reading ability, a single oral-reading score was formed by standardizing (using z-scores) either the Durrell or GORT measure (whichever was applicable for the subject).

Procedure

Implementation.   Our implementation of the program followed quite closely that prescribed by Slavin (Slavin, Madden, Karweit, Dolan, & Wasik, 1992), including the following elements: (a) a developmentally appropriate kindergarten, (b) eclectic reading programs, (c) 8-week assessments, (d) one-to-one reading tutoring for students experiencing difficulty, (e) a family support team, and (f) a program facilitator. These elements are briefly described in the following. See Slavin (this volume) for a more detailed description.

The SFA program calls for a half-day prekindergarten and a full-day kindergarten. Due to budget constraints, the experimental school had no prekindergarten and only a half-day kindergarten, whereas the control schools had half-day kindergarten and prekindergarten programs. This fact put our experimental students at a disadvantage. The kindergarten program that we implemented followed the Johns Hopkins guidelines by offering a literature-based program, beginning the Reading Roots component, as described later, half-way through the year.

As soon as reading problems were evident, students in Grade 1 were assigned to one-to-one tutoring so that they could catch up to their class level. One-to-one tutoring has been identified as an extremely effective form of instruction because tutors are able to respond to the individual child's needs and provide instant feedback on their progress (Wasik & Slavin, 1993). Due to budget constraints only one of the tutors was a certified teacher, the other two were paraprofessionals. There were not enough tutors to cover all students who required tutoring; therefore, priority was given to Grade 1 students.

The experimental school had a half-time program facilitator who was responsible for the achievement of program goals. The facilitator assisted the principal, teachers, and tutors and managed the 8-week student assessments.

The program was introduced in two stages. The kindergarten to Grade 3 students began in February 1995, and the Grade 4 through 6 students began in September 1995. A steering committee, composed of researchers from

Concordia University, administrators from the school board, the school principal, facilitator, and teacher representative, was formed to guide the implementation and research.

Testing.   Corresponding to the gradual implementation, pretesting was administered in three sessions in 1995. The first session, consisting of students from kindergarten to grade three, was conducted in February 1995, while the second session of Grade 4 through Grade 6 students was administered in spring 1995. New kindergarten and other students new to the schools were tested in fall 1995. All students were posttested on the corresponding pretest measures in spring 1996.

Analysis

The analysis of the data collected in this study addresses two questions. First, what is the 1-year effect on reading achievement through the implementation of SFA? This first analysis has 2 parts, asking the question for each year of implementation. The second question considers a 2-year effect of SFA on reading achievement considering the first 2 years of implementation together.

Group inequivalencies create difficulties in statistically comparing the means of the experimental and control samples, even with statistical techniques such as covariate analysis (Cook & Campbell, 1979; Huitema, 1980). The analytic method we selected examines effects of the treatment at different level of student capabilities using a two-way multivariate analysis of covariance (MANCOVA) on participants blocked to be in a common range on a composite pretest-achievement measure. We selected this statistical tool for several reasons. First, the four outcome measures (described above) used for the analysis are not independent or orthogonal. In order to maintain our Type I error rate (alpha) at $p < .05$ for assessing group differences, a multivariate analysis was essential. However, we also examined univariate Fs to further report group differences.

Second, as we were particularly interested in effects for at-risk children, we selected the ability ranking of the child as a second factor in the analysis. A participant's score according to a composite pretest achievement score determined whether the student was in the lower 25% or the upper 75% of their respective age group for the treatment condition. This two-way factorial method aptly partitions variance attributed to the treatment condition and to participants' at-risk determination, clarifying for whom the treatment may be more effective. In addition, as we were more interested in the particular effects of the treatment for low-ability students, we also report the results of an analysis for this subset of the participants.

Third, owing to discussed substantial group inequivalencies and characteristic differences between the conditions, we selected to first loosely block participants into a common pretest achievement range and employ an analysis of covariance model using pretest scores and other covariates. A description of the blocking procedure and covariates follows.

Blocking.   Owing to group differences and a multivariate analysis in which we cannot fully model the regression of pretest variables on to posttest variables, we selected to loosely block the participants from both samples to better equate the groups and reduce the likelihood of heterogeneity of regression lines between the conditions. This loose blocking procedure selected a subset of the participants who had a common range on a composite achievement score formed from a principle component analysis of pretest achievement measures, pretest age, and aptitude. That is, participants in the experimental sample who had a composite achievement score lower than the lowest score of the control sample were removed from the study. This method was likewise applied to the control participants who were above the range of the experimental scores.

It should be noted that any procedure that selects portions of a sample for the analysis should be applied with caution due to potential statistical regression effects (Cook & Campbell, 1979). In our case, however, the experimental group contained scores lower than the control group and we dropped the lowest of the experimental scores and the highest of the control scores. Consequently, any statistical regression that operates would work against the experimental condition and favor the control condition. That is, we would expect statistical regression to decrease the means of the experimental group and increase the means of the control groups.

Covariates.   We used numerous covariates to mitigate initial reading ability inequivalencies between the two groups. First, the respective pretest of each posttest measure of reading ability was used as a covariate (four pretest measures in all). Second, the PPVT was used to control for variance due to aptitude. Finally, the age of the participant at the time of both pretest and posttest was used to control both variance due to age and to differential time between pretest and posttest measures. We needed to account for the latter as the initial pretests were administered over a period of 8 months whereas the posttests were administered in a short (less than two months) period of time. Covariate analysis introduces the heterogeneity of regression lines for different cells as a new threat to validity and interpretation of results of analyses. Although it is difficult to establish heterogeneity of regression in a multivariate analysis with multiple covariates, we examined series of bivariate plots between outcome measures and covariates and between outcome measures and predicted values based on multiple regression. In particular, we looked for grossly heterogeneous regression lines and for repeated heterogeneous lines across multiple bivariate relations. Only one of these regression lines was grossly heterogeneous, and it is discussed in the following. Consequently, we conducted the multivariate analysis on the assumption of homogeneity of regression lines.

RESULTS

Overall, the results indicate that students who participated in the SFA program significantly improved their reading achievement over both years of participation.

Question 1

What are the 1-year effects of SFA during the first year of implementation? (The analysis for the first year data is a reanalysis of data reported in Chambers, Abrami, Massue, & Morrison, 1999). On the reading measures MANCOVA, we found a strong and significant multivariate difference between the SFA and control groups, $F(4, 254) = 3.70, p = 0.006$. A follow-up univariate analysis indicated that these group differences were present on three of the four measures: the Word Identification and Word Attack subtests of the Woodcock measures $F(1, 257) = 7.57, p < .006, F(1, 257) = 11.14, p < 0.001$ respectively) and the Durrell Oral Reading Inventory $F(1, 257) = 3.97, p < 0.048$). However, no significant differences were indicated for the Passage Comprehension subtest of the Woodcock measure $F(1, 257) = 1.61, p > .205$). The adjusted means of all four measures showed that the difference favored the SFA students over the control students (see Table 5.1).

These results support a main effect for the condition. We found no indication of any interaction effects between the treatment and pretest achievement range. Multivariate $F(4, 254) = .70746, p = .587$. In other words, there was no evidence in the multivariate analysis to suggest that the lower 25% of the SFA sample responded to the reading program any better or worse than the upper 75% of the sample, when compared to their control counterparts.

Question 2

What are the 2-year effects of SFA during the first two years of implementation? We repeated the same analysis as per question 1, except that we used

TABLE 5.1

Adjusted Means, Standard Deviations, and Effect Sizes for
Reading Achievement, 1995–1996 (End of Year 1)

	SFA (N = 129)	Control (N = 140)	Effect Size
Word Identification	60.67 (19.70)	57.39 (14.64)	+.22*
Word Attack	22.58 (11.22)	20.02 (10.86)	+.24*
Passage Comprehension	30.07 (10.46)	28.97 (8.85)	+.12
Durrell Grade Equivalency	3.51 (1.27)	3.26 (1.28)	+.20*

*p < .05.

spring 1997 rather than spring 1996 test scores as the posttest measure. On the MANCOVA, again we found a significant multivariate difference between SFA and the control samples: $F(4, 160) = 2.84, p = .026$. Furthermore, we found there was univariate significance on all the measures: Word Identification $F(1, 163) = 4.22, p = .041$; Word Attack $F(1, 163) = 4.35, p = .039$; Passage Comprehension $F(1, 163) = 9.59, p = .002$; and Oral Reading $F(1, 163) = 5.20, p = .024$. The adjusted means are reported in Table 5.2. As with the results from Question 1, there was no multivariate significance on the interaction of the treatment with pretest achievement levels, suggesting the treatment worked equally well for all participants: $F(4, 160) = .84, p = .501$.

To determine whether there was a Hawthorne effect in this implementation of SFA, we conducted another analysis of the second-year data separately. We repeated the same analysis technique: blocked the subjects to a common range on the pretest achievement composite (in this case the spring 1996 measures) and performed a MANCOVA using condition and achievement split as factors.

However, we used the end of Year 1 (spring, 1996) posttests as pretests for Year 2. Because these posttests were significantly higher in the SFA school than in the Control school, using them as pretests removes the first-year effect to allow examination of the unique contribution made by the second year of implementation. Although there was no multivariate main effects for SFA ($F[4, 206] = 1.40, p = .234$), we found evidence of interaction between group and achievement on the Word Identification and Passage Comprehension subtests of the Woodcock. $F(1, 209) = 6.33$,

TABLE 5.2

Adjusted Means, Standard Deviations, and Effect Sizes for
Reading Achievement, 1995–1997 (End of Year 2)

	SFA (N = 88)	Control (N = 87)	Effect Size
Word Identification	63.18 (15.45)	60.51 (13.11)	+.20*
Word Attack	22.43 (9.45)	20.47 (9.23)	+.21*
Passage Comprehension	32.83 (9.17)	30.30 (8.13)	+.31*
Standardized Oral Reading Score (GORT/Durrell)	-.21 (0.92)	-.45 (0.89)	+.27*

*p < .05.

$p < .05$ and $F(1, 209) = 5.24, p < .05$, respectively. For the lower 25% of the sample, there was a significant effect of the treatment on Passage Comprehension $F(1, 209) = 6.46, p = 0.012$ with the mean for the SFA condition (35.65) higher than the control condition (32.48; ES = +.46). For the upper 75% of the sample, there was a significant difference on Word Identification $F(1, 209) = 5.84, p = .017$, favoring the control condition (66.64 vs. 64.52, ES = +.23).

DISCUSSION

The first Canadian implementation of SFA made a significant impact on the reading achievement of these disadvantaged, at-risk children for both the first and second year of implementation. Our findings provide additional support for the use of a pervasive school-restructuring program to decrease the high rate of school failure for at-risk children. The results corroborate those found by Slavin and his colleagues (Madden et al., 1993; Nunnery et al., 1996; Slavin et al., 1996).

Although effect sizes remain relatively constant for Word Identification and Word Attack (between +.20 and +.24), albeit decreasing slightly from the spring 1996 to spring 1997 testing period, the effect size dramatically increases for Passage Comprehension (from + .12 [nonsignificant] to + .31) and for Oral Reading (from +.20 to +.27). These changes in effect size may indicate that it takes longer to have a substantial impact on higher level reading skills such as comprehension than on decoding skills. As the beginning reading component of SFA focuses on phonics, it is not surprising that the subtests that measure these skills demonstrate effects of the program earlier than the higher level abilities.

The effects for Year 2 alone corroborate these findings for the lowest achieving students. As we were particularly interested in the lower achieving students, we analyzed the data for the lower 25% and higher 75% of students separately. In the first year, the two groups were similar in their differences over the control students. However, for the second-year data, we found that the lower achieving students made significantly greater increases in the area of Passage Comprehension than similar control students. Again, it may be that it takes a longer time to learn those higher level skills.

There was little indication of a Hawthorne effect with the separate second-year analyses favoring the higher achieving control students on only one subtest (Word Identification). One may also question this finding as the particular cell for this high-achieving group regresses differently than any other cell for this subtest, adjusting downward their posttest scores and underestimating any treatment effect. Overall, these findings further support Slavin's findings that differences increase with more years in the program.

Limitations of the Study

Our study was limited to only one experimental school, a school that is somewhat different than most elementary schools in Canada today. The higher percentage of special-needs students at the experimental school is not typical of the composition of most schools; therefore, we cannot say definitively that the findings would generalize to most schools in Canada. The Quebec Ministry of Education has a policy of integration and therefore most schools have fewer than 15% of children with special needs.

Although special needs was added as a covariate, it did not fully remove bias against the experimental condition that was due to the relatively higher proportion of special-needs children in this group. This higher proportion was pervasive in both achievement levels (low and moderate to high). We would expect that special-needs children learn at a slower rate than those children not so classified. If the conditions were more balanced in terms of the proportion of special needs to total sample, we would expect experimental gains to be still more substantive. Furthermore, we need to be cognizant of peer effects. In a school with a significant proportion of children with learning and behavioral difficulties, there are fewer models of high-achieving behaviors for the low-achieving students to emulate, biasing the findings in favor of the control students.

We were very conservative in our analytical approach; however we were missing a considerable amount of data and used analysis of covariance, so our results need to be viewed with caution. Our findings are biased to underestimate the effect because statistical regression may be working differentially in favor of the control group due to the nature of the blocking procedure used. By eliminating the lowest extreme of the experimental group and the highest extreme of the control group, we would expect that the mean of the experimental group at the posttest to regress downward and the mean of the control to regress upward. Such differential regression would comparatively weaken any gains made by the experimental group.

Implementation Issues

The enthusiasm of the parents, the feedback from the implementation checks, and the initial progress of the children with the SFA program helped surpass some of the teachers' initial apprehension. Several of the teachers who had been the most skeptical became the program's strongest proponents. Due to budget constraints, the school board planned to merge the experimental school with one of the control schools. In large part because of the success of the SFA program, the teachers and parents from the experimental school protested so vehemently that the board reversed their decision.

The debate between whole language and phonics instruction seems to be abating with the mounting evidence that young children learn to read much more readily when they are introduced to reading through structured phonemic awareness instruction (Castle, Riach, & Nicholson, 1994). Only when we come to see that it is children that we are teaching—not a method—will we will be able to get on with providing whatever it takes to get a child to read, something that SFA promotes.

The procedural challenges were surmounted by patience, communication, creative scheduling, and physical organization of the classes. The teachers' reluctance to being observed for the implementation checks was eliminated by listening to the teachers' concerns, reassuring them that the goal of the observations was to provide them with feedback to help them implement the program effectively. The head of the teacher's union, who was supportive of the program, helped reassure the teachers that the implementation checks would not have any ramifications for their jobs. The scheduling problems were solved by having the Reading Wings component of the program divided into two time slots, one just before recess and one after. The Grade 1 through 3 classes were situated in close proximity to each other to reduce the transition time to the Reading Roots classes.

In order to overcome the financial problems, funding for the program was obtained from the school board's general operating funds augmented by research grants and a special grant from the Quebec Ministry of Education. However, if the program is to expand within Canada, school boards will need to find ways of integrating it into their operating budgets and provincial departments of education will have to reprioritize their budgets. Canada currently lacks the Title I funding for disadvantaged students that largely supports SFA in the United States.

In our present research, we are developing a computer-supported tutoring program to enable tutors who have no teacher education to offer a higher level of tutoring than they normally would without incurring the costs of having certified teacher tutors (Morrison, Aslin, Chambers, & Abrami, 1998). If this form of tutoring proves effective it could bring program costs more in line with Canadian realities. In one of our next studies various forms of tutoring, including cross-age tutoring and computer-assisted tutoring will be compared to see if we can reduce the costs of SFA without decreasing its effectiveness.

In the larger context, the promise of SFA means dramatically reduced costs for society in the long term. If social service agencies were to work more closely with the education sector, the extra costs for the school might be met. Canadian school systems need to undertake systematic schoolwide restructuring rather than piecemeal reforms so that a significant improvement in all children's achievement can be realized.

CONCLUSION

With creativity and perseverance, the initial difficulties in implementing *Success for All* in a Canadian context were overcome. The political issues revolving around the debate between whole language and phonics instruction is rapidly coming to a close as the evidence mounts that most children benefit from focused phonics instruction. The financial barriers will be overcome when the Canadian provincial governments realize that there are solutions to the illiteracy problem (Slavin & Fashola, 1998).

Success for All increased the reading achievement for the Canadian children in our sample, many of whom had serious learning problems. Based on the Canadian experiences and those of other countries in this issue, Slavin (Slavin et al., 1994) can claim with greater confidence that we can achieve success whenever and wherever we choose.

ACKNOWLEDGMENTS

The implementation and research for this project was funded by the Quebec Ministry of Education, the Social Sciences and Humanities Research Council of Canada, the Chawkers Foundation, and the Seagram Fund for Academic Innovation. We would like to express our appreciation to the staff, administration, and the students of the schools that participated in our study. Correspondence concerning this chapter should be addressed to: Dr. Bette Chambers, Success for All Foundation, 200 W. Towsontown Blvd., Baltimore, MD 21204. Electronic mail may be sent to: bchambers@successforall.net.

REFERENCES

Bodilly, S. J., Purnell, S., Reichhardt, R., & Schuyler, G. (1998). *Lessons for New American Schools' scale-up phase: Prospects for bringing designs to multiple schools*. Washington, DC: RAND Institute on Education and Training.

Castle, J. M., Riach, J., & Nicholson, T. (1994). Getting off to a better start in reading and spelling: The effects of phonemic awareness instruction within a whole language program. *Journal of Edcational Psychology, 86*, 350–359.

Chambers, B., Abrami, P. C., Massue, F., & Morrison, S. (1999). Success for All: Evaluating an intervention program for children at risk of school failure. *Canadian Journal of Education, 23*, 357–372.

Conference Board of Canada (1992). *Dropping out: The cost to Canada*. Ottawa, ON: Author

Cook, T., & Campbell, D. (1979). *Quasi-experimentation: Design and analysis issues for field study*. Chicago: Rand McNally.

Dunn, L. M., & Dunn, L. M. (1981). *Peabody Picture Vocabulary Test—Revised: Forms L & M*. Circle Pines, MN: American Guidance Services.

Durrell, D. D., & Catterson, J. H. (1983). *Durrell analysis of reading difficulty* (3rd ed.). San Antonio, TX: The Psychological Corporation.

Frymier, J., Barber, L., Carriedo, R., Denton, W., Gansneder, B., Johnson-Lewis, S., & Robertson, N. (1992). *Assessing and predicting risk factors among students in school*. Bloomington, IN: Phi Delta Kappa.

Hrimech, M., Théoret, M., Hardy, J., & Gariépy, W. (1993). *Sharing responsibility: An action program for the prevention of school dropouts on the Island of Montreal*. Montreal, QC: Montreal Island School Council Foundation.

Huitema, B. (1980). *The analysis of covariance and alternatives*. New York: Wiley.

Madden, N. A., Slavin, R. E., Karweit, N. L., Dolan, L. J., & Wasik, B. A. (1993). Success for All: Longitudinal effects of a restructuring program for inner-city elementary schools. *American Educational Research Journal, 30*, 123–148.

Morrison, S., Aslin, L., Chambers, B., & Abrami, P. (1998, May). Reading CAT please: A case study in progress. Paper presented at the annual conference of the EvNet, Montreal, Quebec.

New American Schools. (1998). *Blueprints for school success: A guide to New American Schools designs*. Arlington, VA: Educational Research Services.

Nunnery, J., Ross, S., Smith, L., Slavin, R., Hunter, P., & Stubbs, J. (1996, April). *An assessment of Success for All program component configuration effects on the reading achievement of at-risk first grade students*. Paper presented at the annual meeting of the American Educational Research Association, New York.

Ross, S. M., Smith, L. J., Casey, J., & Slavin, R. E. (1995). Increasing the academic success of disadvantaged children: An examination of alternative early intervention programs. *American Educational Research Journal, 32*, 773–800.

Slavin, R. E., & Fashola, O. S. (1998). *Show me the evidence! Proven and promising programs for America's schools*. Thousand Oaks, CA: Corwin.

Slavin, R. E., Madden, N. A., Dolan, L. J., Wasik, B. A., Ross, S. M., & Smith, L. J. (1994). 'Whenever and wherever we choose': The replication of 'Success for All'. *Phi Delta Kaplan, 75*, 639–647.

Slavin, R. E., Madden, N. A., Dolan, L. J., Wasik, B. A., Ross, S., Smith, L., & Diana, M. (1996). Success for All: A summary of research. *Journal of Education for Students Placed at Risk, 1*, 41–76.

Slavin, R. E., Madden, N. A., Karweit, N. L., Dolan, L. J., & Wasik, B. A. (1992). *Success For All: A relentless approach to prevention and early intervention in elementary schools*. Arlington, VA: Educational Research Service.

Statistics Canada (1996). *Reading the future*. Ottawa, ON: Canadian Government.

Wiederholt, J. L., & Bryant, B. R. (1992). *Gray Oral Reading Tests* (3rd ed.). Austin, TX: PRO-ED.

Wasik, B. A., & Slavin, R. E. (1993). Preventing early reading failure with one-to-one tutoring: A review of five programs. *Reading Research Quarterly, 28*, 178–200.

Woodcock, R. W. (1987). *Woodcock Reading Mastery Tests—Revised: Forms G & H*. Circle Pines, MN: American Guidance Services.

6

A Longitudinal Evaluation of the Schoolwide Early Language and Literacy Program (SWELL)

Yola Center
Louella Freeman
Gregory Robertson
Macquarie University, Sydney, Australia

Current concern with difficulties in reading largely stems from rising demands for literacy, rather than from declining absolute levels of literacy (Snow, Burns, & Griffiths, 1998). Consequently, in this technological age, the fact that a significant minority of students are leaving school without the ability to critically comprehend text poses a major problem for educators.

Most educators would agree that classroom instruction in the early years of school must be geared toward teaching children to read unfamiliar words in meaningful texts and to write unfamiliar words in meaningful messages (Tunmer, Chapman, Ryan, & Prochnow, 1998). However, agreement about the most effective way of achieving this objective has not yet been reached. For many children, the resolution of this instructional dilemma is not problematic. They will emerge as fluent readers and comprehenders of text, irrespective of the instructional programs that they receive. However, for approximately 25% of students at risk of literacy failure through social, cultural, or neurological disadvantage, exposure to the most effective literacy instruction, from the point of school entry, is essential to guarantee them a successful future in a competitive society.

Over 30 years of converging research data from cognitive psychologists, psycholinguists, neurospsychologists, neurophysiologists, and educators have established the prerequisites for success in literacy acquisition. Essentially, to get started in alphabetic reading, a child must be able to map the letters and spellings of words on the speech units that they represent. Failure to master word recognition will impede text comprehension and consequently decrease motivation for continued text reading, the ultimate goal of reading instruction. Although many children will induce sound–symbol correspondences simply from exposure to text, others will need much more systematic teaching to achieve the same goal. That is why explicit instruction in phonemic awareness and phonological recoding to draw a child's attention to the sound structure of oral language and to crack the alphabetic code must assume primacy in beginning reading acquisition. If early literacy instruction is primarily geared toward contextual guessing in order to achieve word recognition before sufficient sound–symbol translations have been acquired, many children may fail to grasp the alphabetic principle.

However, although an early code emphasis in literacy instruction has been clearly found to have a positive effect on skilled word recognition (Share, 1995; Share & Stanovich, 1995), attention needs to be also directed to another component of reading success. If we are to accept the simple view of reading as proposed by Gough and Tunmer (1986), empirically tested by Hoover and Gough (1990), and refined by Chen and Vellutino (1997), then we must accept that reading can be divided into two component parts: one that is unique to reading, namely word recognition and one which is shared with spoken language, namely comprehension (Gough, Hoover, & Peterson, 1996). Thus in order to be a skilled reader, an individual must be proficient both at the word level and at abstracting meaning from text, whether it be spoken or written. As it is probable that some at-risk readers will have difficulties in both domains, whereas others may have specific problems at the word level or in listening comprehension (Cain, 1996; Oakhill & Patel, 1991; Oakhill & Yuill, 1996), good quality prevention programs in the early school years should adopt a balanced approach to teaching early literacy by including instruction in comprehension as well as in word recognition.

Recent U.S. research into exemplary early literacy programs for students considered to be at risk of literacy failure has consistently demonstrated that explicit instruction in phonemic awareness and phonological recoding achieves better results in word recognition skills than programs targeting word recognition in a more implicit way (Foorman, Francis, Fletcher, Schafschneider, & Mehta, 1998; Hanson & Farrell, 1995; Vellutino et al.,

1996). There is also some evidence that explicit programs aimed at improving listening comprehension have proved effective for at-risk learners (Cain, 1996; Oakhill & Patel, 1991; Slavin, Madden, Karweit, Dolan, & Wasik, 1992). Because most children come to school with relatively well-developed oral-language skills relative to their word recognition skills (Gough et al., 1996), listening comprehension strategies, in the context of quite sophisticated interactive storytelling, can help children acquire knowledge about written-language structures and story grammar, increase their vocabulary, and develop their inferential strategies (Kerr & Mason, 1994). Furthermore, strategies specific to extracting meaning from spoken or written text can be taught alongside word-recognition skills in the early grades in order to facilitate efficient reading comprehension in the higher grades (see Cain, 1996; Oakhill, 1982, 1983; Oakhill & Patel, 1991, for a full description of teaching strategies for poor listening comprehenders).

Our interest in these two components of early literacy derives from determining optimal instructional practice in both word recognition and in comprehension for young at-risk learners. In a large number of low socioeconomic schools in New South Wales (NSW), Australia, we have been implementing and evaluating (Center & Freeman, 1994, 1996a, 1996b, 1997; Center, Freeman, & Robertson, 1998, Center, Freeman, & Robertson, in press) a whole-class early literacy program, derived from the U.S. program, Success for All (SFA; Slavin & Madden, in press). This program has been significantly adapted and extended for use with Australian school children in collaboration with researchers at Johns Hopkins University in Baltimore and is known as Schoolwide Early Language and Literacy (SWELL).

Like SFA, SWELL is a whole-class program based on an interactive-compensatory model of reading acquisition. The interactive-compensatory reading theory that underpins SWELL assumes that both psycholinguistic (top-down) and phonological processes (bottom-up) are carried out simultaneously and complement each other (Andrews, 1989; Pratt, Kemp, & Martin, 1996; Stanovich, 1980, 1984) but that the dominant role of each process occurs at different times during instruction, because reading acquisition is not equivalent to speech acquisition. Although the theory acknowledges the importance of semantic and syntactic processes in skilled readers (top-down), it recognizes the primacy of phonological and orthographic processors (bottom-up) in early reading acquisition. The bottom-up emphasis on explicit instruction in phonological awareness and decoding, particularly for at-risk students in the initial stages of reading acquisition, has been shown to be essential, although not sufficient, in avoiding literacy failure for this group of students (Adams, 1990; Stanovich, 1994).

Unlike SFA, the SWELL program spans only the first 3 years of school, from kindergarten to Year 2, and consists of three stages. The first focuses on the development of oral-language skills, listening comprehension, and early phonological awareness (Supporting Emergent Literacy), the second on the acquisition of phonemic awareness and word recognition in context through explicit instruction, as well as continuing comprehension instruction (Becoming Literate), and the third specifically targets the acquisition of listening and reading comprehension strategies (Towards Literacy Competence). Furthermore, whereas the one-to-one tutoring provided to low-progress readers in SFA schools is based on the SFA program, in NSW schools it is generally provided by Reading Recovery, a widely accepted individualized intervention for low-progress students.

The aim of this chapter is primarily to present a summary of results from all experimental evaluations of the three stages of the SWELL program. It also aims to provide some information about the interface of SWELL and Reading Recovery because these two programs appear to be less congruent theoretically than the whole-class programs operating in schools before the introduction of SWELL.

An overview of typical programs operating in non-SWELL classrooms, the components of the SWELL program and a precis of the Reading Recovery Program are presented next and are followed by the methodology used in each evaluation study.

EARLY READING PROGRAMS OPERATING IN NON-SWELL CLASSROOMS

In order to obtain information about reading programs operating in non-SWELL classrooms, teachers were interviewed by the current authors, and syllabus documents provided to all teachers by the Department of Education and Training were examined.

In their interviews, most teachers indicated that, in their first year of teaching, they had very little theoretical or practical knowledge about reading acquisition and were guided by the approach of other staff members as well as by syllabus and support documents. An examination of these documents indicates that, at least until 1994, the theoretical orientation adopted for reading acquisition was aligned more closely with a whole-language approach (top-down processes) than with the interactive one (alternating between bottom-up and top-down processes) that underpins the SWELL program. Reading was characterized as *the process of constructing meaning from texts*, and teachers were to use the following understandings about reading in order to structure their students' learning experiences.

- Learning to read should proceed from the whole text to consideration of the parts.
- Approaches to the teaching of reading should focus on the reader's quest for meaning.
- Students' views of what reading involves and its purpose are shaped by the kinds of written texts they encounter and by the contexts in which they experience them at home, in the broader community and at school.
- Effective readers concentrate on constructing meaning, employing a range of strategies to self-correct miscues when meaning is disrupted during the reading process.
- These strategies can be described as a cycle, involving sampling the print, drawing on cues to make predictions, confirming and correcting these predictions on the basis of subsequent semantic, syntactic, and graphophonic cues.

In 1994, the NSW Board of Studies published a new English K–6 Syllabus and Support Document (Board of Studies, 1994), which provided teachers with many more guidelines for literacy teaching than had been available before. However, the syllabus did not specify a developmental sequence for these outcomes, or systematic or explicit teaching procedures for their acquisition.

Thus, in non-SWELL classrooms, at the time the evaluation studies were being carried out:

- Teachers did not necessarily adopt a developmental sequence for teaching curriculum outcomes, as is specified in the SWELL program.
- Teachers were unaware of the importance of phonological recoding as the primary means for initial printed word learning, which is characteristic of the SWELL program, and tended to use syntactic, semantic, and pragmatic information in surrounding text.
- Teachers used shared book reading from Big Books to discuss grapheme-phoneme correspondences when they occurred in context (implicit instruction), rather than using individual phonically constrained stories for students to practice recently taught phoneme-grapheme correspondences in context (explicit instruction), as occurs in the SWELL program.
- Teachers did not undertake systematic assessment in reading accuracy and reading fluency (prerequisites for reading comprehension) as well as in spelling so that students could be grouped according to their rate of acquisition of these concepts, a mandated feature of the SWELL program.
- Teachers would not typically undertake performance grouping of students, or continuous accelerating and slowing of lesson material to accommodate chil-

dren's different rates of decoding acquisition, which is specified in Stage 2 of SWELL.

THE COMPONENTS OF THE SWELL PROGRAM

In contrast to the predominantly psycholinguistic (top-down) orientation of non-SWELL classrooms, the SWELL program stresses the need to alternate between top-down and bottom-up processes at different stages of literacy learning. An emphasis on a top-down approach characterizes the first few months of school as language and listening comprehension concepts together with early phonological awareness abilities are developed (Stage 1). The emphasis is then transferred to a bottom-up approach as explicit instruction in phonemic awareness and phonological recoding is instituted (Stage 2). When most sound–symbol correspondences have been taught and practiced in connected text, the emphasis is redirected to extracting meaning from print when skills and strategies in listening and reading comprehension are explicitly taught (Stage 3).

Stage 1: Emergent Literacy (Focus on Top-Down Processes)

- *Storytelling and Retelling (STaR):* In the first 3 months of the regular kindergarten year, a structured interactive program of storytelling and group and individual retelling program, of 20 minutes' duration, takes place four times per week.
- *Learning About Print:* Connections between Speech and Print and Concepts about Print (Clay, 1985) are taught systematically through Big Book activities and generalized in the STaR component.
- *Early (Shallow) Phonological Awareness:* Concepts such as recognition and production of rhyme and alliteration are systematically introduced in context through Big Book activities and generalized in the STaR component.
- *Syntactic Awareness:* Syntactic awareness is developed through the use of oral cloze and jumbled sentence procedures using familiar words and sentences from Big Book and STaR stories.
- *Expressive and Receptive Language Development:* The Peabody Language Development Program (Dunn, Smith & Dunn, 1981) or Classroom Listening and Speaking (CLAS) Program (Plourde, 1995) is used for 20 minutes daily to provide additional models for language use and expression as well as for development of specific vocabulary skills.
- *Emergent Writing:* Emergent Writing is a regularly programmed activity—accepting drawings, scribble, nonphonetic letter strips, and invented or conventional spelling as valid communication, and follows storytelling activities.

- *Intervention:* Listening comprehension activities are systematically monitored and assessed during the individual-retell sessions and small-group remediation in listening comprehension is delivered twice weekly by a volunteer as necessary. Children with difficulties in early phonological awareness also receive small-group assistance twice weekly by a trained teacher.

Thus all students who start Stage 2, Becoming Literate, will have had every chance to master the emergent literacy prerequisites prior to the systematic introduction of deeper level phonemic awareness skills and phonological recoding in context. Furthermore, receptive and expressive language activities are continued, and an extended version of STaR with emphasis on higher order comprehension skills as well as a writing program is added in Stage 2 to maintain students' comprehension, emergent writing, and vocabulary skills.

Stage 2: Becoming Literate (Focus on Bottom-Up Processes)

Becoming Literate is generally introduced in Term 2 of the kindergarten year and continues until almost the end of Year 1. It is suggested that for this stage of the program, the kindergarten and Year 1 classes are categorized in groups that are organized by reading performance for the 50-minute Becoming Literate lesson, with an extra small class being created for the most at-risk students.

A brief description of the components of Becoming Literate follows:

- *Sound–Symbol Correspondence (Phonological Recoding):* Sound–symbol correspondence is introduced systematically to help students crack the alphabetic code and is practiced in specially written (phonically constrained) shared stories.
- *Phonemic Awareness:* Later (deeper) phonemic awareness concepts of blending, segmenting, and phoneme manipulation are systematically developed and practiced through the use of known sounds.
- *Exception or Irregular Words:* Exception or irregular words are taught systematically to promote reading fluency and to enlarge reading vocabulary.
- *Shared Stories:* These are specially written stories to accommodate research indicating that students learn to read in meaningful contexts while systematically acquiring metalinguistic and phonological decoding skills.
- *Writing:* Writing as a communicative skill is included in the program, because reading and writing, being mutually supportive, are connected at each step to the learner's knowledge of the system of written language.
- *Spelling:* Spelling is taught concurrently with reading because they develop in parallel when the two are intertwined in a literacy curriculum. To enhance

children's knowledge about the orthographic structure of English, students are briefly introduced to orthographic constraints using pseudowords (Treiman, 1993).

- *Comprehension:* Comprehension strategies are developed through listening comprehension activities based on stories (at higher textual levels) and through reading comprehension activities based on Shared Stories (at lower textual levels).
- *Intervention:* Assessments are carried out at the end of every 10 lessons to check on students' accuracy and fluency in reading connected text and on their spelling. This allows for a regular rearrangement of groups for students.

In the Becoming Literate program in Year 1, the use of daily, individualized literacy intervention for at-risk students is suggested, using one-to-one instruction to complement the classroom program. Lack of funds prevented most of the experimental schools from implementing this procedure for its lowest achieving students in any systematic way. As an alternative, classes were grouped by reading performance for the 50-minute literacy lesson (the usual arrangement for SWELL) but the most at-risk students were placed in one or two smaller groups than the more able children, in order to receive more individualized attention. All children who were classified as having mild intellectual difficulties and most first-phase English as a Second Language (ESL) children were included in these smaller groups and, where possible, peer tutoring was also organized. When Reading Recovery was implemented in SWELL classrooms, it was used as the daily individualized intervention. These limitations to the optimal implementation of the SWELL program must be borne in mind when the results are being discussed.

Becoming Literate normally ends toward the end of Year 1 when most necessary grapheme-phoneme correspondences have been mastered. However, any at-risk students in Years 1 or 2 can avail themselves of Becoming Literate, either in class groups or in individual tutoring if they have not yet become unglued from print (Chall, 1983).

Stage 3: Toward Literacy Competence

The third component of the SWELL program is called *Toward Literacy Competence* and is designed specifically to address comprehension skills. It marks the transition from learning to read to reading to learn (Chall, 1983), and covers both curriculum and classroom organizational procedures. It is typically introduced in the latter part of Year 1 or the beginning of Year 2 and continues for about four school terms. It consists of Listening Together, a whole class program, Reading Together, where children are divided into performance groups (and where some children may still be completing Becoming Literate prior to starting Reading Together), and Reading Time, a whole class program. A brief description of these three sections appears below.

- *Listening Together:* During Listening Together (20 minutes daily), teachers and students are involved in the interactive listening comprehension of literary, factual, and procedural texts. Listening Together is subdivided into four sections:
  1. *Facilitating Comprehension:* In this section, teachers facilitate comprehension through developing specific comprehension strategies, such as activating background knowledge, discussing relevant vocabulary, providing a purpose for listening, and encouraging students to make predictions about the text.
  2. *Teaching Comprehension:* In this section, teachers teach, through direct instruction, more general comprehension strategies such as the difference between literal and inferential comprehension, text structure of literal, factual, procedural texts, and cognitive strategies such as representational visual imagery and the verification of predictions. Teachers also model metacognitive strategies, such as monitoring for meaning, as they read the text to their students.
  3. *Assessing Comprehension:* Assessment of both literal and inferential comprehension is conducted through the joint construction of story maps, where literal and inferential questions are posed about the text. In this section, grammatical concepts relevant to the text under discussion are also introduced and developed.
  4. *Extending Comprehension:* This section deals with higher order questioning about the text, including application, evaluation, and elaboration. Semantic webbing for literary texts and word categorization for factual texts are undertaken with students to extend their spoken and written vocabulary. Opportunities are also made in this section to expose students to the beauty and diversity of written language.
- *Reading Together:* In Reading Together (55 minutes daily), these listening comprehension strategies are applied through student partner work in the context of lower level text. Writing activities to parallel both Listening Together and Reading Together are introduced in this component, as are spelling activities to complement Reading Together. A number of at-risk students will not yet have finished the Becoming Literate component of SWELL and will be still completing this component while the other students are engaged in Reading Together.
- *Reading Time:* In Reading Time, the last 15 minutes of the comprehension program are devoted to students' independent reading of books that have

been matched to each student's independent reading level. During this time, the teacher listens to about three or four of the most at-risk students reading individually from their Reading Together book or from their Becoming Literate book if they have not yet joined a Reading Together group.

- *Assessment:* Summative assessment in Toward Literacy Competence is carried out once per term for an entire week at the end of 10 weeks of Towards Literacy Competence lessons. Formative assessment is undertaken at the end of each Reading Together lesson.
- *Intervention:* The lowest progress students will continue in a small group, either completing Becoming Literate or beginning Reading Together, and will be having individual assistance related to the mechanics of reading accuracy and fluency. In addition, twice a week, they will be receiving additional small group assistance, as in Emergent Literacy and Becoming Literate, with listening comprehension strategies that are linked to the whole-class Listening Together component.

A Short Overview of Reading Recovery

Reading Recovery is an individualized daily early intervention program designed to bring struggling readers who have failed to benefit from 12 months of reading tuition to the level of their regular peers (see Shanahan & Barr, 1995 for a full overview of the program). Although Reading Recovery is not considered by its practitioners to have a whole-language orientation, it does emphasize the constructive as well as the strategic process involved in extracting meaning from print during early reading acquisition. In general terms, its overall philosophy parallels the one articulated in syllabus documents followed by NSW primary schools until 1996. Klein, Kelly, and Pinnell (1997), in their chapter on Reading Recovery, quote Clay's (1991, 1993) statements that:

> "Children learn to read by reading and writing, and an environment that engages young children in a rich array of literacy activities supports children taking on the behaviors of good readers and writers. Writing is an analytic activity that requires close attention to print. It is through writing that children learn about the conventions of print, visual features of print, and how the sounds of speech are coded in print" (p. 163).

Further in the same chapter, the authors indicate that "in literacy learning, too, children construct their own understandings, but lean on the social context to weave meaning around their first interactions with written language" (p. 169).

As it has been clearly stated (Smith-Burke & Jagger, 1994) that Reading Recovery is only enhanced and supported in those schools in which Reading Recovery teachers and classroom teachers share a common theoretical perspective on literacy development, the question of whether its theoretical mismatch with SWELL will adversely its implementation in SWELL classrooms remains to be answered.

METHODOLOGY FOR THE FOUR EVALUATION STUDIES

Evaluation Study 1 (After 12 Months of SWELL): Stage 1 and Early Stage 2

In 1994, four Department of Education and Training elementary schools from two low-socioeconomic districts in NSW, Australia, were chosen to take part in a pilot evaluation study of the first two stages of SWELL. One school in each district, which had adopted SWELL as its early literacy program, was selected as an experimental school, whereas the other school in each district, matched as closely as possible for size and socioeconomic status, which had not changed its kindergarten literacy program, was designated as a control school. There were 87 students in experimental schools and 69 students in control schools with a mean student age of 72 months. Pretesting and posttesting of all students were undertaken in February 1994 (the commencement of the Australian school year) and November 1994 (the end of the school year), respectively. The tests used in the evaluation included a measure of reading connected text, a measure of reading real words in isolation, a pseudoword reading test, and a test of developmental spelling. (For full details of testing materials, participants and procedures, see Center & Freeman, 1997).

Evaluation Study 2 (After 18 Months of SWELL): Stage 1 to Mid/End Stage 2

For the second evaluation study in 1995 and 1996, six Department of Education and Training elementary schools in three low-socioeconomic districts in NSW, Australia, who had chosen to implement SWELL in 1995 were selected. Testing in all six schools was carried out at the end of 12 months, but the 18-month study, which is described here, is based on four schools only, as two schools withdrew from the evaluation after a change of executive staff. Results from the 12 month study were used as covariates for the 18-month evaluation and are fully described in Center, Freeman, & Robertson, 1998.

The 18-month evaluation was a within-school study, since testing was carried out in the same schools on Year 1 students (non-SWELL) in August, 1995 and on Year 1 students who had undertaken the SWELL program in August, 1996. As it was not possible to pretest kindergarten children in each of the schools before the implementation of SWELL to control for equivalence of subjects, the assumption was made that by aggregating the results of all participating schools in the comparison and the experimental year in a within-school study design, the effects of pupil and teacher variability would be partialled out as far as is possible in a study of this kind. (Furthermore, school effects were entered as an independent variable into the analysis). While these procedures obviate the difficulties inherent in a between-school design in terms of matching schools, the weaknesses in study design by this assumption of kindergarten equivalence must be acknowledged.

The final effective sample for the 18 month evaluation consisted of 134 students in the comparison group and 220 students in the experimental group. Mean chronological age was 78 months for the comparison group and 79 months for the experimental group. Tests used in the 18 month evaluation included a test of pseudoword reading, a reading connected text measure, a standardized test of reading, and a developmental spelling test. For full details of testing materials, participants and procedures for the 18 month evaluation, see Center, Freeman, & Robertson, 1998.

Evaluation Study 3 (After 24 Months of SWELL):
Stage 1 to End Stage 2

The third evaluation study was designed to see whether SWELL students maintain a literacy advantage over non-SWELL students at the end of Year 1 (after 24 months of school). In addition, by selecting schools for this evaluation which were using Reading Recovery as an intervention program for low-progress students in Year 1, we were also able to determine whether the two different classroom contexts, SWELL (code-oriented), and non-SWELL (psycholinguistically oriented) differentially affected the literacy performance of at-risk readers selected for the Reading Recovery Program.

This evaluation again used a within-school design, with Year 1 students in the same schools being tested in two subsequent years (1996 and 1997), before and after the introduction of SWELL as the regular classroom program. Three middle-income, non-Departmental elementary schools, which had been using Reading Recovery for at-risk Year 1 students in both the comparison and experimental year, were involved. The final effective sample contained 163 students in the comparison group and 150 students in the experimental group, with a mean age of 86.7 months and 87 months respectively. There were 18 students in each group who had received Reading Recovery. Tests used at the end of Year 1 for both the whole sample and the Reading Recovery students included a standardized measure of reading, a reading connected text measure, a test of pseudoword reading and a developmental spelling test. For full details of testing materials, participants and procedures, see Center, Freeman, & Robertson, in press.

Evaluation Study 4 (After 36 Months of SWELL): Stage 1 to End of Stage 3

The final evaluation study was undertaken in February, 1998, when all students in SWELL classrooms had completed Year 2, the third year of school, and most had also completed the last stage of the SWELL program (Toward Literacy Competence). In this study, six low-socioeconomic schools in NSW, Australia were selected for participation, four of which were Catholic schools and two of which were schools administered by the Department of Education and Training.

This evaluation also used a within-school design and compared students in the same schools before and after the implementation of SWELL. The comparison students consisted of all students at the end of Year 2 in the six selected schools who had not been exposed to the SWELL program for any part of their schooling. The experimental students consisted of all students in the six schools who had commenced school 1 year later than their comparison peers and had thus all experienced 3 years of SWELL. As classroom teachers administered the group tests (the standardized reading test and the spelling test) on two different occasions to all present and eligible children, and the remainder of the tests were administered on one occasion to a two-third sample, there were differing numbers of children for some of the measures (see results section).

It was not possible to pretest the comparison children at the commencement of their kindergarten year (1994) to gauge the equivalence of comparison and experimental subjects. The assumption was made, however, that by aggregating the results of the six schools in both the comparison and the experimental years in a within-school design and by using school as a covariate measure, the effects of pupil variability would be partialled out as far as is possible in a study of this kind. In addition, there were no obvious major changes in the neighborhoods that could have led to a shift in cohort level of early literacy. Although the procedures that have been used obviate the difficulties inherent in a between-school design in terms of matching schools, the weaknesses in study design by this assumption of kindergarten equivalence must once again be acknowledged.

RESULTS

Evaluation Study 1 (After 12 Months of SWELL):
Stage 1 and Early Stage 2

Table 6.1 shows the means, adjusted means and standard deviations for kindergarten classes in control and experimental schools on the four early literacy measures used at the end of the kindergarten year.

A Multivariate Analysis of Covariance (MANCOVA), using the pretest scores on the phonemic awareness test as the covariate, revealed an overall significant effect ($F_{4,154} = 9.55, p < .000$). Inspection of the univariate results indicated that only the Passage Reading Test, (reading connected text accurately and fluently), was significant, ($F_{1,157} = 12.91, p < .000$). The test of Developmental Spelling just failed to reach significance ($F_{1,157} = 3.06, p = .082$). There was no significant difference between the two groups on the other two tests of early literacy, the Burt Word Reading Test (real word reading in isolation) and the Word Attack Skills Test (reading pseudowords). These results indicate that the experimental group was significantly better than the control group in reading connected text both accurately and fluently, and there was a trend for better performance on the test of Developmental Spelling.

Because the experimental students in kindergarten classes had not yet finished the Becoming Literate Program (Stage 2) at the end of year testing, an error analysis of the Word Attack Skills Test was undertaken for the most at-risk students (the lowest quartile) in both experimental and control schools. The analysis indicated that 28% to 48% of experimental students were able to correctly read all words containing taught sounds, but none of these students could read pseudowords containing sounds that had not yet been covered in the lessons. The most at-risk students in the control group, however, were not able to read any pseudowords at all, suggesting that they had not yet acquired even minimal grapheme-phoneme correspondences.

Evaluation Study 2 (After 18 Months of SWELL):
Stage 1 to Mid/End Stage 2)

Table 6.2 shows the means, standard deviations, and means adjusted for both school and three measures taken at the end of the kindergarten year for all Year 1 experimental and comparison students on the four early literacy measures.

Multivariately, there was a significant difference between experimental and comparison groups ($F_{3,344} = 16.54, p < 0.01$). Univariately, the experimental group performed significantly better than the comparison group on

TABLE 6.1

Means, Adjusted Means, and Standard Deviations for
Kindergarten Control and Experimental Students on Four Early
Literacy Measures (12-Month Evaluation)

Measure	Comparison Group (n = 69)	Experimental Group (n = 87)
Expressive Word Attack Skills Test		
M	5.77	6.60
M (adjusted)	5.55	6.85
SD	7.15	6.30
Reading Connected Text (PRT)		
M	16.32	23.49
M (adjusted)	15.72	24.09
SD	19.12	17.39
Developmental Spelling Test		
M	42.44	44.53
M (adjusted)	41.08	44.89
SD	17.02	13.43
Reading Real Words (BURT)		
M	11.14	11.60
M (adjusted)	10.79	11.98
SD	10.18	10.60

TABLE 6.2

Means, Means Adjusted for School and 12-Month Measures, and
Standard Deviations for Year 1 Comparison and Experimental
Students on Four Early Literacy Measures (18-Month Evaluation)

Measure	Comparison Group (n = 134)	Experimental Group (n = 220)
Expressive Word Attack Skills Test		
M	4.51	7.21
M (adjusted)	4.50	7.24
SD	4.73	4.36
Passage Reading Test		
M	29.63	36.27
M (adjusted)	29.52	36.52
SD	28.65	26.13
Diagnostic Reading Test*		
M	22.19	25.57
M (adjusted)	22.16	25.59
SD	8.55	6.65
Developmental Spelling Test	(N = 47)	(N = 84)
M	18.55	22.30
M (adjusted)	18.38	22.22
SD	7.48	4.75

*Raw scores on the Diagnostic Reading Test indicated a reading age of 7 years, 2.5 months for the experimental group and 6 years, 10 months for the control group.

the Expressive Word Attack Skills (EWAS) test, measuring pseudoword reading ($F_{1,346}$ = 38.02, p < 0.01), the Diagnostic Reading test ($F_{1,346}$ = 31.62, p < 0.01) and the PRT test, measuring reading connected text ($F_{1,346}$ = 4.07, p < 0.05). The experimental group was also significantly better than the control group on the Diagnostic Spelling test ($F_{1,122}$ = 12.73, p < 0.01).

These results indicate that the experimental group still continued to significantly outperform the comparison group in mid-Year 1 on standardized reading measures, a test of decoding and spelling measures, even after controlling for their initial superiority at the kindergarten level.

We also examined the performance of the lowest quartile of students in both groups separately with respect to two critical early literacy measures. Because of the predictive power of pseudoword decoding (EWAS) for future literacy success (Byrne & Fielding-Barnsley, 1995), we looked more closely at the 18-month results of the pseudoword test for the lowest progress comparison and experimental students. Of the 30 lowest progress students examined in the comparison group, 26 (86%) were unable to decode the simplest phonically regular single syllable word consisting of consonant, short vowel and consonant. The remaining four students were able to decode just one simple consonant/vowel/consonant (cvc) word. Of the 54 lowest progress students examined in the experimental group, only 14 or 26% could not decode a single cvc word. The other 40 students ranged from being able to read from 1 word to 10 words accurately, with some students achieving mastery over more complex cvc words, cvcc words, and ccvc words.

As children's invented spellings serve as an indication of their current level of linguistic awareness (Tangel & Blachman, 1995), we also examined the differences between the spelling productions of each word of the lowest quartile of experimental and comparison children on the Developmental Spelling Test. It must be borne in mind that the lowest quartile of children in the comparison group is based on a 25% sample only, so that the number of children represented is very small, containing only 9 comparison students.

Table 6.3 shows the results on the five individual words on the Developmental Spelling Test for the lowest progress comparison and experimental groups.

Independent t-tests indicated that on three of the words, *lap* (t = -2.33, p < .05), *train* (t = -3.35, p < .01) and *pretty* (t = -4.96, p < .01), the experimental group evidenced a significantly higher level of spelling sophistication than the comparison group. On the word *sick*, and the word *elephant*, which is developmentally the most difficult word (see Tangel & Blachman, 1995), only a positive trend was observed in favor of the experimental group. Inspection of group means on individual words and an analysis of actual spelling productions indicated that the comparison group of at-risk spellers was able to access only the first letter of each word. Some children in

TABLE 6.3

Mean Developmental Levels of Low Progress Control
and Experimental Groups on 5-Word Developmental Spelling
Test (18-Month Evaluation)

Individual Words	Control Group (n = 9)	Experimental Group (n = 19)
lap		
M	1.67	3.26
SD	1.58	1.91
sick		
M	1.44	2.37
SD	1.13	1.46
elephant		
M	1.22	1.68
SD	0.97	1.16
train		
M	0.56	2.00
SD	0.88	1.37
pretty		
M	0.67	2.79
SD	1.12	0.92

the experimental group, however, were able to spell all three letters in *lap* and the blend in *train*, as well as approximate the phonemic structure of both *elephant* and *pretty*.

Evaluation Study 3 (After 24 Months of SWELL): Stage 1 to End Stage 2

Table 6.4 shows the means, adjusted means, and standard deviations for all Year 1 comparison and experimental students on the four early literacy measures at the end of Year 1.

Table 6.5 shows the means, adjusted means and standard deviations for all experimental and comparison regular (non-RR) and RR students on the four early literacy measures at the end of Year 1.

Multivariately, both the SWELL ($F_{4,3064} = 12.37$, $p < 0.000$) and the Reading Recovery ($F_{4,304} = 11.82$, $p < 0.000$) treatments effects were significant (the former positively, the latter negatively), whereas the SWELL by Reading Recovery interaction was not ($F_{4,304} = 0.16$, $p > 0.05$). A similar pattern was found in each of the four univariate analyses.

In the first univariate analysis, the experimental group containing all SWELL students performed significantly better than the comparison group containing all non-SWELL students (see Table 6.4) on the pseudoword decoding test (EWAS; $F_{1,307} = 40.87$, $p = 0.000$), test of reading words in connected text Passage Reading Test (PRT) ($F_{1,307} = 26.11$, $p<.0.01$), the standardized Diagnostic Reading Test ($F_{1,307} = 29.49$, $p < 0.000$) and the Developmental Spelling Test ($F_{1,307} = 37.16$, $p < 0.01$). Effect sizes, based on the Glass formula, ranged from $+.56$ to $+.69$.

The second univariate analysis indicated that all Reading Recovery students, whether comparison or experimental, performed significantly worse than students not receiving Reading Recovery (see Table 6.5) on the EWAS ($F_{1,307} = 23.31$, $p < 0.01$), the PRT ($F_{1,307} = 36.60$, $p < .0.01$), the Diagnostic Reading Test ($F_{1,307} = 44.62$, $p < 0.01$) and the Developmental Spelling test ($F_{1,307} = 23.47$, $p < 0.000$). Effect sizes, based on the Glass formula, ranged from $+.71$ to $+1.04$.

These results suggest that the reading proficiency of all students (both regular students and those receiving Reading Recovery) in SWELL classes was significantly higher than that of all students in non-SWELL classes. However, the results also show that all Reading Recovery students, whether in experimental or comparison classes, were significantly below the mean scores of all regular classroom students not receiving Reading Recovery. Thus Reading Recovery students did not reach the mean level of their peer group (as predicted by program developers) at the end of Year 1 when measured by the four early literacy tests used in this study. The absence of any

TABLE 6.4

Means, Adjusted Means, and Standard Deviations for All Year
1 Comparison and Experimental Students on the Four Early
Literacy Measures at the End of Year 1 (24-Month Evaluation)

Measure	Comparison Group (n = 163)	Experimental Group (n = 150)
Expressive Word Attack Skills Test		
M	9.08	12.68
M (adjusted)	7.18	11.18
SD	6.27	3.71
Passage Reading Test		
M	62.10	83.41
M (adjusted)	45.64	68.86
SD	41.56	36.11
*Diagnostic Reading Test		
M	31.14	35.08
M (adjusted)	27.62	32.38
SD	7.74	7.50
Developmental Spelling Test		
M	46.58	51.87
M (adjusted)	43.56	49.97
SD	9.28	7.11

*Raw scores on the Diagnostic Reading Test indicated a reading age of 7 years, 9 months (7y, 4m—adjusted) for the control group and 8 years, 1 month (7y, 10m—adjusted) for the experimental group.

TABLE 6.5

Means, Adjusted Means, and Standard Deviations for All
Reading Recovery (RR) Students (Experimental and
Comparison) and Non-RR Students (Experimental and
Comparison) Students on the Four Early Literacy Measures at
the End of Year 1 (24-Month Evaluation)

Measure	RR Students (n = 36)	Non-RR Students (n = 277)
Expressive Word Attack Skills Test		
M	6.97	11.30
M (adjusted)	6.99	11.36
SD	4.18	5.40
Passage Reading Test		
M	37.11	76.89
M (adjusted)	37.19	77.3
M	25.97	33.94
M (adjusted)	25.94	34.07
SD	5.53	7.62
Developmental Spelling Test		
M	43.19	49.88
M (adjusted)	43.22	49.97
SD	8.33	8.40

*Raw scores on the Diagnostic Reading Test indicated a reading age of 7 years, 3 months for the RR students and 8 years, 0 months for the non-RR students.

significant SWELL by Reading Recovery interaction indicates that there were no differential program effects. The SWELL program was of equal benefit to both regular students and to those students selected for Reading Recovery.

Table 6.6 shows the means, adjusted means and standard deviations for all Year 1 comparison and experimental Reading Recovery students on the four early literacy measures at the end of Year 1.

It is clear from the data shown in Table 6.6 that the experimental group of Reading Recovery students outperformed the comparison group on all four literacy measures, recording an 8-month difference in favor of the experimental Reading Recovery students on the standardized Diagnostic Reading Test. In addition, when the Diagnostic Reading Test was examined in more detail, the results indicated that 8 of 18 comparison Reading Recovery students were one standard deviation below their mean chronological age of 7 years, 3 months, compared with only 2 of 18 experimental Reading Recovery students. Thus, despite the mismatch between the theoretical orientation of SWELL and Reading Recovery, the SWELL program was better able to support its low-progress readers than a more psycholinguistically oriented program.

Evaluation Study 4 (After 36 Months of SWELL): Stage 1 to end Stage 3

Because not all students in this evaluation study were tested on all measures, and one school did not return results for the Diagnostic Reading Test for its experimental children, the efficacy of the SWELL program over 3 years was assessed through three separate analyses. Two separate univariate analyses of variance were performed on the Diagnostic Test of Reading and the Diagnostic Spelling measure, and a MANOVA was performed on the decoding measure and the listening and reading comprehension tests.

Table 6.7 shows end-of-year means, standard deviations, and effect sizes for all Year 2 comparison and experimental students on the five literacy measures.

The two univariate analyses indicated that the experimental group of SWELL students significantly outperformed their comparison non-SWELL peers on both the Diagnostic Test of Reading ($F_{1,422} = 17.94, p < 0.01$) and the Developmental Spelling test ($F_{1,569} = 30.07, p < 0.01$). As there was a significant multivariate effect ($F_{3,456} = 5.89, p < 0.01$) on the MANOVA, follow-up univariate testing revealed that the experimental group also scored significantly higher than the comparison group on the decoding measure ($F_{1,458} = 5.11, p = 0.024$), on the listening comprehension test ($F_{1,458} =$

TABLE 6.6

**Means, Adjusted Means, and Standard Deviations for All Year 1
Comparison and Experimental Reading Recovery Students on
the Four Early Literacy Measures at the End of Year 1**

Measure	Control RR Group (n = 18)	Experimental RR Group (n = 18)
Expressive Word Attack Skills Test		
M	4.72	9.22
M (adjusted)	4.76	9.23
SD	4.16	2.84
Passage Reading Test		
M	24.50	49.72
M (adjusted)	24.40	49.99
SD	12.05	25.43
*Diagnostic Reading Test		
M	23.11	28.83
M (adjusted)	23.19	28.70
SD	5.03	4.51
Developmental Spelling Test		
M	39.67	46.72
M (adjusted)	39.70	46.75
SD	10.11	3.82

[*]Raw scores on the Diagnostic Reading Test indicated a reading age of 6 years, 11 months for the control RR group and 7 years, 7 months for the experimental group.

TABLE 6.7

Means, Standard Deviations, and Effect Sizes for All Year 2 Comparison and Experimental Students on Five Early Literacy Measures at the End of Year 2 (36-Month Evaluation)

Measure	Comparison Group	Experimental Group	Effect Size
Expressive Word Attack Skills Test	(N = 221)	(N = 198)	
M	19.87	21.78	+0.21
SD	9.04	8.31	
*Diagnostic Reading Test	(N = 230)	(N = 198)	
M	37.93	40.94	+0.37
SD	8.09	6.00	
Developmental Spelling Test	(N = 300)	(N = 276)	
M	51.88	55.03	+0.42
SD	7.54	5.27	
**Listening Comprehension Test	(N = 244)	(N = 244)	
M -0.14	0.15	+0.35	
SD	1.04	0.94	
**Reading Comprehension Test	(N = 244)	(N = 244)	
M	-0.14	0.15	+0.28
SD	0.98	0.94	

*Raw scores on the Diagnostic Reading Test indicated a reading age of 8 years, 4 months for the comparison group and 8 years, 8 months for the experimental group.

**Standardized scores.

13.79, $p < 0.01$), and on the reading comprehension test ($F_{1,458} = 9.36, p = 0.002$).

These results indicate that the superiority of the experimental group, at the word level, not only continues at least until the end of their third year at school, but that SWELL students now also show to advantage on tests of both listening and reading comprehension.

In a subsequent analysis, the question of whether the better reading comprehension of the SWELL students was due to their better listening and decoding ability was examined. Following the simple view of reading (Hoover & Gough, 1990), an analysis of covariance was undertaken to see whether the difference between experimental and comparison students on reading comprehension, adjusted for school, still remained after further adjustment for decoding, listening comprehension, and the decoding x listening comprehension interaction term. Using the unique sums of squares approach, the results indicated that both decoding ($F_{1,455} = 35.2, p > 0.01$) and listening comprehension ($F_{1,455} = 91.4, p < 0.01$) were significantly related to reading comprehension, but the interaction term in our sample was not ($F_{1,455} = 0.24, p = 0.624$). Moreover, there were no longer any differences between the two groups of students on adjusted reading comprehension scores.

DISCUSSION

The results of all four evaluation studies indicate that children undertaking the SWELL program outperform their peers in non-SWELL classes on early literacy measures at every stage of the SWELL program. After 12 months in the program, when children had completed Stage 1 and were being explicitly taught to crack the alphabetic code in Stage 2, students in SWELL classes were significantly ahead of comparison students on a test of reading connected text, although only a trend towards better spelling skills and no differences at the word level on the part of the experimental group was evident at this point.

For children at risk, making the transition from home to school, this could well be an important result. The acquisition of automaticity in word recognition is a necessary, but not sufficient, prerequisite to reading for meaning. This is because automatic word recognition enables more cognitive resources to be allocated to higher level processes of text integration and comprehension (Stanovich, 1993, 1994). Early success with print is more likely to lead to greater involvement with reading related activities that will further increase proficiency at the word level (Stanovich, 1993, 1994). These positive early literacy encounters provide a natural progression to reading for text meaning, which, in turn, facilitates general cognitive development. Such successful experiences, early in a child's school's career, may prevent the negative spiral of cumulative educational disadvantage to which at-risk children are frequently prone.

Although the results pertaining to reading connected text discriminated significantly between experimental and control students, only trends in favor of the experimental group were observed on tests measuring the reading of pseudowords and real words in isolation. No doubt constant exposure to connected text, sequenced at the correct instructional level, was directly responsible for the greater success of the experimental students on the story-reading measure. However, it must also be stressed that, at the time of testing, toward the end of the kindergarten year, not all phoneme-grapheme correspondences had been covered in the Becoming Literate Program, which typically continues for another 6 to 9 months, until the middle of Year 1. The experimental children, therefore, had not yet developed a full repertoire of word attack skills, which would militate against great success in reading words in isolation. In connected text, on the other hand, context cues could have assisted word recognition for students with developing analytic skills in the experimental group. For many of the control students, however, who had experienced less systematic instruction in phoneme-grapheme correspondences, context cues, in the absence of pictorial cues, would have been less effective. The fact that the most at-risk students in the experimental group were benefitting from explicit instruction in decoding in comparison to their counterparts in the control group was clearly demonstrated when an error analysis of the pseudoword test was undertaken for the lowest quartile in each group. Twenty eight to 48% of low-progress students, after 6 months of SWELL, were able to read pseudowords in isolation, provided that they contained taught sounds. None of these students could read pseudowords containing sounds which had not yet been taught. In contrast, none of the low-progress students from the control group could read any pseudowords at all. This suggests that mere exposure to sound–symbol correspondences, which is the hallmark of most early literacy programs, had not been effective for this group of students.

By the middle of Year 1, after 18 months in the program, most children had completed Stage 2, with its emphasis on phonemic awareness and phonological recoding. The results of the second evaluation study indicated that children in SWELL classes were significantly outperforming the comparison group on a standardized reading measure, a test of decoding and a spelling measure, even after controlling for their initial superiority at the kindergarten level. However, after controlling for 12 month measures, the experimental group did not outperform the comparison group on reading connected text at the 1% level of significance.

This finding is consistent with that of Byrne and Fielding-Barnsley (1995), who found that there was an ordering of phoneme identity training effects from nonwords to regular words. The authors argued that this could arise from the need to rely on phonologically mediated decoding processes as against direct access on the basis of sight-word acquisition, which is more characteristic of reading real words in context than of pseudoword decoding. By August of first grade, when the children were assessed, the Becoming Literate program had been almost completed by most students, apart from those in the lowest progress groups. Consequently, children had been directly instructed in most of the common sound–symbol correspondences and were more successful, as a group, in paying progressively greater attention to the internal structure of the printed word than their peers receiving less systematic phonological instruction. This detailed analysis of the internal structure of printed words is likely to result in increasingly explicit and more fully specified orthographic representations, which promote greater word recognition (Share & Stanovich, 1995) and lead to greater text comprehension.

The superior results of the experimental group on the Developmental Spelling Test at the 18 month evaluation may also be explained by their more detailed analysis of internal word structure, which is particularly critical to accurate spelling (Frith, 1985). These results are consistent with those from other studies, which have shown an effect on spelling of phonological awareness training and explicit letter training (Bradley & Bryant, 1983; Tangel & Blachman, 1995). Indeed, they are remarkably similar, in terms of both means and standard deviations, to those reported by Tangel and Blachman, when corrected for the additional spelling word used by Tangel and Blachman in their assessment of spelling achievement for students midway through their first year. However, they are not consistent with spelling results obtained in a study completed by Byrne and Fielding-Barnsley in 1995, or with our own 12-month study, detailed here and in Center and Freeman (1997). Byrne and Fielding-Barnsley (1995) explain their failure to find significant spelling effects in Year 1 as resulting from an absence of letter training in their early phonological awareness training program. Our failure to find significant differences on spelling measures at the end of kindergarten in our first evaluation study may possibly be explained by the children's mastery over too few sound–symbol associations so early in the program, resulting in a less detailed analysis of internal word structure. The most important consideration of the significant spelling results midway through Year 1 for the experimental group, however, is that the shallow phonological awareness skills introduced in Emergent Literacy, followed by segmentation training and alphabetic coding instruction in Becoming Literate, enabled the experimental group both to sequence sounds properly and to use correct orthographic patterns in their spelling attempts more often than their control counterparts (Ehri & Wilce, 1985).

The fourth early literacy measure used at the 18-month evaluation was a standardized diagnostic reading test (Waddington, 1988), which measured sentence comprehension as well as word acquisition. The results of the MANCOVA indicated that the experimental group, as a whole, significantly outperformed the comparison group on this test. When raw scores were converted into reading ages, it appears that the experimental group had achieved a reading age of 7 years 2 to 3 months, whereas the control group had reached a reading age of 6 years 10 months, not an inconsiderable difference after only 18 months of schooling.

Although it appears that the SWELL program can enhance the early literacy abilities of children from the disadvantaged schools studied, we were also interested in its effect on the lowest progress children in the cohort, specifically those students who appear to be most intractable to implicit instructional practices. When the bottom quartile was isolated, it included only 19% of experimental children and almost 47% of comparison students. Furthermore, it was evident that this smaller experimental group had benefitted considerably from systematic instruction. At the 18-month evaluation, the experimental group was significantly ahead on the pseudoword decoding measure and the standardized reading test but not on reading connected text.

A qualitative analysis of the performance of the lowest quartile of each group on two critical early literacy measures, however, is perhaps more instructive than observation of quantitative differences. An examination of the separate performance of the lowest progress comparison and experimental groups on pseudoword decoding indicates that only 25% of students in the experimental group were unable to even partially decode, as compared with 86% in the comparison group. In addition, even the most successful children in the comparison group could only decode the very simplest cvc words, whereas some of the lowest progress children in the experimental group were correctly sounding out and blending ccvc and cvcc words. There is converging evidence (Share & Stanovich, 1995; Vellutino et al., 1996) that only phonological recoding offers a viable means for learning the large number of low-frequency words that cannot be recognized on a visual basis. Furthermore, although dual route theorists of word acquisition (Coltheart, 1978, cited by Andrews & Scarratt, 1996) distinguish between lexical and rule-based procedures for retrieving word forms, we would argue that Ehri's (1992) alternative view that skilled readers have developed lexical representations that 'amalgamate' the visual and phonological components of words is equally valid. Because SWELL students tended to outperform the comparison group on lexical awareness (as measured by reading connected text), the phonological recoding superiority on the part of the experimental group shown in this study suggests that the SWELL program is successfully promoting the acquisition of the independent word reading skills that are critical to reading comprehension (Andrews & Scarratt, 1996).

An analysis of results on the Developmental Spelling Test also reveals another interesting comparison between the lowest progress children in each group. When all five spelling words were examined separately, it was clear that the lowest quartile of children in the experimental group evidenced a higher level of spelling sophistication on four of the words than their counterparts in the comparison group with a positive trend only observed for the fifth word. It appears that the phonological/phonemic awareness training in Emergent Literacy and Becoming Literate received by the SWELL students together with their significantly greater ability to recode phonologically as a result of the Becoming Literate Program enhanced their accurate phonological representations of regular words. (It must also be remembered that this at-risk group was progressing more slowly on Becoming Literate, had not yet covered a number of grapheme-phoneme correspondences, and were only rarely receiving individualized instruction, unless they had been selected for Reading Recovery).

The third measure, which showed a continuing significant difference between the lowest group of children, was the Diagnostic Reading Test. Thus it is apparent, from both curriculum-based measures and results on a general standardized measure of reading, that the most at-risk students in the SWELL program are experiencing more positive encounters with literacy related activities and developing more analytic abilities than the low-progress children in more psycholinguistically oriented classrooms. The more efficiently a child can process spelling to sound conversions, the richer will be the orthographic lexicon developed by that child through a greater number of successful self-teaching trials (Jorm & Share, 1983). Such positive learning trials lead to the amalgamation of both orthographic and phonological representations in memory (Ehri, 1984, 1987, 1989, 1991), and the amalgamated orthographic representation is what eventually enables rapid and efficient lexical access (Share & Stanovich, 1995). Consequently, for our most vulnerable children, who may have not been necessarily equipped with the prerequisites and corequisites of reading acquisition at school entry, the SWELL program appears to have been successful in developing these critical word-acquisition skills.

The third evaluation study provides more converging data on the positive effects of the SWELL program for literacy proficiency in the early years, not only in disadvantaged schools but in schools that have a higher socioeconomic level. At the end of Stage 2, when all children had spent 24 months in the SWELL program and most low-progress students were finishing Becoming Literate, the literacy proficiency of all students in SWELL classes was significantly higher than that of all students in non-SWELL classes on all measures employed. The experimental group recorded significantly higher scores on tests measuring decoding, reading connected text, and developmental spelling as well as on a standardized diagnostic reading measure.

Once again, our particular interest was directed at those students most at risk of literacy acquisition, who were receiving Reading Recovery as their tutorial intervention program. The results of the third evaluation study indicated that those low-progress children receiving Reading Recovery in SWELL classes outperformed their at-risk peers receiving Reading Recovery in non-SWELL classes in the same way as had their regular classmates on all the four measures used, recording an 8-month advantage over non-SWELL Reading Recovery students on the standardized Diagnostic Reading Test by the end of Year 1. As the theoretical orientation of the Reading Recovery program tends to be more psycholinguistic than that of SWELL, there was always the possibility that the SWELL program to which low progress students were returned after intervention would not be as sensitive to their needs as the more psycholinguistic oriented non-SWELL classroom programs. As Shanahan and Barr (1995) in their review of Reading Recovery, stated, "an intervention may accelerate the progress of children, but if instruction is not responsive to the higher achievement shown by children, the promise of the intervention may not be realized" (p. 980).

The results of this study seem to contradict current views often held about the incompatibility of Reading Recovery, which has a psycholinguistic orientation, and progress like SWELL, which stresses phonemic awareness and phonological recoding in the early years of school. Not only did Reading Recovery students outperform their counterparts in non-SWELL classes on all early literacy measures, a qualitative analysis also indicated that they took less time in the Reading Recovery Program before discontinuation. This result is similar to the one found by Iversen and Tunmer (1993) in their modified Reading Recovery intervention that supported their hypothesis that children with reading problems will be remediated more quickly if they receive systematic instruction in sound–symbol relatedness. In the study cited earlier, this training was incorporated into the Reading Recovery intervention. In our third evaluation study, this instruction was a part of the regular SWELL classroom program. A number of researchers (Center et al., 1995; Iversen & Tunmer, 1993) have suggested that phonemic awareness instruction through reading as well as spelling sequences and more explicit code instruction in the Reading Recovery program could lead to greater reading proficiency. It does not seem to be adventitious that the Reading Recovery students from SWELL classrooms, where these prerequisite variables were explicitly taught, significantly outperformed students from non-SWELL classrooms where they were not. The most recent research on literacy acquisition for hard-to-teach students has indicated the need for explicit instruction in these skills as a necessary but not sufficient condition for remediation (Torgesen, Wagner, & Rashotte, 1997). A number of successful early intervention programs have already included these components (Slavin, et al., 1992; Slavin & Madden, in press; Vellutino et al., 1996). We agree with Shanahan and Barr (1995) when they suggested that Reading Recovery should also consider modifying its strategies to encompass those that have been found to enhance early literacy acquisition.

It is perhaps unduly optimistic to believe that children with specific phonological difficulties and those with a combination of phonological and general cognitive deficiencies, who are typical candidates for Reading Recovery, can be returned to their classrooms as full participants after a single period of intervention (see also Ross, Smith, Casey, & Slavin, 1995). It is quite evident, from our study, that Reading Recovery students, as a group, had not reached the level of their regular peers at the end of Year 1, irrespective of the programs operating in the classrooms to which they were returned. There is no doubt that some students who are experientially impoverished will only need a quick fix in order for them to rejoin their peers successfully. Others, however, with problems of a more constitutional origin, will need ongoing individualized intervention to avoid Matthew effects (Stanovich, 1986). Our results and those from other recent studies (see, e.g., Chapman, Tunmer, & Prochnow, 1998, 1999) particularize the point made by Shanahan and Barr (1995) when they suggested that it would be an unwise strategy to shift all resources for remediation to Reading Recovery because some students would be likely to require some additional support.

There is always the possibility that some criticism, particularly from whole-language theorists, may be directed at the choice of reading tasks in these three evaluations, as there was a concentration of measures at the word acquisition level rather than at the level of comprehension. There is no doubt that the ultimate goals of reading are the comprehension and enjoyment of printed language. However, for kindergarten and Year 1 children, who are reading connected text at about 30 to 35 words a minute, it would be difficult to find a suitable standardized reading comprehension test, aside from the Diagnostic Reading Test, to administer, particularly for those students most at risk (see Scanlon & Vellutino, 1997, for a good discussion of this issue). Furthermore, there is sufficient research evidence available to be able to state that the accuracy with which first- and second-grade children can read words in isolation accounts for 75% to 80% of variation in reading comprehension (Bowey, 1995; Hansen & Bowey, 1994b). In addition, if the Simple View of reading comprehension (Gough et al., 1996) is accepted, reading comprehension can be conceptualized as the product of decoding and listening comprehension. Consequently, although there is no denying that the skills of listening comprehension must be systematically instructed, the mastery of decoding skills is also essential.

This is why we find the results of the fourth and final evaluation particularly encouraging, in view of the criticism sometimes directed at the early code emphasis of the SWELL program. By the end of Stage 3, when most students had completed Toward Literacy Competence, which targets the explicit instruction of listening and reading comprehension strategies, students in SWELL classes were outperforming their non-SWELL peers not only at the word level, but also on comprehension measures. Experimental students were significantly ahead of their comparison counterparts on tests of decoding and spelling and on a standardized measure of reading, as well as on two curriculum-based measures of listening and reading comprehension.

As the third stage of SWELL includes explicit training in listening- and reading-comprehension strategies such as inference making, visual imagery training, and story event structure (see Center, Freeman, Robertson & Outhred, 1999), we anticipated that our program would be of particular benefit to low-listening comprehenders who have been found to be deficient in these areas (see Oakhill, 1982, 1983; Cain, 1996, for a full discussion of these issues). If we accept the dual-coding theory of Paivio (1971, 1991, cited in Gambrell & Jaywitz, 1993) that verbal and nonverbal information is processed in distinct, but interconnected mental subsystems, it is possible that explicit instruction in representational mental imagery stimulates the nonverbal system specifically. Thus it may be that our training program resulted in better organization in the nonverbal system by the formation of holistic nested sets of information (Gambrell & Jaywitz, 1993). What visual imagery instruction may have provided for poor comprehenders is a nonverbal conceptual peg, on which associated information is hooked for storage and retrieval and that can compensate to some extent for weaker phonological integration skills.

Furthermore, the combination of visual imagery instruction and narrative event structure training, which is a feature of Toward Literacy Competence, reduced the task difficulty for low comprehenders in a similar fashion to that found by Cain (1996) when she provided picture prompts to elicit storytelling. She reported that when stories were elicited by a sequence of picture prompts, less skilled comprehenders were aided most by this type of prompt and produced more integrated stories than in the topic prompt condition. It thus appears that teaching visual imagery together with story grammar is particularly effective for students with poor comprehension skills, as the mental model provided to such students may well reduce their processing load.

It should be emphasized that all the results discussed in these four evaluation studies apply only to a small number of schools and to the specific classrooms under review. However, despite this caveat, the results do suggest that the three stages of SWELL, which alternate between top-down approaches (early language and listening skills), bottom-up approaches (phonemic awareness and phonological recoding), and top-down approaches (listening and reading comprehension strategies) will raise the literacy levels of more students than the less structured classroom programs, more closely aligned with a whole-language approach, which operated in our control and comparison schools. It appears that explicit instruction at the word level, together with implicit and explicit instruction at the comprehension level in the first 3 years of school, will be of considerable benefit to both regular and at-risk students in both disadvantaged and middle-income schools. When we examined whether the better reading comprehension of SWELL students in the final evaluation study was due to their better listening comprehension ability or to their better decoding ability, we found that both variables were significantly related to reading comprehension, although the interaction of the two did not contribute any unique variance, thus supporting the simple view of reading, first enunciated by Gough and Tunmer (1986).

Furthermore, these results also indicate that a whole-class systematic program of reading instruction such as SWELL, with an explicit approach to the teaching of the essential prerequisites of literacy in context, appears to work better in combination with an individualized program like Reading Recovery for more students than the programs with a greater psycholinguistic orientation that operated before the implementation of SWELL. It thus appears that there does not necessarily need to be a theoretical match between classroom and tutorial program in order to achieve the best literacy results for low-progress students. This is not to say that other classrooms programs may not work even better when combined with Reading Recovery. It is also not to deny that an individualized intervention program, based on the components of SWELL and instituted for as long as necessary from the point of failure (as mandated in SFA), may work even better with SWELL than the Reading Recovery Program.

Our overall results are not altogether surprising because SWELL, though significantly modified for Australian conditions, has been modeled on SFA, a whole-class program for disadvantaged students, which has been systematically monitored for at least 10 years (Slavin & Madden, in press). The data presented by these authors demonstrates graphically that substantially greater literary success for disadvantaged or delayed students can be routinely ensured in schools through teacher commitment, parent involvement and the best available classroom programs. Of particular interest is the fact that the highest effect sizes are typically found for those students who are in the bottom 25% of their classes. Furthermore, the longer a school is in the program, the better the effects on reading performance seem to be for the whole grade. The results of our detailed investigations, carried out in a different social and educational environment, support these findings, both for the whole cohort of children in disadvantaged and some middle-income schools and for those designated most at-risk at the point of school entry. The SWELL program appears to have been instrumental in significantly reducing the early reading failure to which too many children in need have been prone. While we acknowledge cross-cultural difficulties when transposing a program from one country to another, we feel we have addressed local curriculum and organizational differences in our program, while maintaining the essential theoretical basis of SFA, which is consonant with all recent research in early literacy.

Finally, we must acknowledge a number of weakness of these evaluation studies. These include the nonestablishment of equivalence for the whole cohort of children at school entry in the second, third, and fourth evaluation study and the consequent aggregation of results for schools to partial out entry difference; the small sample size, particularly for children most at-risk; the fact that not all teachers in all schools had received a full in-service in SWELL; and the absence of a part-time facilitator in schools (as is customary in SFA schools) to ensure the smooth operation of the SWELL program. However, despite these shortcomings in study design and optimal implementation of the SWELL program, we feel that our four evaluation studies have contributed to our understanding of the most effective early classroom programs, and combination of tutorial and whole-class programs for at-risk students, with important implications for early literacy policy makers in Australia and elsewhere.

REFERENCES

Adams, M. J. (1990). *Beginning to read*. Cambridge, MA: The MIT Press.

Andrews, S. (1989). Psycholinguistics and reading acquisition the argument for decoding. *The NSW Journal of Special Education, 10*, 15–20.

Andrews, S., & Scarratt, D. R. (1996). Using lexical experts to investigate orthographic processes in reading. *Australian Journal of Psychology, 48*, 141Ÿ148.

Board of Studies (1994). *English K–6 syllabus and support documents*. Australia: Author.

Bowey, J. A. (1995). Socioeconomic status differences in pre-school sensitivity and first-grade reading achievement. *Journal of Educational Psychology, 87*, 476–487.

Bradley, L., & Bryant, P. E. (1983). Categorizing sounds and learning to read: A causal connection. *Nature, 30*, 419–421.

Byrne, B., & Fielding-Barnsley, R. (1995). Evaluation of a program to teach phonemic awareness to young children: A 2- and 3-year follow-up. *Journal of Educational Psychology, 87*, 488–503.

Cain, K. (1996). Story knowledge and comprehension skill. In C. Cornoldi & J. Oakhill (Eds.), *Reading comprehension difficulties* (pp. 167–192). Mahwah, NJ: Lawrence Erlbaum Associates.

Center, Y., & Freeman, L. B. (1994). *Emergent literacy manual*. North Ryde, Australia: Macquarie University.

Center, Y., & Freeman, L. B. (1995). *Becoming literate manual.* North Ryde, Australia: Macquarie University.

Center, Y., & Freeman, L. B. (1996a). *Towards literacy competence manual,* North Ryde, Australia: Macquarie University.

Center, Y., & Freeman, L. B. (1996b). *The SWELL tutor manual.* North Ryde, Australia: Macquarie University.

Center, Y., & Freeman, L. B. (1997). A trial evaluation of SWELL (Schoolwide Early Language and Literacy Program for at-risk and disadvantaged children. *International Journal of Disability, Development and Education, 44,* 21–39.

Center, Y., Freeman, L. B., & Robertson, G. (1998). An evaluation of Schoolwide Early Language and Literacy (SWELL) in six disadvantaged schools. *International Journal of Disability, Development and Education, 45,* 143–172.

Center, Y., Freeman, L. B., & Robertson, G. (in press). The relative effect of a code-oriented and meaning-oriented early literacy program on regular and low-progress Australian students in Year 1 classrooms using Reading Recovery.

Center, Y., Freeman, L. B., Robertson, G., & Outhred, L. (1999). The effect of visual imagery training on the reading and listening comprehension of low listening comprehenders in Year 2. *Journal of Research in Reading, 22,* 241–256.

Chall, J. S. (1983). *Stages of reading development.* New York: McGraw Hill.

Chapman, J. W., Tunmer, W. E., & Prochnow, J. E. (1999). *Success in Reading Recovery depends on the development of phonological processing skills.* New Zealand: Massey University.

Chapman, J. W., Tunmer, W. E., & Prochnow, J. E. (1999). *An examination of the effectiveness of Reading Recovery. A longitudinal study.* New Zealand: Massey University.

Clay, M. M. (1985). *The early detection of reading difficulties.* Exeter, NH: Heinemann.

Clay, M. M. (1991). *Becoming literate: The construction of inner control.* Portsmouth. NH: Heinemann.

Clay, M. M. (1993). An observation survey of early literacy achievement. Portsmouth. NH: Heinemann.

Chen R. S., & Vellutino, F. R. (1997). Prediction of reading ability: A cross-validation study of the simple view of reading. *Journal of Literacy Research, 9,* 1–24.

Coltheart, M. (1978). Lexical access in simple reading tasks. In G. Underwood (Ed.), *Strategies of information processing* (pp. 151–216). New York: Academic Press.

Dunn, L. M., Smith, J. O., & Dunn, L. M. (1981). *Peabody Language Development Kits* (Rev. Ed.). *Revised.* Circle Pines, MN: American Guidance Service.

Ehri, L. C. (1984). How orthograhy alters spoken language competencies in children learning to read and spell. In J. Downing & R. Valtin (Eds.), *Language awareness and learning to read* (119–147). New York: Springer-Verlag.

Ehri, L. C. (1987). Learning to read and spell words. *Journal of Reading Behavior, 19,* 5–31.

Ehri, L. C. (1989). The development of spelling knowledge and its role in reading acquisition and reading disabilities. *Journal of Learning Disabilities, 22,* 356–365.

Ehri, L. C. (1991). Development of the ability to read words. In R. Barr, M. L. Kamil, P. Mosenthal & P. D. Pearson (Eds.), *Handbook of reading research* (Vol. 2; pp. 383–417). New York: Longman.

Ehri, L. C. (1992). Reconceptualising the development of sight word reading and it relationship to decoding. In P. B. Gough, L. C. Ehri, & R. Treiman (Eds.), *Reading acquisition* (pp. 107–144). Hillsdale, NJ: Lawrence Erlbaum Associates.

Ehri, L. C., & Wilce, L. S. (1985). Movement into reading: Is the first stage of printed word learning visual or phonetic? *Reading Research Quarterly, 20,* 163–179.

Foorman, B. R., Francis, D. J., Fletcher, J. M., Schafschneider, C., & Mehta, P. (1998). The role of instruction in learning to read: Preventing reading failure in at-risk children. *Journal of Educational Psychology, 90,* 37–55.

Frith, U. (1985). Beneath the surface of developmental dyslexia. In K. Patterson, J. Marshall & M. Coltheart (Eds.), *Surface Dyslexia* (pp. 301–330). Hillsdale, NJ: Lawrence Erlbaum Associates.

Gambrell, L. B., & Jawitz, P. B. (1993). Mental imagery, text illustrations, and children's story comprehension and recall. *Reading Research Quarterly,* July/August/September, 265–273.

Gough, P. B., & Tunmer, W. E. (1986). Decoding, reading, and reading disability. *Remedial and Special Education, 7,* 6–10.

Gough, P. B., Hoover, W. A., & Peterson, C. L. (1996). Some observations on a simple view of reading. In C. Cornoldi & J. Oakhill (Eds.), *Reading comprehension difficulties* (pp. 1–13). Mahwah, NJ: Laurence Erlbaum Associates.

Hansen, J., & Bowey, J. A. (1994). Phonological analysis skills, verbal working memory, and reading ability in second-grade children. *Child Development, 65,* 938–950.

Hanson, R. A., & Farrell, D. (1995). The long-term effects on high school seniors of learning to read in Kindergarten. *Reading Research Quarterly, 30,* 908–933.

Hoover, W. A. & Gough, P. B. (1990). The simple view of reading. *Reading and Writing, 2,* 127–160.

Iversen, J. A., & Tunmer, W. E. (1993). Phonological processing skills and the Reading Recovery program. *Journal of Educational Psychology, 85,* 112–125.

Jorm, A. F., & Share, D. (1983). Phonological recoding and reading acquisition. *Applied Psycholinguistics, 4,* 103–147.

Juel, C. (1988). Learning to read and write: A longitudinal study of 54 children from first through fourth grades. *Journal of Educational Psychology, 80,* 437–447.

Kerr, B. M., & Mason, J. M. (1994). Awakening literacy through interactive story reading. In F. Lehr & J. Osborn (Eds.), *Reading, language, and literacy.* Hillsdale, NJ: Lawrence Erlbaum Associates.

Klein, A. F., Kelly, P. R., & Pinnell, G. S. (1997). Teaching from theory: Decision-making in Reading Recovery. In S. A. Stahl & D. A., Haynes (Eds.), *Instructional models in reading* (pp. 161–179). Mahwah, NJ: Lawrence Erlbaum Associates. Oakhill, J. V. (1982). Constructive processes in skilled and less-skilled comprehenders. *British Journal of Psychology, 35A,* 441–450.

Oakhill, J. V. (1983). Instantiation in skilled and less-skilled comprehenders. *Quarterly Journal of Experimental Psychology, 54,* 31–39.

Oakhill, J. V., & Patel, S. (1991). Can imagery training help children who have comprehension problems? *Journal of Research in Reading, 14,* 106–115.

Oakhill, J. V., & Yuill, N. M. (1996). Higher order factors in comprehension disability: Processes and remediation. In C. Cornoldi & J. Oakhill (Eds.), *Reading Comprehension Difficulties,* pp 69–92. Mahwah, NJ: Lawrence Erlbaum Associates.

Paivio, A. (1971). *Imagery and verbal processes.* New York: Holt, Rhinehart, & Winston.

Paivio, A. (1991). Dual coding theory: Retrospect and current status. *Canadian Journal of Psychology, 45,* 255–287.

Plourde, L. (1995). *Classroom Listening and Speaking* (CLAS). Arizona: Psychological Co-operation.

Pratt, C., Kemp, K., & Martin, F. (1996). Sentence context and word recognition in children with average reading ability and with a specific reading disability. *Australian Journal of Psychology, 48,* 155–159.

Ross, S. M., Smith, L. J., Casey, J., & Slavin, R. E. (1995). Increasing the academic success of disadvantaged children: An examination of alternative early intervention programs. *American Educational Research Journal, 32,* 773–800.

Scanlon, D. M., & Vellutino, F. R. (1997). A comparison of the instructional backgrounds and cognitive profiles of poor, average and good readers who were initially identified as at-risk for reading failure. *Scientific Studies of Reading, 1,* 191–215.

Shanahan, M., & Barr, R. (1995). Reading Recovery: An independent evaluation of the effects of an early instructional intervention for at-risk learners. *Reading Research Quarterly, 30*(4), 958–996.

Share, D. L. (1995). Phonological recording and self-teaching. Sina qua non of reading acquisition. *Cognition, 55,* 151—218.

Share, D. L., & Stanovich, K. E. (1995). Cognitive processes in early reading development: A model of acquisition and individual differences. *Issues in education: contributions from Educational Psychology, 1,* 1–57.

Slavin, R. E., & Madden, N. A. (in press). *One million children: Success for All*. Thousand Oaks, CA: Corwin.

Slavin, R. E., Madden, N. A., Dolan, L. J., Wasik, B. A., Ross, S. M., & Smith, J. S. (1994). 'Whenever and wherever we choose.' The replication of Success for All. *Phi Delta Kappan, 75*(8), 639–647.

Slavin, R. E., Madden, N. A., Karweit, N. L., Dolan, L., & Wasik, B. A. (1992). *Success for All: A relentless approach to prevention and early intervention in elementary schools*. Arlington, VA: Educational Research Service.

Smith-Burke, M. T., & Jagger, A.M. (1994). Implementing Reading Recovery in New York: Insight from the first two years. In Hiebert, E. H., & Taylor, B. M., (Eds.), *Getting reading rights from the start* (pp. 63–84. Boston, MA: Allyn & Bacon.

Stanovich, K. E. (1980). Toward an interactive-compensatory model of individual differences in the development of reading fluency. *Reading Research Quarterly, 16*, 32–71.

Snow, C. E., Burns, M. S., & Griffin, P. (Eds.). (1998). *Preventing reading difficulties in young children*. National Research Council Washington, DC: National Academic Press.

Stanovich, K. E. (1984). The interactive-compensatory model of reading: A confluence of developmental, experimental and educational psychology. *Remedial and Special Education, 5*, 11–19.

Stanovich, K. E. (1986). Matthew effects in reading: Some consequences of individual differences in the acquisition of literacy. *Reading Research Quarterly, 21*, 360–407.

Stanovich, K. E. (1993). Romance and reality. *The Reading Teacher, 47*(4), 280–290.

Stanovich, K. E. (1994). Constructivism in Reading Education. *The Journal of Special Education, 3*, 259–274.

Tangel, D. M., & Blachman, B. A. (1995). Effect of phoneme awareness instruction on the invented spelling of first-grade children: A one-year follow-up. *Journal of Reading Behavior, 27*, 153–185.

Torgesen, J. K., Wagner, R. K., & Rashotte, C. A. (1997). Prevention and remediation of severe reading disabilities: Keeping the end in mind. *Scientific Studies of Reading, 1*, 217–234.

Tunmer, W. E., Chapman, J. W., Ryan, H. A., & Prochnow, J. E. (1998). The importance of providing beginning readers with explicit training in phonological processing skills. *Australian Journal of Learning Disabilities, 3*, 4–14.

Treiman, R. (1993). *Beginning to spell*. New York: Oxford University Press.

Vellutino, F. R., Scanlon, D. M., Sipay, E. R., Small, S. G., Pratt, A., Chen, R., & Denckla, M. B. (1996). Cognitive profiles of difficult-to-remediate and readily remediated poor readers: Early intervention as a vehicle for distinguishing between cognitive and experiential deficits as basic causes of specific reading disability. *Journal of Educational Psychology, 88*, 601–638.

Waddington, N. J. (1988). *Diagnostic reading and spelling tests*. Ingle Farm, Australia: Waddington Educational Resources.

7

Success for All:
A Community Model
for Advancing Arabs
and Jews in Israel

Rachel Hertz-Lazarowitz
University of Haifa, Israel

INTRODUCTION: SUCCESS FOR ALL
AND ALASH: LITERACY IN COOPERATIVE LEARNING
IN THE ISRAELI CONTEXT

This chapter presents a community model of implementation and evaluation research on Success for All (SFA) and ALASH, an Israeli adaptation of Bilingual Cooperative Integrated Reading and Composition (BCIRC; Calderon, Tinajero, & Hertz-Lazarowitz, 1992) in Acre, an Arab-Jewish mixed ethnic community in Israel. These two cooperative learning (CL) methods are best known as powerful innovations for literacy development for all students, especially for at-risk students, from kindergarten through elementary school. The programs create a school-wide commitment to give all children the skills, tools, and hopes to become competent readers and effective writers, and thus become literate citizens in society (Slavin, Madden, Dolan, & Wasik, 1996). The potential of these programs to advance children, teachers, schools, and communities are the focus of this chapter.

More than 1,500 schools are working in the United States following the vision and practice of SFA with its various subprograms. In Israel the term SFA refers to a program used in the United States in the early years of elementary school. ALASH follows the SFA Language Arts program for the third to sixth grades. The two programs were adopted and implemented in Israel, building on the long tradition of CL in Israel. In recent years, SFA has created an international movement in many countries around the world, both in direct application and in influencing similar developments. Since 1993, SFA and ALASH have been implemented in Israeli schools (Hertz-Lazarowitz, Schaedel, Calderón, & Tinajero, 1993; Hertz-Lazarowitz & Schaedel, 1997).

Cooperative learning methods have been prominent within the Israeli educational context and its culture for half a century. Its roots were in the ideology of communal cooperation and equality of the Kibbutzim and the Zionist movement. Small group work in schools was widely present during the years 1920 through 1950. In 1948, with the establishment of the State of Israel and the creation of the *Melting Pot* ideology, direct whole-class teaching became the prominent form of schooling (Hertz-Lazarowitz & Zelniker, 1995, 1999). In the 1970s, two books criticized the disappearance of small group teaching (SGT) from Israeli schools and called for reestablishing CL methods in the classrooms (Sharan & Hertz-Lazarowitz, 1978; Sharan & Sharan, 1974).

In July 1979, educators and researchers from many countries met in Tel-Aviv and founded the International Association for the Study of Cooperation in Education (IASCE). Since then the dialogue between researchers and educators of CL from different cultures and countries has made CL a global educational movement backed with theory, research, and implementation. Since the 1980s, CL methods in Israel and elsewhere were developed, refined, and creatively adapted to the Israeli context (see Lazarowitz & Hertz-Lazarowitz 1998; Sharan, 1994; Sharan & Hertz-Lazarowitz, 1981).

CL was implemented in Israel until the early 1990s mainly in the upper elementary grades and junior high schools, language arts, social studies, math, and science (Lazarowitz, 1995; Rich & Ben-Ari, 1994; Sharan & Shachar, 1988). In 1995, SFA was introduced for reading and writing instruction in first grade in one school in Acre, after ALASH had been in the schools for 2 years. In Israel, entering first and second grades with new programs was a daring endeavor. The window of opportunity opened when Acre, a Jewish-Arab mixed city in northern Israel, became a part of a holistic educational project funded by the Israeli Ministry of Education.

Its overall goal was to empower the educational community to unite to make a difference in their schools and in the city. Acre chose SFA and ALASH as their primary pedagogy (Hertz-Lazarowitz, 1999b). The significance of the work in Acre derived from the city's decision to become a SFA cooperative learning community.

This chapter presents and discusses two important issues. One relates to the different stages of building an SFA community with a city-wide research and evaluation model. The second is to present the development and use of evaluation that measured academic outcomes in a long-term research process. This process gradually included all the children in Acre.

Two long-term sets of research are presented, one reading and writing in Arabic and Hebrew of third to sixth graders from 1993 through 1996, and later the academic outcomes of almost all first graders in Acre in reading and writing. This research gives strong support to the power of SFA and ALASH to advance children from diverse cultural background in literacy development in two languages: Hebrew as a first language (L1) for Jews and as a second language (L2) for Arabs, and Arabic as L1 for Arab students. The chapter concludes with perspectives on how to build communities for SFA.

BACKGROUND OF ACRE

The city of Acre is one of the most ancient ports on the Mediterranean. It is a beautiful city with a history going back 4,000 years. It has survived many ruling nations, has seen the rise and fall of the empires of Greece and Rome, battles between Muslims and Christians, and in the modern era the war between the Ottoman empire and the British crown. Before 1947, Acre was mainly an Arab city with a small but stable Jewish community. After the war of independence in 1948, the population composition changed and Acre became a multinational, multiethnic, and multireligious city, embraced by an ancient wall, but also divided by many social, national, and political groups.

The 22 schools in Acre are fully segregated by national and religious boundaries; Jewish children attend only Jewish schools in three sectors: secular, religious, and orthodox, in which Hebrew is the first language of instruction. Arab children attend only Arab schools, where Arabic is the language of instruction. Beside these four main school divisions by sectors and religion, there is also a private Arabic school run by the Catholic Church. Even within sectors there is often wide variation in socioeconomic status and other factors. This educational tapestry of Acre, composed of 50,000 inhabitants, 15,000 school students, and 1,000 educators, was a challenge for this community-wide project.

The Acre school system mirrors the multicultural and sometimes conflictual context of the socioeconomically mixed city. In interviews with city residents, two major concerns were salient. One was the flight of people from the city, and the other was the changing population composition of the city. The following quotations are taken from interviews with Acre educators (Eden, Hertz-Lazarowitz, & Ben-Shushan, 1998; Hertz-Lazarowitz, 1999b). One teacher said, "The population is leaving the city to neighboring small cities." Another said, "The Arab population is growing in Acre, in numbers that will make Acre in 10 years the major Arab city in northern Israel." Whereas Jews were concerned with decreasing numbers of Jews in the city, the Arabs were critical about their growing poverty and the unequal allocation of resources such as housing, jobs, and education.

Many of the people we talked to were quite doubtful about the chance of the holistic project to make a difference, but also wanted to hang on to some hope. Two statements were frequently heard. One recalled the history of Acre: "Acre is a tough and stubborn city, even Napoleon could not conquer the city with his guns." The other was: "there is so much to do here, and even small changes will be a huge success."

Although the socioeconomic and political context of Acre were perceived as gloomy, everyone in the city spoke with respect about the educational system, more for the preschool and elementary level than for the secondary level. The Jewish educational system was perceived as being much better then the Arab one. Most of the school principals and community leaders denied or ignored the severity of the socionational problems in Acre. It was one of the secrets everyone knew but no one talked about. It touched deep anxieties of Jews and Arabs regarding the nature of future coexistence in Israel (Eden et al., 1998).

When focusing on the schools in the city, it was evident that the level and function of the educational system in Acre was thought to be much better than the overall functioning of the city. The schools were "the diamonds of the city." However in order to get resources for their schools, principals had to work with the political leadership, and they did so by being "lonely wolves," as one principal put it. Principals indeed tried to maximize gains for their schools, with constant battles based on tough competition and rivalry for assigning children to their schools because the population is in decline. They fought to get resources from a political system that was not fully predictable or stable, while trying to pursue academic excellence in a highly heterogeneous population, with academic outcomes in decline. Both in the Arab and the Jewish sectors, many classrooms have 50% to 70% percent of students from low socioeconomic levels. In the Jewish sector many students are recent immigrants to Israel.

The principals reported being isolated and separated within each sector, secular and religious, and between the Jews and the Arabs. One principal said, "We are all in a bus that is stuck. Everyone thinks only of his or her school, so no one will help to pull this bus out, so we go nowhere."

SFA AND ALASH: ACRE CHANGE PLAN

Cooperative learning methods for literacy development were suggested to the schools in Acre. Those included Success for All (SFA) (Slavin & Madden, in press), and ALASH Cooperative Learning and Literacy (Hertz-Lazarowitz et al., 1993), an Israeli extension of BCIRC (Calderon, Hertz-Lazarowitz, & Slavin, 1998; Calderon et al., 1992).

The implementation of CL in Acre was based on long-term experience and research in school change in diverse context. The systemic approach guided the development of the project at the level of the classroom, the school, the community, and the district. The model suggested the connections and coordination among those systems.

The classroom was observed as the core system for change following the six interrelated mirrors of the classroom model (Hertz-Lazarowitz, 1992): physical organization of the classroom, the learning task, teacher instructional behavior, teacher communicative behavior, student academic behavior, and student social behavior (see Fig. 7.1). The metaphor *mirrors* is used to express the view that the dimensions that characterize the classroom setting are interrelated; structures and activities in one dimension or /mirror are reflected in each dimension. The relationships can range from maximum coordination to minimum coordination and disharmony. When the classroom is functioning on similar levels of complexity in each of the dimensions, it is perceived as harmonious. It is suggested that when this harmony takes place at a high level of complexity, such as in the ALASH cooperative classroom, student academic and social behavior become more interactive, and a rich array of thinking, teaching and learning takes place in the group. This affects the level of academic and social outcomes.

The working assumption that the mirrors of the classroom are interrelated and function simultaneously was first confirmed by observing many types and contexts of classrooms. A line of research using an observational instrument based on this model confirmed the model's assumptions that harmony of mirrors in cooperative contexts relates to academic and social outcomes in observed behaviors (Hertz-Lazarowitz 1983, 1989, 1992; Hertz-Lazarowitz, Baird, Webb, & Lazarowitz, 1984). In addition, paper and pencil measures were taken for the academic and social outcomes. The model of the classroom became a significant part in the professional development of the teachers in Acre.

This process of implementing a project with a systemic concept was gradual and by choice. All schools participated in the teachers' staff development in the city in different intensity, with variations that reflect the decisions that each school made. The transition from the traditional to the

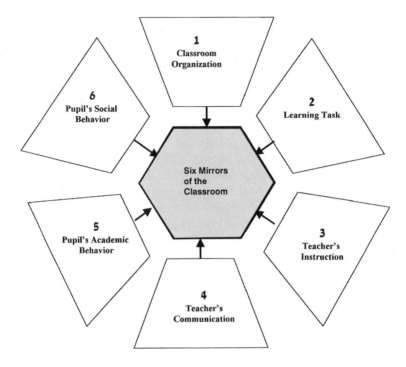

FIG. 7.1   Six mirrors of the learning–teaching environment.

cooperative classroom was based on the six mirror model. The transition to
the cooperative school, and then to the cooperative community and the cooperative district followed a seven-stage model (see Fig. 7.2). The model
was inspired from work in El Paso, Texas where several schools participated
in long-term projects in BCIRC from 1989 through 1995 (Hertz-Lazarowitz
& Calderon, 1994). The model was elaborated in Acre to include four leading concepts: cooperation, investigation, literacy, and community.

In Acre the model was expanded to work within each school, across all elementary schools, to a stage in which the city of Acre became a community
of CL schools with a strong impact on the district. Teachers and principals
formed whole communities for various staff development, learning and
evaluation, coaching, and open-house activities. One principal said, "In one
year principals have visited each other's schools more then they did in the
past 15 years."

This statement was the outcome of the active participation and cooperation of several Investigation Task Forces (ITF) in the holistic project

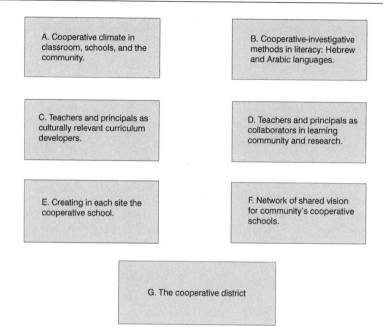

FIG. 7.2   Building the CILC model: Cooperation, investigation, literacy, and community—The Holistic Project in Acre, Israel.

(Hertz-Lazarowitz, 1999b). Within these ITFs many of the city educators and leaders developed a shared vision, with a strong commitment to prevent failure and bring school children to academic achievement. Most important was the fact that SFA and ALASH was supported as a city-wide goal, so elementary school principals created a forum in which they studied SFA and ALASH, coordinated its implementation, and decided on policies and strategies for quality implementation, including a decision to conduct city-wide evaluation research. Within-school and cross-school professional teams met biweekly to develop the pedagogical programs, and a special task force was established for evaluation.

From the very beginning of ALASH, and later of SFA, schools created models of literacy teaching and learning and practices to support children and families that made a noticeable change in the schools. In Acre the word that SFA and ALASH were working very well motivated other schools to join in the programs. In the school years 1993 through 1997 thirty schools joined the programs. First ALASH was adopted in several schools in Acre and in the Northern District, and in 1995 SFA entered first grade in Acre. The school year of 1997 was the year that 9 of the 10 state elementary schools implemented SFA in the early school grades and ALASH in third to sixth grade (Hertz-Lazarowitz & Schaedel, 1997).

A COMMUNITY RESEARCH AND EVALUATION MODEL

Following the conceptual framework that was developed in Acre, emphasizing cooperation, investigation, literacy, and community (Hertz-Lazarowitz, 1999a), an evaluation and research task force was created to plan the research and evaluation that would accompany SFA and ALASH implementation. The heart of the task force was the within-school facilitators and coordinators of SFA and ALASH from each school. This group included approximately 20 educators who carried on the evaluation procedures with the inspiration, support, challenge, and help of all levels of the community.

The model consisted of several groups of participants (see Fig. 7.3). The first group was the leadership in the community. The role of these members was threefold: to decide and empower others as to the needs and importance of research and evaluation (the steering committee); to bring to the community experts' knowledge (from Haifa University); and to assist with budget, regulation, and policy (with the Ministry of Education, Culture, and Sport superintendents). The facilitators then formed a task force that met twice a month to regulate the implementation of SFA and ALASH in all participating schools. This task force worked within and across schools to develop curricula, learning materials, and community-wide activities, and to facilitate and regulate evaluation processes.

During these years the facilitators and the principals, with the leadership of university experts, developed various evaluation schedules. The on-going eight-week evaluation measures were developed in Arabic and in Hebrew. Readiness tests for entry to first grade were developed and administered in Arabic and Hebrew to all first graders in the city in the beginning of the school year (Hertz-Lazarowitz, Schaedel, & Lerner, 1996). In addition, the task force developed the research and evaluation agenda and policies for literacy development in all grade levels, in Hebrew and in Arabic. Unfortunately, in Israel, unlike the United States, national standardized tests are not available, and nation-wide evaluations are very rare. District-wide evaluations are more consistent, with evaluation schedules that vary among the six districts of the State of Israel. Thus the task force in Acre became a pioneer and a leader in the community's evaluation model. This team is still at work in Acre.

School principals joined the facilitators and coordinators once every 6 weeks to work with the evaluation team. Representatives of teachers and parents were also included in the evaluation task force for consultation and

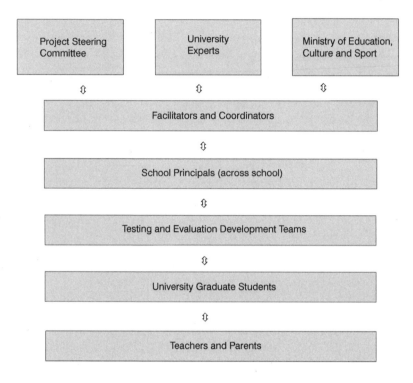

FIG. 7.3 SFA and ALASH in Israel: A community research and evaluation model.

sharing information. One additional element of the model was the participation of graduate students from the Faculty of Education at Haifa University. These students participated in the research as part of their academic
requirements in a research seminar on SFA and ALASH. Their role was to
observe classrooms, assist in the data collection, and carry out data analysis.
They became involved in the holistic project in Acre and gained knowledge
and practice. In the sequence of the task-force work, many members of the
community became active and interested participants in the development
of reading and writing of the children. Intensive family–school programs developed in the city. The research and evaluation was a powerful tool to reach
every child, every family, and every school.

RESEARCH AND EVALUATION OF ALASH

As mentioned earlier, ALASH preceded SFA in Israel, so here the research
on ALASH is presented prior to the research on SFA. Since 1993, cooperative learning has become one of the leading methods in elementary schools
in the Northern District of Israel, which includes the city of Acre. The educational system in Israel is divided into six districts, and the northern district is the largest in Israel, with more than 50% of all Arab schools. Based
on prior work with cooperative learning mainly in the Jewish sector
(Hertz-Lazarowitz & Zelniker, 1995, 1999), we looked for methods that
were sensitive to diverse cultures and languages because we planned to
work for the first time with the Arab sector. The CIRC Cooperative Integrated Reading and Composition program (Madden et al., 1988), which
was further developed as the BCIRC program (Calderon et al 1992;
Calderon, Hertz-Lazarowitz & Slavin, 1998), for Mexican-American children in El Paso, Texas, served as the foundation for the Hebrew and Arabic
program of ALASH, namely literacy via cooperative learning
(Hertz-Lazarowitz, in press; Hertz-Lazarowitz et al., 1993).

Starting in 1993, ALASH was implemented in third to sixth grades in
Arab and Jewish schools in the northern district of Israel. In 1995 we introduced the program to first and second grades, naming it Success for All in
Hebrew and Arabic. Currently SFA and ALASH are one sequence of our
educational interventions, and the program follows generally the U.S.
model with contextual adaptations to Israel. Obviously, the curriculum materials were different in Israel due to the different languages, but instructional procedures were very similar to the U.S. model.

Since 1993, we have been conducting research in two avenues, one focusing on literacy development in third to sixth grades in Acre and elsewhere in the northern district of Israel. This research is on reading and
writing in Arabic and Hebrew as L1 and L2. Arab children study Arabic as
L1, and it is mandatory for them to begin the study of Hebrew as L2 in third
grade. Jewish children do not have the same mandatory policy, and very few
schools offer Arabic as L2 at the elementary level, because the main focus of
L2 learning is on English. The second avenue of the research was the focus
on Acre as a city-wide evaluation model. However, because in Acre we have
only one large Arabic school (over 1,400 students), we implemented and
studied ALASH in other Arab schools in the district. The following section
describes and presents four studies in third to sixth grades.

From 1993 through 1998, research and evaluation of ALASH were an integral and consistent part of the implementation project (Hertz-Lazarowitz

& Schaedel, 1998). The studies measured academic outcomes mainly in reading comprehension and composition writing, in Hebrew as L1 and L2 and in Arabic as L1. Social outcomes were assessed by measures of classroom learning climate and peer relationships attachment, but are not presented here (see Hertz-Lazarowitz, 1999a; Hertz-Lazarowitz, Lerner, & Schaedel, 1996; Scharf & Hertz-Lazarowitz, 1999).

Academic outcomes included comparison of experimental SFA and ALASH methods to other methods of learning. The experimental and comparison design was based on careful matching of schools and classrooms according to background variables. We chose schools that implemented other innovative methods, such as active learning or various forms of group work. We felt it was important to compare schools that had some innovative work in the classrooms, so that the comparison would not be conducted between schools that have and have not in terms of resources for innovations.

The typical procedure used in our research was to develop a set of tests based on literature selections separate from the classroom text, but on school-related themes. Each test was composed of 8 to 10 open-ended questions assessing comprehension, inference making, language skills, main-idea identification, elaborated writing, and creative writing. The test evaluated on a scale from 0 to 100 basic literacy comprehension (up to 20%), elaborated literacy development (up to 30%), language skills (up to 20%), and writing (up to 30%). Categories and criteria for scoring were developed by a research team composed of evaluation experts from the field and graduate students from the University of Haifa. The tests were first piloted in a few schools in a different district and administered to the research sample only after an inter-rater reliability of .85 was established.

During those years a large set of tests in Hebrew and Arabic were developed, accompanied by a detailed scoring manual for all elementary school grades. The tests covered various genres of texts: informative texts, fables, stories, poems, and folk stories (Schaedel & Hertz-Lazarowitz, 1998).

ACADEMIC OUTCOMES FROM THIRD THROUGH SIXTH GRADES

The first cohort of ALASH was composed of four schools. These schools and their comparison schools were tested twice, at the end of the 1993 and 1994 school years. One school was an Arab school in the city of Acre and the other three schools were Jewish schools, secular and religious, elsewhere in the northern district.

The First Study

In 1993, a total of 434 students were tested on a folk story shared by the two cultures, "The Wise Farmer and His Sons." The story tells about an old farmer who told his sons before he died that a treasure was hidden in his vineyard. In searching for the treasure, the sons worked and cultivated the vineyard, so that gave them a lot of fruit. The test asked nine questions: (1) What was the instruction the father gave to his sons?; (2) What did the sons think?; (3) Did the father lie to his sons?; (4) Did they find the treasure?; (5) What is the main idea of the story?; (6) Compose a new title to the story; (7) Identify the genre of the story; (8) Write a sentence to show the meaning of two words; and (9) Write a story about a mother who for good intentions does not tell the truth to her daughter. This writing task stimulated many interesting and intriguing stories (Hertz-Lazarowitz et al., 1996). Figure 7.4 summarizes the research in 1993, 1994, and 1996.

The tests were administered in Hebrew as L1 to third and fourth graders in the Jewish schools ($n = 244$, of which 115 were from comparison classrooms). The same test was administered to fourth and fifth graders in the Arab schools as L2 ($n = 190$, of which 60 were from comparison classrooms). The tests in Hebrew were always administered to older students in the Arab sector because it is their L2. The outcomes showed significant gains for the ALASH students, both for the Arabs and the Jews, in comparison to their matched counterparts in control schools.

ALASH Jewish students' mean score was 70.32 (18.88), whereas the comparison mean score was 65.38 (16.66). ($F = 4.31\,p < 03$). ALASH Arab students' mean score was 61.33 (22.50), whereas the comparison mean score was 51.06 (21. 91), ($F = 9.39\,p < .003$). As expected, Jews were higher than Arabs in their scores in Hebrew, which is the Jews' first language. Arabs start formal learning of Hebrew, their L2, in third grade. Thus ALASH was very effective in increasing achievement in Hebrew as L1, and even more so for Arabs as their L2 (Hertz-Lazarowitz & Schaedel, 1996; see Fig. 7.4).

The Second Study

In 1994, ALASH was extended to third through sixth grades in these four schools, so more classrooms studied in the method. A total of 681 students were tested: The experimental group included 445 students, of which 189 were Arabs. The comparison group included 236 students, of which 86 were Arabs. The Arab and Jewish students were tested in Hebrew, as L1 and as L2, respectively. The Arab students were also tested in Arabic, on a different text, reported in the following:

The tests in Hebrew introduced a poem as a new text "An Hour Between Green and Purple," by a well-known female poet in Israel, Mira Meir. This text and the test that followed were administered to fourth and fifth graders in the Jewish schools and to fifth and sixth graders in the Arab schools. The students in the fourth grade in the Arab schools (the new cohort of the Arab students) were tested on "The Wise Farmer and His Sons."

The overall result in the Hebrew tests showed significant interaction effects for methods and nation, with gains for the ALASH students in each sector ($F = 30.84 p < .001$). In the Jewish sector, students in the experimental classroom scored significantly higher then the comparison students ($M = 71.28$ vs. $M = 66.82$). In the Arab sector, students in the experimental classroom scored 17 points higher then the comparison ($M = 63.12$ vs. $M = 46.84$). The results showed that learning in ALASH narrowed the gap be-

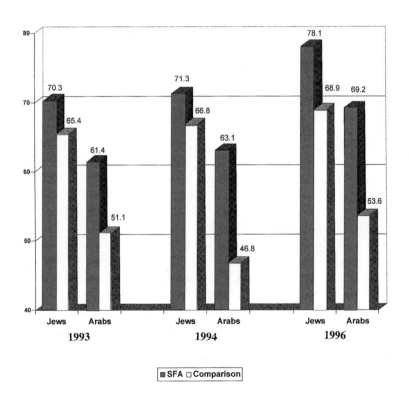

FIG. 7.4 Reading and writing achievement: Summary of outcomes.

tween Jews and Arabs, whereas learning in non-ALASH schools maximizes this gap. Moreover, Arabs in ALASH scored at a level similar to Jews in comparison classrooms (66.82 vs. 63.12). This can be viewed as an outstanding achievement, considering that for the Arabs, Hebrew is L2. The data also showed that girls in each sector achieved higher scores then boys (see Fig. 7.4).

The Third Study: Tests in Arabic

In 1994, the second year of the project, tests in Arabic were developed for the project by the Jewish–Arab research team. For the first time, Arab educators and experts on evaluation and testing selected four stories for each grade level (third, fourth, fifth, and sixth) and created tests with adequate validity and reliability to assess literacy development. These tests were piloted in the Arab school in Acre, in ALASH and comparison classrooms. Overall the tests did not show significant differences between ALASH and comparison classrooms within the same school except for higher writing scores in the ALASH sixth grade. However, we did find that the comparison classrooms within this school were adopting some strategies of ALASH (Hertz-Lazarowitz, in press).

The Fourth Study

In 1995–1996, the project was further extended and included 17 schools, of which 12 were Arab schools. In this year, four schools were in Acre, our pioneer Arab school and three additional Jewish schools. At the end of 1996, we tested Arab fourth graders in Arabic and sixth graders in Hebrew (as L2). This enabled us to evaluate the progress of the students in the new cohort in the end of the second year and also to make comparisons between students and classrooms who were in the program 1 or 2 years.

In Arabic the 4th-grade students were tested on a short folk story, "The Prince and His Sense of Humor." The sample included 845 students, 600 in ALASH schools, and 245 in comparison schools. Among the 600 ALASH students, 222 studied with this method for the second year. Overall results showed higher scores for ALASH students ($M = 58.43$; 22.10) than for comparison ($M = 51.76$; 23.01). ANOVAs indicated a tendency toward significance for the group effect (F [df 3,804] $= 2.46$; $p < .11$). Gender effects (F [df3,844]) $= 25.32$, and the interaction of gender and group (F [df 3,844]) $= 6.30$ were significant beyond the .05 level.

Students who spent two years in ALASH scored the highest ($M = 63.75$; 20.22). This was significant (F [df 3,331] $= 18.25$ $p < .000$). As consistently found before, girls outscored the boys (Schaedel, Ali Said, & Hertz-Lazarowitz, 1997), (see Fig. 7.5).

In Hebrew as a L2, 707 Arab sixth graders were tested. The sample included 461 students in ALASH schools and 246 in comparison schools. Among the 461 ALASH students, 201 studied 2 years in ALASH. The tests were based on two poems related to friendship, "A New Friend" by Shlomit Cohen-Asaf, and "I Want A Friend" by Hagar Shenhav. The test also asked students to compare the two poems. Results of a two-way ANOVA testing for group and gender indicated that ALASH students scored significantly higher than the comparison students (M = 60.22 [26.33], M = 53.53 [23.79] respectively (F [df 3,706] = 11.56, p < .001). Girls scored 6 points higher than boys, a significant effect for gender, but there was no significant interaction effect. Students who were two years in the program scored the

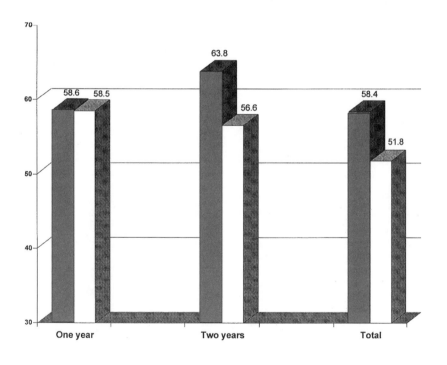

FIG. 7.5   Reading and writing achievement in Arabic (fourth grade, 1996).

highest in Arabic as L1, and in Hebrew as L2 (Schaedel & Hertz-Lazarowitz, 1997; see Fig. 7.6).

In 1996, the Jews were tested in Hebrew in fourth grade on the same two poems used with Arab students in sixth grade. Two-hundred-sixteen students took the test, 102 in the comparison schools and 114 in the experimental schools. Of these, 107 were the second year in the study. Results indicated that overall, ALASH students scored significantly higher than comparison students, both for the Jews (M = 78.09 [12.55], M = 68.85 [13.99], F [df1,216] = 23.54 p < .000) and for the Arabs (M = 69.20 vs. 53.55;F[3,322] = 40.49 p < .001; see Fig. 7.4).

The results of the four studies indicate that ALASH was effective in promoting literacy development of Arabs and Jews. For the Arab students, ALASH was very effective in promoting their competence in Hebrew as L2, and even more effective in promoting reading and writing in Arabic (see Figs. 7.4 and 7.6).

Achievements in reading and writing in Hebrew were visible from the first year and improved from 1993 through 1996 for both sectors (see Fig. 7.4). Furthermore, the development of the SFA and ALASH project gave a sense of empowerment and pride to the Arab teachers, principals, trainers, and su-

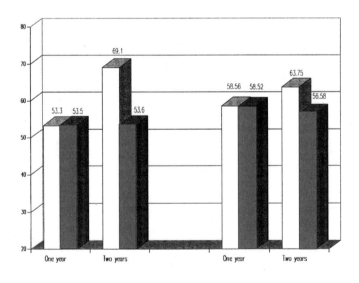

FIG. 7.6   Reading and writing achievements in Hebrew (L2) and Arabic (L1), 1995–1996 (fourth through sixth grades).

pervisors. The development of achievements in the Arabic language increased among Arab students mostly in their second year in the program. This can be explained by the fact that the project started with Hebrew as L1 for Jews and L2 for Arabs, so more time and knowledge were required for training, curriculum development, and test construction for the Arab sector.

SUCCESS FOR ALL IN ACRE

SFA was first implemented in the United States in 1987. The program is a culmination of 20 years of development of cooperative learning and language arts in schools. The program implemented in Israel is connected to the international network in the United States, Australia, Canada, Mexico, and the United Kingdom.

Israeli educators and university staff adopted the main goals and elements of the SFA program. In Acre, the challenge of using prevention and intensive early intervention to ensure the success of all children in learning to read became a crucial issue. Indeed it became the most important issue from the social, educational, and political angles. The program in Israel did not include the prekindergarten and kindergarten programs, due to structural constrains. However, the content of the program, such as the focus on oral-language development, using thematic units, the Story Telling and Retelling (STaR) program, and the use of a variety of curriculum supplements, were part of the program in first grade. The Reading Roots curriculum was implemented in the beginning of first grade. It emphasizes language skill, the use of interesting shared stories that students work on cooperatively, auditory discrimination, and sound blending. The Beyond the Basics-Reading Wings curriculum was called SFA from the first grade to the end of second grade and ALASH from third grade through sixth grade. ALASH was based on BCIRC and emphasized reading and writing using the school's or district's basal or literature series, or on novels. It also included cultural themes and social studies. Certified teacher-tutors provided one-to-one tutoring in most schools on different levels. Some schools used community resources for tutoring, such as girls in the army, not certified teachers. However, the model of providing 20-minute blocks each day to each eligible student was in place. The component of heterogeneous grouping for homeroom most of the school day was the practice in the schools. However the regrouping of the students during 90-minute reading periods across Grades 1 through 3 was difficult to implement in Acre. The best schools did was to create homogeneous reading levels within classrooms in first and second grade, and assign two teachers for each 90-minute reading period in the classroom. There was no way to create reduced class size below 20 students (most of our first grade classrooms are 40 students). All students were assessed every 8 weeks in order to make new reading group and tutorial placements. The full-time facilitator was another element the school could not fulfill in the way typical of SFA schools in the United States. Instead, we had two teachers, one expert for first and second grades, and one for the ALASH program from third through sixth grade, each having 2 to 3 hours per week to work with teachers to implement and monitor the program use. The family support team was already part of many schools before entering with SFA, and was working to help support parents in ensuring the success of their children. The team focused on attendance, coordination of outside social services, parent involvement, and student behavior. The advisory committee was established within schools and between schools as described earlier in the chapter. It helped to shape program policies and guide program development with a community vision. Grade-level teacher teams were an ongoing part of the program. In the Jewish schools in Acre there were only two to three teachers at each grade level. The only exception was the Arab school where each grade-level team consists of six to seven teachers. In most schools they met at least every two weeks to allow the faculty to problem solve and support one another. Staff development was provided prior to and during the program, for several years. Schools in Acre had the commitment to reduce special-education referrals and there is no student retention. They made scheduling adjustments to accommodate grouping and tutoring activities, and supplemented their libraries to address the needs of the reading curriculum.

The initiative to implement SFA was suggested by university faculty, without the support of a center or major grants. In Israel the methods of teaching reading are fully controlled by the Minister of Education, Culture, and Sport. Thus SFA was adjusted to the structure of existing teaching-learning reading methods (Feitelson, 1988; Shimron, 1994). No curriculum materials or new methods had been developed especially for SFA schools before the project began. The existing reading methods and materials were implemented and updated to meet SFA program components.

For example, in Acre we introduced very early original and high-quality children's literature books for the STaR component of the program. These books also served for enrichment and language development. We emphasized writing as a process from an early stage in first grade. The children read and wrote every day in their first language, Arabic or Hebrew, as part of their life in the classroom. These two foci were also integrated with the evaluation model of reading and writing.

Budget constraints were a major issue because SFA was implemented with very few additional funds. Thus special roles, such as the facilitators, were much more modest than in the United States. Small reading groups in the

90-minute block were partially implemented because of shortage of staff and problems in scheduling. However children were engaged in writing and reading at least 90 minutes each school day. Despite these constraints, the basic and significant components of SFA for first and second grades were introduced, with less investment in the upper grades. Most importantly, schools and the whole community had the commitment to promote children's literacy development without creating separation and tracking in the school.

RESEARCH AND EVALUATION OF SFA IN ACRE

In September 1994 our first experimental SFA cohort included five schools in Acre. Of those, three schools had already been working with us for 2 years implementing ALASH. The schools voluntarily joined the program and participated in the staff development offered by the Center for Research on the Education of Students Placed at Risk (CRESPAR) staff of Johns Hopkins University in the summer of 1994. Five additional schools in Acre did not join the program, and they served as the comparison schools. Within the Arab school we had two SFA first-grade classrooms and four comparison classrooms. Gradually, schools joined the program. By 1997, we had all schools except one in the program. The comparison schools for the studies were then from a neighboring city a few miles away from Acre, with similar socioeconomic backgrounds.

During these years our research design was a mirror of the changes in the city and in the project. It was a challenge to study an entire city with such diversity in population, ethnicity, and culture. A 3-year evaluation schedule was developed with the expansion of the project. In this chapter we describe studies completed at the end of the 1996 and 1997 school years.

FIRST GRADE READING AND WRITING OUTCOMES

Study 1: Arabs and Jews Write a Book

The first study of SFA was conducted in June 1996. In this study, 505 Jewish and Arab first-grade children in SFA and comparison classrooms received an envelope with four separated pictures, glue, crayons, and an empty booklet with a colored cover. The children were asked to write a story based on the pictures. Scoring categories were developed by a group of experts. Those included: book and print awareness, writing conventions, story quality, and teacher holistic evaluation. University graduate students assessed all the storybooks for reliability following the scoring of the teachers. Reliability was .90.

SFA children, both Jews and Arabs, scored higher than comparison students in story writing quality in their L1 (see Table 7.1). Effect sizes were higher for the Arabs (+.54 vs. +.29; Hertz-Lazarowitz & Schaedel, 1997; Hertz-Lazarowitz, Schaedel, Lerner, & Tov-Lee, 1997). All the students loved the task and were capable of composing one- to six-page storybooks and then read or tell the story to their teacher. Those books, in Hebrew or in Arabic, are sometimes funny, often complex, and tell us about children's thoughts, feelings, and reflections. Two examples of their writing follow on the next page.

Study 2: Composing a Poem

In the 1997 school year, 547 Jewish first graders from 11 schools in 22 classrooms participated. Of these, 454 were in eight SFA schools and 93 were in three comparison schools. The sample included 260 boys and 287 girls.

TABLE 7.1

Measures of Writing a Picture Book in First Grade (1996)

	Jewish			Arab		
	SFA (N = 204)	Comparison (N = 117)	F p	SFA (N = 66)	Comparison (N = 118)	F p
Story quality	36.28	33.86	6.62	24.86	20.72	14.93
	(7.72)	(8.34)	.01	(7.71)	(6.90)	.00
Writing conventions	20.53	22.00	11.32	18.59	19.00	n.s.
	(3.81)	(3.66)	.00	(3.19)	(3.10)	
Book-print awareness	10.22	8.16	42.51	13.20	11.26	3.04
	(2.76)	(2.60)	.00	(7.25)	(7.29)	.08
Teacher evaluation	6.98	6.26	12.71	5.97	5.74	n.s.
	(1.61)	(1.88)	.00	(2.57)	(2.12)	
Total	74.00	70.29	3.29	62.62	56.72	4.82
	(12.56)	(14.04)	.04	(19.11)	(17.32)	.03

Note.   n.s. = not significant

Story 1
Me and the basketball
Vasam went up the ladder so he can hang a basket.
A bird arrived and gave him a nail, Vasam fixed the basketball
so he can play with it.
And then Vasam came to play and Vasam saw the bird's nest in the basket.
And than Vasam felt sad and he went into the house as he was sad and his
mother said:
Why are you sad and crying my son?
And then Vasam said: because the bird built a nest on the basketball.
Language: Arabic
School EA
Grade A5
Boy—M. H.

Story 2
Achmed and the bird
Achmed went out of the house he was happy that he has a ball.
He went to the yard climbed on the ladder and found a bird sitting
in the basket.
The bird sang and he is fixing the basket.
Achmed was happy and he and the bird became friends.
Language: Arabic
School EA
Grade A4
Girl—H. G.

The test was based on a poem entitled "The Gift" written by Yehuda Amichai, a famous poet in Israel. The poem is about the gifts nature gives us and the idea that fathers (Dad) and mothers (Mom) are gifts for children. The poem was written in a puzzle form of questions and answers. The poem was not part of the literature children read in the classroom, but it was related to the family, a topic that was part of their curricula. Parts of the poem are presented here in free translation:

What is the evening's gift
For a little girl?
The moon and the stars
And sweet dreams …
What is the night's farewell gift?
The sun and its light
And the day.
What is the gift of Dad
For a little girl?

Her Mom.
And what is the gift of Mom?
Dad.
There is a Mom for the day
And a Dad for the day,
There is a Mom for the night
And a Dad for the night,
There are many Moms and many Dads
And all of them together

The children received the text and they were asked to read the poem and answer six open-ended questions. Four of the questions were based on the text, and asked for reading comprehension, such as "What is the gift that Dad gives the girl?" Two questions were elaboration of the text, for example, "The poet writes that Dad and Mom are gifts, explain why." The children were asked to write a story or a poem about a gift they received, or a gift they wished to receive. They were also asked to draw a picture.

The scoring manual was developed following the model described earlier with the help from experienced teachers outside of the schools involved in the study. Detailed categories for scoring were developed; those were pretested by the graduate students in other schools. Reliability of scoring based on 145 children in five classrooms was .90. The scoring was in the range of 0 to 100. In the reading comprehension part (Questions 1 to 4), the child could get up to 30 points, according to the criteria for each question. For the elaboration questions (5 to 6), children could get up to 20 points. The writing scoring was a maximum of 50 points in the following sections: structure—based on sequence of content, background, plot, and cohesiveness (up to 15 points); quality—based on coherence, creativity, complexity, rich language, and level of interest (up to 15 points); readability—based on the format of the written text and its level of readability (up to 10 points); and drawing—evaluated in terms of the connection to the text the child either read or wrote, and its artistic level (up to 10 points).

The test was administered to all first graders in a 1-hour sitting in the regular school day, during the last month of the school year, June 1997. Each child received a four-page booklet with the poem, the question with space for answers, a page for the writing part, and a page for the drawing. The graduate students helped to administer the tests. The text and the scoring were not known to the teachers before. The booklets were collected and scored first by the teachers, after they received training in the scoring program the same day of the test. After the teachers completed their scoring, all tests were gathered in the university.

From each classroom, 20% of the tests (5 to 8 children) were randomly picked and scored by an expert, blind to former scoring. The reliability coefficient between teachers and university students and experts was .90 in total score and .80 to 100 in different categories. If reliability of the two scores was less then .80, the whole class was rescored in the University. In this study we rescored only three classrooms. This procedure showed that teachers, after being trained in the coding system, were highly reliable in their scoring.

Two separate MANOVA analyses were conducted to test the effects of group (SFA vs. Comparison) and gender. The first was conducted on the three measures of literacy development: reading comprehension, elaboration, and writing. The second analyzed writing components: structure, quality, readability and drawing. In addition, ANOVA's were conducted to test differences in the total score of the test.

The ANOVA indicated group main effect on the total score, where SFA children scored significantly higher then the comparison children (M = 72.63 vs. 66.58). The effect size for this difference was +.30, and the F = 5.46, $p < .02$, (df 1,543 for all analyses).

The first MANOVA yielded significant interaction on group and gender for all literacy measures. The girls in SFA were higher in all measures, especially in writing, which contributed to their higher total score (see Table 7.2). The second MANOVA was conducted on the measures of writing: structure, quality, readability, and drawing. A similar pattern emerged in this analysis, SFA children were significantly higher in structure and quality of

TABLE 7.2

Reading and Writing in First Grade (1997)

Text: The Gift (Poem)	SFA		Comparison		F^*
	Boys	Girls	Boys	Girls	p
	(N = 215)	(N = 239)	(N = 45)	(N = 48)	
Reading comprehension	21.63	22.77	19.47	17.19	3.32
	(7.87)	(7.28)	(9.75)	(8.57)	.05
Elaboration	12.97	14.56	14.56	12.98	5.08
	(6.50)	(5.90)	(4.68)	(7.03)	.02
Writing	34.26	38.51	36.09	33.10	6.47
	(14.23)	(11.72)	(8.87)	(10.59)	.01
Total	69.05	75.85	70.11	63.27	7.66
	(24.04)	(20.30)	(17.87)	(19.85)	.006

*Interaction affect.

compositions, and SFA girls were especially high in composition structure (see Table 7.3).

Most of the children wrote stories and not poems. They wrote about birthday parties, and receiving presents from families and friends. Many of them wrote about wishing to receive bicycles, and about presents such as Barbie dolls. Translated examples of the children's writing appear here:

Example 1: A boy, a newcomer to Israel, wrote:

> Once Dad bought me a bicycle.

TABLE 7.3

Structure, Quality, Readability, and Drawing of First Grade Writing (1997)

| Composition: The gift | SFA | | Comparison | | F* |
	Boys (N = 215)	Girls (N = 239)	Boys (N = 45)	Girls (N = 48)	p
Structure	9.93	11.03	9.80	8.52	5.44
	(4.87)	(4.32)	(3.81)	(4.05)	.02
Quality	9.07	10.32	8.91	7.56	6.65
	(4.47)	(4.41)	(3.47)	(3.72)	.01
Readability	7.69	8.40	8.31	8.38	n.s.
	(3.27)	(2.84)	(2.25)	(2.55)	
Drawing	7.57	8.76	9.07	8.65	4.78
	(8.83)	(2.84)	(2.21)	(2.94)	.02

* Interaction affect.

Example 2: A boy wrote:

> The present I wish to get
> Yoram (a boys' name) has a birthday party on Friday.
> Yoram wanted for his birthday to get a bicycle. Yoram always dreamt about bicycle.
> His Dad knew that Yoram dreams only of bicycle and said: I'll buy him bicycles. The day of the birthday arrived, and everyone made him a surprise. Yoram saw the bicycle and was so happy, and said to his father thank you!

Example 3: A girl wrote:

> The present I wish to get
> I wanted my present to be a Barbie and I met her, and I played with her, and I laugh and we slept together and in the morning I went to school and I played with my friends.

Example 4: A girl wrote:

> The present I wish to get
> Is the land of sweets,
> And the land of snakes
> And also the land of dogs
> And the present I received
> Is a library full of books
> And I was happy
> Because this was a surprise!
> The end of the story.

PERSPECTIVES AND DISCUSSION

The studies presented in the chapter are examples of the city-wide research and evaluation process in Acre. These studies were part of a long term research program that involved all levels of the city as presented in Fig. 7.3. They used an experimental-comparison design, within the Arab sector, within the Jewish sectors, and between the Arab and Jewish sectors, in the same community. In a period of 5 years the studies on literacy development in reading and writing in all elementary school grade levels became a consistent part of the pedagogy of Acre. They showed mostly higher achievements for the SFA and ALASH schools and classrooms (Hertz-Lazarowitz, & Schaedel, 1997; Schaedel & Hertz-Lazarowitz, 1994).

The community of Acre and of the northern district developed accountability and efficacy in their work and pride in the children's outcomes. The consistent findings that the program had such an impact of reading and writing gave power to the principals and teachers in the program. One parent told her daughter's first-grade teacher:

> This is my third child in this school. My older children were very good students, they did well in the elementary school and in the high school.... This one is our baby, we are all amazed at her achievements, it is nothing like what we saw before, she reads well after three months in school, she writes stories, she is glued to books.... SFA is just unbelievable.

The school year of 1997 was the first year we had all (but one) of the schools in Acre within the SFA program. Since then we have kept the model of SFA and comparison schools with some consistency and comparability. The fact that for two years we had the willingness of schools, which did not formally join SFA to serve as comparison schools is quite significant. On one hand, the comparison principals wanted to prove that they "will do as well as the SFA schools," and were daring enough to expose their students to the tests. On the other hand they were exposed to all changes that SFA brought to the community and later decided to join the program. Since 1997 we had to use for comparison matching schools from a nearby area.

In Israel there is no culture of open information on school outcomes and test scores. On the contrary, there is a strong resistance to national or district evaluation. Test scores are still kept a secret. The fact that the evaluation model was highly professional and developed good measures, and was accompanied by feedback in a secure and empowering way to the school personnel, made a change in the schools. No doubt that the participation in the study as a comparison school motivated school principals to join the SFA program. We had one principal who refused to be part of the evaluation, but he did implement SFA.

Thus, the schedule of evaluation in Acre was a rare model within an organic educational community that voluntarily participated in the research and evaluation process. The function of the task force and the principal's forum was very significant. We worked on three dimensions: Work within schools, work across schools, and work from the school into the community (Hertz-Lazarowitz, 1999a). Because literacy was the focus of SFA, it reflects the vision that in Acre, respect for differences, in culture and languages, and tolerance for conflicting beliefs and ideologies could best be promoted by the innovative and critical pedagogy of cooperative literacy via language development.

Through SFA elements, including school–family partnership, we could be sensitive and responsive to the needs of the community and touch every child, every family, and his or her national and social being through teaching and learning in the school. The contribution of SFA to children's reading and writing, in Hebrew and in Arabic, was backed with data of what good schools do, and what other schools could do in order to increase student success. This was coupled with data gathered from school observations between school visitation and knowledge shared and built during the learning–training workshops. The results of every year analyses, and initial longitudinal analysis, were presented annually to school principals, the SFA facilitators, teachers, and district and city administrators of the programs. The evaluation was perceived and used by them as a challenge and a resource for further decision making about budget and planning for future improvements of the programs. In this way a sense of ownership for SFA children was shared by the entire community.

·ACKNOWLEDGMENTS

Thanks to Dr. Bruria Schaedel, the field director of ALASH and SFA, the educators, leaders, principals, teachers, consultants, and children of Acre and other communities in northern Israel who participated in the project reported here.

REFERENCES

Calderon, M. (1999). Teacher learning communities for cooperation in diverse settings. *Theory Into Practice, 38*(2), 94–99.

Calderon, M. E., Hertz-Lazarowitz, R., & Slavin, R. (1998). Effects of Bilingual Cooperative Integrated Reading and Composition on student transition from Spanish to English. *Elementary School Journal, 99*(2), 153–165.

Calderon, M. E., Tinajero, J. V., & Hertz-Lazarowitz, R. (1992). Adapting Cooperative Integrated Reading and Composition (CIRC) to meet the needs of bilingual students. *The Journal of Educational Issues of Language Minority Students, 10*, 79–106.

Center for Research on the Education of Students Placed at Risk (CRESPAR). (1996, November). *Research and development report* (No. 1). Baltimore, MD: Johns Hopkins University.

Eden, D., Hertz-Lazarowitz, R., & Ben-Shushan, N. (1998, July). *The political power of school principals.* Paper presented at the 6th International Conference on Work Values and Behavior. Istanbul.

Feitelson, D. (1988). Facts and fads in beginning reading: A cross language perspective. Norwood, NJ: Ablex.

Hertz-Lazarowitz, R. (1983). Prosocial behavior in the classroom. *Academic Psychology Bulletin, 5*, 319–339.

Hertz-Lazarowitz, R. (1989). Cooperation and helping in the classroom: A contextual approach. *International Journal of Research in Education, 13*(1), 113–119.

Hertz-Lazarowitz, R. (1992). Understanding students' interactive behavior: Looking at six mirrors of the classroom. In Miller, N., & Hertz-Lazarowitz, R. (Eds.), *Interaction in cooperative groups: The anatomy of group learning* (pp. 71–102). New York: Cambridge.

Hertz-Lazarowitz, R. (1999a, September). *The six mirrors of the cooperative classroom as a context for development*. Paper presented in the 9th international conference of Developmental Psychology, The Island of Spetses, Greece.

Hertz-Lazarowitz, R. (1999b). Cooperative learning and group- investigation in Israels' Jewish and Arabs schools: A community approach. *Theory Into Practice, 38*(2), 105–113.

Hertz-Lazarowitz, R. (in press). *Cooperative learning for literacy development*. Haifa, Israel: Ach Publications.

Hertz-Lazarowitz, R., Baird, H., Webb, C., & Lazarowitz, R. (1984). Student–student interaction in science classrooms: A naturalistic study. *Science Education, 68*(5), 603–619.

Hertz-Lazarowitz, R., & Calderon, E. M. (1994). Implementing cooperative learning in the elementary schools: The facilitative voice for collaborative power. In S. Sharan (Ed.), *Handbook of cooperative learning methods* (pp. 300–317). New York: Greenwood.

Hertz-Lazarowitz, R., Lerner, M.., & Schaedel, B. (1996, July). *Learning in the ALASH classroom: Jewish and Arab students in cooperative-literacy based classroom*. Paper presented at the 10th conference of SCRIPT, Special Committee for Research in Processing of Text, Ma'ale Hahamisha, Israel.

Hertz-Lazarowitz, R., & Schaedel, B. (1997, March 24–28). *Success For All (SFA) in Acre-Israel. Effects of Hebrew and Arabic Reading and Writing: Initial findings*. In R. Slavin (symposium organizer), International Adaptation of Success For All. American Educational Research Association meeting. Chicago.

Hertz-Lazarowitz, R., & Schaedel, B. (1998, April). *ALASH—Cooperative learning and literacy development in Jewish and Arab schools in Israel*. Paper presented at the American Educational Research Association (AERA), San-Diego, CA.

Hertz-Lazarowitz, R., Schaedel, B., Calderon, M., & Tinajero, J. (1993). Literacy development via cooperative learning: CIRC-ALASH Project: The beginning of the Israeli project. *Helkat Lashon: The Israeli Journal of Linguistic Education, 11/12*, 6–21 (Hebrew).

Hertz-Lazarowitz, R., Schaedel, B., & Lerner, M. (1996, July). *Assessment of literacy in cooperative learning (ALASH) in its second year*. Papers presented at the 11th Conference of SCRIPT, Special Committee for Research in Processing of Text, Ma'ale Hahamisha, Israel.

Hertz-Lazarowitz, R., Schaedel, B., Lerner, M., & Tov-Lee, E. (1997, August). *Success for all (SFA) in literacy and writing development in first year grade*. Paper presented at the 7th European Conference for Research on Learning and Instruction, European Association for Research on Learning and Instruction (EARLI), Greece.

Hertz-Lazarowitz, R., & Zelniker, T. (1995). Cooperative learning in the Israeli context: Historical, educational and cultural perspectives. *International Journal of Educational Research, 23*, 267–285.

Hertz-Lazarowitz, R., & Zelniker, T. (1999). Alternative methods in teaching: Cooperative learning in Israel. In E. Peled (Ed.), *Fifty years of Israeli education* (Vol. 2; pp. 349–367). Israel: Jerusalem Ministry of Education, Culture, and Sport.

Lazarowitz, R. (1995). Learning biology in cooperative-investigative groups. In J. E. Pedersen & A. D. Digby (Eds.), *Cooperative learning and secondary schools: Theory, Models and Strategies* (pp. 185–227). New York: Garland.

Lazarowitz, R., & Hertz-Lazarowitz, R. (1998). Cooperative learning in science curriculum. In B. J. Fraser & K. G. Tobin (Eds.), *International handbook of science education* (pp. 449–471). Netherlands: Kluwer.

Madden, N., Farnish, A. M., Slavin, R., & Stevens, R. (1993). *CIRC Cooperative Integrated Reading and Composition-Teacher's manual writing*. Center for social organization of schools. Baltimore: Johns Hopkins.

Rich, Y., & Ben-Ari, R. (1994). *Teaching methods for the heterogeneous classroom*. Tel-Aviv, Israel: Ramot.

Schaedel, B., Ali-Said, M., & Hertz-Lazarowitz, R. (1997, July). *Achievement in reading and writing in Arabic: Effects of two years in ALASH*. Paper presented at the 11th Conference of SCRIPT, Special Committee for Research in Processing of Text, Ma'ale Hahamisha, Israel.

Schaedel, B., & Hertz-Lazarowitz, R. (1997, July). *Reading and writing in Hebrew as a second language in Arabs schools—ALASH and comparison.* Papers presented at the 11th Conference of SCRIPT, Special Committee for Research in Processing of Text, Ma'ale Hahamisha, Israel.

Schaedel, B., & Hertz-Lazarowitz, R. (1998). *Writing and Reading Tests in Arabic and Hebrew.* University of Haifa, ALASH Project. Israel.

Scharf, M., & Hertz-Lazarowitz, R. (1999). *Social networks in the school context: Effects of culture and gender* (manuscript submitted for publication).

Sharan, S. (Ed.). (1994). *Handbook of cooperative learning methods.* Westport: Greenwood.

Sharan, S., & Hertz-Lazarowitz, R. (1978). *Cooperation and communication in schools.* Tel Aviv: Schocken (Hebrew).

Sharan, S., & Hertz-Lazarowitz, R. (1981). *Changing schools: The small group teaching (SGT) project in Israel.* Tel Aviv: Ramot Publishing, Tel Aviv University.

Sharan, S., & Shachar, H. (1988). *Language and learning in the cooperative classroom.* New York: Springer.

Sharan, S., & Sharan, Y. (1974). *Small Group Teaching.* Tel Aviv: Schocken.

Shimron, J. (1994). The making of readers: The work of Professor Dina Feitelson. In D. K. Dickinson (Ed.), *Bridges to literacy: Children, families, and schools* (pp. 80–90). Cambridge, MA: Blackwell.

Slavin, R. E., Madden, N. A., Dolan, L. J., & Wasik, B. A. (1996). *Every Child, Every School: Success for All.* Newbury Park, CA: Corwin.

8

Success for All in Mexico

Margarita Calderón
Johns Hopkins University

This chapter describes the implementation process, challenges, and student outcomes from the first years of implementation of Success for All (SFA) programs in Mexico. The pilot program was implemented in one prekindergarten and kindergarten school, one 1st through 6th grade school, and two 7th through 9th grade middle schools. Due to testing restrictions, only end-of-the-year data from the state's student achievement tests were collected and compared to the previous year's data. Within this limited sample and analysis, significant differences were noted in achievement and attendance. Other data demonstrated what has perhaps become the cornerstone for critical change in the Mexican schools: increased parental involvement, changes in the school's infrastructure, and a new view of professional development. Unfortunately, the one barrier yet to overcome is the district- and state-level support for scaling up the program.

WHY SFA IS NEEDED IN MEXICO'S BORDER SCHOOLS

SFA is not only an effective and comprehensive literacy program (Slavin et al., 1996) but also a means to restructure school funding and resources, upgrade teachers' and administrators' skills, and invite parents to more meaningful school participation. It is designed to address the needs of disadvantaged children. It is also an enrichment program that can provide

179

instruction in one or two languages, adjusting easily to a variety of bilingual programs.

Schools on the northern border of Mexico such as Cuidad (Cd.) Juárez, Chihuahua, have long been interested in bilingual education. Therefore, we felt that SFA, with its Spanish adaptation called Éxito Para Todos (EPT), could serve as a vehicle for dual language instruction. The SFA schools across the border in El Paso, Texas could serve as models and catalysts for creating binational staff-development opportunities for teachers on both sides of the border.

Another more immediate reason for Cd. Juárez schools to adopt SFA is the city's recent immense influx of people from the interior of Mexico and Central and South America. Most come from extreme poverty, seeking jobs in the twin plants in Juárez, whereas others come with the hope of crossing the border to a better life in the United States. Many of the children have had little or no education. Because of these and other difficulties, the Juárez schools have many serious problems, such as the following: 49% of 11 year-olds drop out of school (about 10,000 children), about 40% of students are retained at first or second grade because of reading difficulties, 140 elementary schools in Juárez have the lowest performance ratings in the nation (Loera, 1998).

A high mobility rate, a lack of instructional leadership, and a proliferation of private schools for middle-income families, have drained the resources of the Juárez public schools. The demand for more schools has resulted in widespread use of temporary trailers, tents, and even open spaces for year-long use in extreme weather conditions. There is a critical shortage of teachers and most new hires are noncredentialed. We felt that a program such as SFA could help new teachers develop the necessary instructional skills. We also felt that SFA could help the administration develop the infrastructure necessary to support the reforms the new educational programs espouse. And finally, the SFA Family Support program could begin to address the needs of many parents, their children, and the school's efforts to reach out to parents.

Concerned with the low literacy rates and social problems, a group of business men and women formed the Rosario Fernández Foundation to find a way to improve education in the Juárez public schools. After a year of research, they selected the Success for All/Éxito Para Todos (SFA/EPT) program because of its balanced approach to reading and its comprehensiveness: Tutoring, 8-week assessments, Family Support programs, administrators' training, all the materials teachers need, plus a comprehensive staff-development program with peer coaching, implementation visits, and Teachers' Learning Communities (TLCs; For a thorough description of the program see chap. 1, this volume).

The Foundation volunteered to fund the pilot program in the four schools and to support the modification of the materials needed to dovetail the Mexican national text and program essentials. Although SFA had reading materials in Spanish for use in the U.S. bilingual schools, many of the materials (e.g., teachers' manuals, tutoring manuals, and family support manuals) did not exist in Spanish. Seeing the need for research and development, they agreed to fund this development as well. The Foundation is actively involved in the project beyond providing funds. As a joint partnership, the members also learned the program, visit the schools, and negotiate with the local and state administrators to seek support for scaling up after the pilot study. They periodically accompany us to the capital to negotiate implementation logistics with the educational administrators. One of their goals is to make the administration accountable for sharing the cost of the upscale implementation and dissemination once the components are completed. Although the project has only been piloted in four schools thus far, much as been learned about creating positive change in schools in Mexico.

CHALLENGES TO THE IMPLEMENTATION IN MEXICO

The Educational Context in Mexico

Education in Mexico has recently undergone various reform movements as different factions have gained political power. Mexico's 1992 reform called for decentralization of the educational system, supposedly giving more power to the states and local districts. However, 100 years of centralized decision making have made the transition a most complicated matter. On the one hand, the states and local agencies are now empowered to direct the schools. On the other, the central government still manages the funding and dictates the instructional program and the national text.

Decentralization has also run up against a lack of understanding and resistance from some local educational authorities (Andrade de Herrara, 1996). Historically, state educational agencies have been treated as opportunities to reward those who stood by the winning political party. As minority political parties gain territory, they continue to uphold those traditions. Thus, the upper echelons of the administration are rarely filled by those who have a knowledge base or background in education. They do know, however, that they will be in this position for a brief period of time and are hesitant to create significant change.

The national reading text is developed by scholars in Mexico City every 6 years. The grade-level texts rarely fit the interests and needs of border students. They are not sensitive to the realities of students who come to school with diverse funds of knowledge and experiences. There has been ample criticism of the current text (B. Calvo, personal communication, June, 1996). The latest text utilizes a whole-language approach, radically different from the previous phonics system. In most classrooms, students continue to do individual work with the workbooks that accompany this method. Teachers have received little or no training on the use of the texts, much less on the theory and methodology of the approach (Davis & Sumara, 1997). Students work on their workbooks most of the period or try one of the 70 whole-language activity cards that accompany the teacher's text. There is no direct teaching of decoding included in the text. Some teachers resort to the old method whereas others prefer the phonics worksheets that the local administration office sells to supplement the workbooks.

One of our main problems stemmed from a lack of additional personnel to fill the positions of facilitators and tutors. Schools have a staffing ratio of 1 teacher per 45 students or more. The Foundation hired three facilitators for the first year, hoping that the educational agency would pay their salaries the following year. This did not occur, and the primary and elementary schools were left without facilitators. Luckily, the middle school had a coordinator who became the facilitator, and retired teachers happily volunteered as tutors. Whereas the Baltimore SFA Foundation hires the trainers on a full-time basis, the Juárez Foundation begrudgingly voted to give the Juárez EPT trainers a monthly stipend to do the training and the follow-up implementation visits. They felt that trainers should also be sponsored by the educational system, because their preparation as SFA trainers was building capacity at the school district level.

In addition to these problems, there were also hurdles to overcome such as: (a) a lack of appropriate literature books for all the grade levels; (b) extremely limited resources in the schools and low pay for teachers; (c) a history of interruptions during time-on learning; (d) no history of staff-development practices; (e) varying interpretations of administrative support for the innovation; (f) an unrecognized resource in parental support; and (g) an archaic system of measuring student achievement. These are further discussed in the following:

IMPLEMENTATION CHALLENGES

In 1996 we set out to pilot, adjust, and implement the EPT adaptation of SFA. The pilot was initially implemented in a feeder system involving a preschool, elementary school, and secondary school. The task that year was to pilot the little that was in existence in Spanish and to finish developing and translating and modifying the materials to meet the needs of Mexican students. The Spanish prekindergarten and the middle school SFA programs had not been developed in Spanish in the United States, so the Mexican teachers were enlisted to help develop these programs. The 2nd through 9th grade Treasure Hunts had to be developed to match the national textbooks. The advantage of having one national text was that once the materials had been adapted, they could be used throughout the country.

Challenge: Literature Books

One of the biggest challenges was finding a variety of literature books appropriate for teaching phonemic awareness, conventions of print, Story Telling and Retelling (STaR), listening comprehension, and analysis of story elements. Accompanying the national text is a library of about 150 literature books called Rincones de Lectura (Reading Corners) that every school is supposed to receive. We waited an entire year for the pilot school to receive its library, but it never came. Therefore, teachers had very few books for STaR or Listening Comprehension. We shied away from buying literature books in the United States because the cost would be prohibitive in a large-scale implementation. Our search in Mexican bookstores for quality books for each grade level also yielded few choices. Although there are many children's books, very few met the criteria for STaR or Listening Comprehension—a good story plot with a beginning, middle, and end; language difficulty a little above grade level; well developed characters; containing literary devices that can serve as the objective for discussion; and books free from gender and other bias.

After finally receiving the "Ricones de Lectura," from the Secretary of Education (1995), we found that they did not meet the criteria either. These books are either too small (pocket size) or the language is too difficult for prekindergarten and kindergarten. For first grade, the characters are usually not developed enough to analyze, and the plots are weak. We also looked for big books for the prekindergarten shared-reading component and these were even more difficult to find. Mexico does not print big books. Predictable books are rare or not appropriate. Teachers had to put together their own materials to teach phonemic awareness through rhyme and alliteration. We also had to improvise large-print versions of books with good story lines.

The national text also has its limitations. Students at the sixth-grade level are reading stories that are only two or three pages long. They are not accustomed to reading novels or lengthy text. We found classical novels in bookstores appropriate for the upper grades but the schools rarely use them. Cost is probably the strongest reason, although they are less than $2.00 dollars per copy. Because the parents have to pay for all extra materials beyond the national text, including the teacher's chalk and copier paper, these are seen as luxuries.

What Could We Do With This Challenge? We have begun to package novels and their Treasure Hunts at a minimal reproduction cost. One way to scale up the program is for the Fernández Foundation to assist in recruiting local business and industry to support new schools with EPT materials. Each year we also meet with Chihuahua State Agency officials to negotiate their contribution to the schools, hoping each year that their commitment will materialize.

Based on the framework of a Talent Development model (Boykin, 1994), we began to identify, through observation and interview, the talents of the teachers. One of the characteristics of Mexican teachers is that they are very creative storytellers. Capitalizing on this talent, we hired them to write children's stories and their Treasure Hunts. Treasure Hunts are guide sheets for teachers and students to discuss the background of a literature piece, purposes for reading, story elements, authors' craft, new vocabulary, and types of comprehension skills.

Challenge: Limited Resources and Low Teacher Pay   In addition to the decentralization and reformation of content and educational materials, the Ministry of Education also set out in 1992 to reevaluate the teaching function (SEP, 1992), but little has been accomplished since then. The economic situation of teachers has deteriorated over the years to a point that salaries are barely above minimum wage. This situation obligates teachers to meet their financial needs by taking other jobs, which translates to overcommitment and student neglect. Other teachers simply abandon the teaching profession (SEP, 1993). To ameliorate the shortage of secondary teachers, people from other professions with little knowledge of pedagogy have been hired.

The teachers' financial situation is only matched by the lack of resources at the school. One teacher wrote in his journal:

> I arrived at school at 7:30 am. I turned on the small heater in my room so that it would be fairly warm by the time the other teachers arrived. I have the best room for workshops and meetings. The SFA/EPT trainers arrived at the same time to set up their materials for the workshop. They don't want to take off their hats, coats, and scarves. I can see they are wearing two pairs of socks. They were really cold yesterday. Poor things, today the cement floor feels colder because the rain has seeped in and it turned into ice. I have my shovel and mop ready for when this happens. I'll have it cleared in no time, before somebody slips and falls. Last year one of my students broke his elbow when he fell on the ice in our classroom. Our workshop will go from 9:00 to 1:00. At 1:00 the parents are bringing us lunch because from here all of us go on to our 2:00 p.m. jobs and we don't have time to go home and eat. There are days when I don't have time to eat. I have to take two buses to my next job and I don't like to be late (Cesar, November 1997).

The teachers in our study report that they cannot afford to spend even an hour to prepare lessons, spend money buying props, or read. The resilient teachers find ways to learn and sustain their teaching goals. Others find teaching as one more pay check for the family. The group in between finds that resiliency is often overpowered by insufficient energy and family time.

What Could We Do With This Challenge?   This has been the greatest challenge for us: how to rekindle the teaching spirit and help teachers find time for their students, themselves, and their families. Not having all the materials developed at the beginning of the pilot study was very frustrating for teachers. It helped us to see what would be necessary in order to help teachers, with no time to spare or prepare. We refocused our staff development design and added more explanations to the teachers' instructions. Capitalizing on the teachers' excellent memory skills and improvisational skills, we built in opportunities to learn the new methodologies through this mechanism. The teacher-writers benefited most by learning as they wrote. The small amounts of money we paid the writers, editors, and typists also enabled them to drop their more burdensome part-time jobs and concentrate on teaching and learning. Unfortunately, this opportunity could only be offered to a small number of teachers. If the scaling up of the program is to take place, a stronger staff-development system and explicit materials will need to be in place.

Challenge: Schedules, Interruptions, and the Struggle for Time on Task

One of the greatest accomplishments in the pilot schools was to institute schedules: the 90-minute reading block, schedules of sports activities, testing, interdisciplinary blocks, and extracurricular activities. The schools also learned to take attendance. When asked for the attendance average for the previous year, they reported a range between 67% to 85%. We estimate that it might have been closer to the 67%. There had been no record keeping until this past year. Students who participated in sports, contests, or other extracurricular activities were usually pulled out of class without prior notification to the teacher. The first year, state officials and central administrators frequently came unannounced to pilot a test or conduct a social activity. The 90 minutes of uninterrupted EPT time rarely remained 90 minutes. Every Monday there is a mandated 1-hour salute to the flag that is followed by collecting, recording, sorting, and storing every child's savings into their savings accounts. Therefore, Monday's 90-minute reading block was usually moved to an abbreviated time frame later on in the day. We counted four holidays in the month of May with unofficial vacation bridges (extra days off) built around the holidays.

Secondary schools are more problematic than elementary schools when it comes to time on learning. At the secondary schools, each student is required to take 11 subjects in a week, on alternate days, in 45-minute periods. Before the program implementation we observed that at the beginning of each class period it took 7 or more minutes for students to get settled and the teacher to take roll for 45 to 50 students. Each teacher teaches from 1 to 14 classes a week. Their load is scheduled around their other jobs. Some want Friday and Monday off; others want to leave by noon. Some teachers go back and forth between two schools to try to fill their 35-hour load in the morning. In the afternoon, they might go back and forth between two other schools, as they try to maintain a full teaching load in the afternoon as well. This coming and going results in high teacher absenteeism, excessive wait time for students, periods of inactivity, or assignments to keep students busy.

What Did We Do About This Challenge? The secondary school is now piloting 90-minute blocks with some subjects. Teachers and students are still practicing promptness in moving from one classroom to the next. A student monitor is assigned to check attendance and tardiness through charts of students sitting in cooperative teams of four. This enables the monitor to quickly scan for empty seats and record a tardy or absent mark. The counselor picks up and confirms the seating charts. The teacher is freed to initiate instruction.

Master calendars of activities, staff development and holidays have been instituted. However, the problem of central district and state administrators' lack of scheduling is still a problem. The principal and Family Support Team check and keep track of attendance and tardiness. They post monthly results. The parents instituted awards ceremonies for teachers and students with perfect attendance and on-time arrival.

Challenge: A New Culture of Staff Development

Staff development becomes a challenge when the teachers are so tired from trying to keep up with two jobs. Saturdays are out of the question because that is the only day teachers have for their personal and family chores. Weekdays are a burden on everyone's conscience because the students have to stay home, because there are no substitutes.

The only staff development teachers receive is 2 days at the beginning of the year to "hear" about textbook and program guidelines. The teachers were quite used to a transmission model rather than a transformative model of professional development (Barth, 1999). Based on custom, most of the teachers did not take the 3-day initial SFA/EPT workshop seriously. They were not accustomed to follow-up implementation accountability. To complicate matters more, we later learned that half of the faculty in the elementary school was set to retire in November, the official and customary time of retirement. That first year, we did a lot of on-the-job training and retraining of teachers new to the school.

How Did We Begin to Address This Challenge?   EPT staff development had to consider going beyond the SFA initial 3-day workshops and include relearning how to teach and value learning. After the first year's failures of transfer from training and struggles with teacher resistance, we redesigned a 5-day initial workshop. In this workshop we added more theory and practice of cooperative learning, personal and professional change, transfer from training cycles, peer coaching, and Teachers' Learning Communities (Calderón, 1997). Teachers struggled at first with the intensely interactive and learner-centered approach to staff development, but in 5 days they saw the merits. We added another secondary school to test this design, and the impact on teacher attitude and transfer was dramatic in comparison to the first schools. The level of transfer went from 40% appropriate to 80% appropriate with 10% rated as exemplary.

In the second year of piloting we also learned to focus more on the talents of the teachers. Because we were working with only one school, we were able to focus more resources on teachers' learning and contributing through their talents: as writers, story tellers, innovators, organizers, social mediators between parents and school, and peer teachers.

Their innate sociability conveniently opened the door to implementing TLCs. The TLCs are social places for learning. Food, fun, and fanfare make learning possible even under the most oppressing circumstances (Calderón, 1997). The principal arranged for 1-day-a-month release for TLCs. Time was borrowed from "bridges"; extracurricular activities were clustered so that students did not have to stay home; and parents held their Parent Learning Communities at the same time so they could see that these days were spent primarily for the benefit of their children's education.

Activities in TLCs ranged from review of techniques and materials to discussing and solving problems. Writing teams were formed. Experiments with schedules were mapped. Celebrations were planned. The TLCs sustained and improved implementation. Teachers began visiting and inviting their colleagues from the SFA schools across the border in El Paso to join them. They are currently training each other on their strengths—the Juárez teachers conduct monthly workshops in El Paso to help the bilingual teachers with grammar and discourse in Spanish for the SFA components; the El Paso teachers helped their Juárez colleagues in the development of interdisciplinary units, cooperative learning in the content areas, and scheduling. Thus, the binational TLCs came into being. Teachers continue to assist one another across the border.

Challenge: Administrative Support

The 1992 reform has shaken some of the institutionalized norms but not completely destroyed them. Personal politics and power are still at the forefront of most educational agendas. The administration welcomes programs such as EPT because they want the publicity and the limelight. As one administrator admitted "we need to put up a good front and defend our image." There are no formal administrator training programs. Although recently a masters degree has become desirable for newly appointed administrators, the majority rose from the ranks of teacher union leaders or knew someone in a higher position. The nonexistence of administrators' academies or systematic professional development has stifled educational growth in many ways and has created a mind set against change. Our first year of piloting revealed a most complex system of leadership that almost made us give up the project.

How Did We Begin to Tackle This Challenge? The Fernández Foundation became a partner in promoting the program to the state and local administrations. The first 2 years were spent informing officials of the pilot and replication plan and trying to convince the administration of the need to invest in one teacher facilitator per school and a cadre of local trainers. All other expenses would be covered by the Foundation. Just as we were making inroads, the government party changed again, all the officials and top administrators were removed, and we had to start all over again. The new administration demonstrated more interest initially, but no commitment has yet been made. Once again, the Foundation is wondering if all their investments and our efforts will ever be recognized by the system. This year, a new strategy will be identified to seek the state's collaboration, to give it one more try.

Challenge: Parental Involvement and Support

Mexican parents have always been highly involved with their children's schools. They conduct fund raising activities throughout the year and pitch in to clean or paint the school. They walk their children to school and wait around to see if they are needed. They volunteer in the classrooms. They always support the teachers' disciplinary decisions and make sure their children have school supplies, even if they have to go without. The challenge here was to learn how to channel their good will and talents toward school reform.

How Did We Meet this Challenge? The school's Family Support Team, an educational psychologist from Mexico City, the parents, and their children were given the task to develop a family support component for the school. Sections of the SFA Family Support manual were translated and soon thereafter discarded because the Family Support Team felt it was not culturally or contextually relevant. Nevertheless, the key concepts of attendance, early intervention for students with problems beyond instruction, and parental involvement in literacy activities were retained. At the secondary school, 60 parents and their children met monthly in their learning communities with Dr. Trini Berrúm, a prominent psychologist, to brainstorm solutions for each category. They then tested their ideas during the month and reported back on their effectiveness. The Family Support Team recorded ideas, developed forms and processes, the principal removed potential barriers, and the program developers compiled a new Family Support Manual.

The parents' and Family Team's accomplishments went beyond everyone's expectations. They instituted a variety of programs that ranged from the development of the manual to patrolling the neighborhood shopping malls. They took turns patrolling the back of the school yard where students sometimes jumped the 7 foot fence to get away for a midmorning break. Attendance went from about 67% up to 96% by the end of the year. Tardiness diminished 90%. Teachers' attendance and promptness increased dramatically as well. When the students and parents began complaining that the cause of such delinquent behavior was the behavior of the teacher, even the most resistant teachers began to exhibit positive changes. Other activities such as "wake-up calls" to parents or students who did not even have a phone were also creatively instituted. The parents learned about schooling and problem solving through cooperative-learning workshops once a month. The last hour of these workshops was usually shared with student representatives and the faculty. Assignments, goals, and plans were then jointly finalized for the month.

Challenge: Lack of Systematic Student Evaluation

For the first year of the pilot study, we found it very difficult to gather student academic results beyond the EPT assessments. From these, we could see that students were progressing at the equivalent rate of students in new

SFA schools in the United States. We had no baseline data for state exams for attendance because these were not available. The second year, however, students demonstrated significantly higher performance as compared to the students' performance the year before on tests given at the same time each spring (see Figs. 8.1 to 8.3). However, one of the complaints was that these tests were "too old fashioned" and could not reflect all that the students had actually learned.

Teachers reported that in addition to higher test scores, the students were writing better and more complete sentences; their discussions were richer and more profound; their verbal skills and self confidence had increased dramatically; they were reading more; their social and cooperative skills had improved considerably over the year; they were taking on more leadership roles; and they were being responsible for their own learning.

The students themselves reported that they liked learning and reading more; they liked coming to school now; they enjoyed learning in coopera-tive teams; they liked the changes in the teachers; and they liked the changes in their parents.

The parents also reported great enthusiasm that their children were do-ing better in school and behaving better, the teachers were teaching better,

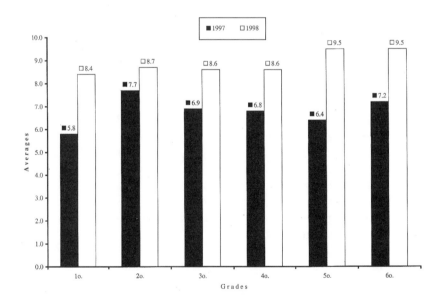

FIG. 8.1   Ciudad Juárez Elementary School percentages of students
passing—all subjects combined.

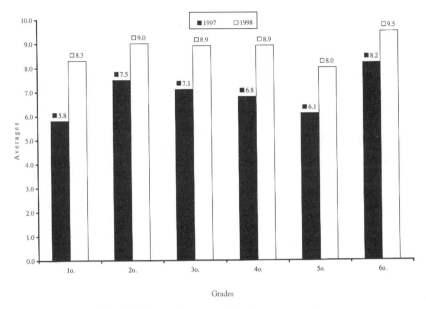

FIG. 8.2   Ciudad Juárez Elementary School percentages of students passing—Spanish reading and writing.

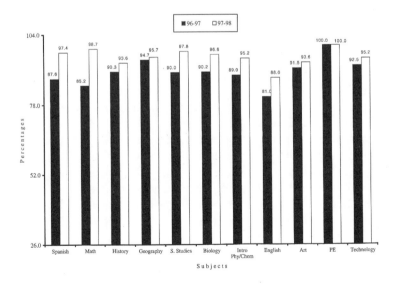

FIG. 8.3   Ciudad Juárez Elementary School percentages of students passing—each subject area.

and that the administration really cared for their children. One parent stated, "I don't know how to read, but I am so happy my children are reading. I just wish I could have had this program, maybe I would have learned" (Sr. Campos, September 1998).

Nevertheless, these new learnings and behaviors are not accorded as much weight as the test scores on the state's tests, which mostly measure recall of book knowledge.

What Happened Next?

We anxiously awaited the second year of implementation to refine the process. However, the principal was promoted to the district=level administration and the school remained without a principal for over half a year. The teachers union began a power struggle over the new leadership appointment, and the program was put on hold as they waited for the political results. This year, there is a new principal who has indicated interest in picking up where we left off.

Because there is no consensus among Mexican scholars, administrators, and politicians as to where the educational system is heading, we find ourselves balancing on that fine line between success and failure. Although the intent of the EPT program was primarily to improve reading and writing, we now find ourselves in a web of complex reform issues.

News of the merits of the program has spread throughout the educational community and there are now 5 kindergartens, 10 elementary schools, and 5 secondary schools wanting to implement EPT in their schools. The question is whether the Foundation or the program developers have the energy, time, and resources to invest in this on-going struggle. Thus far, fundamental structural change has failed due to deep-rooted behavior, beliefs, attitudes, and assumptions of the majority of the educational leaders. Are we too early for fundamental change? Are we on the brink of a powerful breakthrough? Will the experiences with these 20 new schools remove existing barriers and serve as model schools for the rest of the state?

Theories of leadership and change (O'Tool, 1996; Singe, 1996) remind us that timing is important. Drucker's experiences prompted him to ask the questions "Do leaders have a responsibility to act even when the world isn't ready for change? If they do act, are they merely engaging in a quixotic quest?

Much has been accomplished. Much has been developed. The elementary program is now complete. The 1st- and 2nd-grade curriculum and materials for secondary schools are finished. The family support program was rewritten and the manual needs one last component to pilot and add. Half of the prekindergarten and kindergarten program is ready and in need of pilot sites. The five kindergarten schools are anxious to volunteer. The 10 elementary and 5 secondary schools are so willing to adopt the program that they have found their own resources for the five days of training. They are in the process of securing funds for the materials from other sources. They understand the long-term commitments and are willing to tackle the uncertainties of change.

Uncertainties are all that we currently have in Juárez, México. A new presidential election is forthcoming, along with more unrest, major changes in the national textbooks and programs, and another long period of uncertainty that inhibits systemic change. Meanwhile, the student drop out and failure rates continue to increase.

REFERENCES

Andrade de Herrera, V. (1996). Education in Mexico: Historical and contemporary educational systems. In J. Le Blanc Flores (Ed.), *Children of la frontera* (pp. 25–59). Charleston, WV: Clearinghouse on Rural Education and Small Schools.

Barth, R. S. (1991). *Improving schools from within.* San Francisco: Jossey-Bass.

Boykin, W. (1994). *The talent development model.* Baltimore, MD: Johns Hopkins University.

Calderón, M. (1997). Voces de maestros: La construcción de conocimiento en comunidad. In the *Second Binational Conference Proceedings: In Search of A Border Pedagogy.* Baltimore, MD: Johns Hopkins University, CRESPAR.

Davis, B., & Sumara, D. J. (1997). Cognition, complexity, and teacher education. In *Harvard Educational Review, 67*(1) 105–125.

Loera, A. (1998). *Investigaciones sobre la educación en Cd. Juárez.* Presentation to the Rosario Fernández Foundation. Cd. Juárez, Chihuahua.

O'Toole, J. (1996). *Leading change: The argument for values-based leadership.* New York: Ballantine.

Secretaría de Educación Pública (1992). *Dirección General de Información, Capítulo Educación.* Mexico, DF: Author.

Secretaría de Educación Pública (1993). *Dirección General de Información, Informe de Educación.* Mexico, DF: Author.

Secretaría de Educación Pública (1995). *Rincones de lectura.* Mexico, DF: Author.

Singe, P. (1990). *La quinta disciplina: El arte y la práctica de la organización albierta al aprendizaje.* Mexico, DF: Vergara Granica.

Slavin, P., Madden, N. A., Dolan, L. J., & Wasik, B. A. (1996). *Every child, every school: Success for all.* Thousand Oaks, CA: Corwin.

III

Implications for Policy and Practice

9

Disseminating Success for All: Lessons for Policy and Practice*

Robert E. Slavin
Johns Hopkins University

Nancy A. Madden
Success for All Foundation

Never in the history of American education has the potential for fundamental reform been as great. However, it is by no means certain that the potential for reform will be realized. Changes will take place, but will these
changes actually make a difference in the school success of large numbers of
children? For this to happen, the nearly 3 million teachers in U.S. schools
will have to learn and regularly apply very different and far more effective
instructional methods than those they use now. School organization, assessment, grouping, and many other aspects of schooling will have to change.
The systemic changes happening at many levels of government are creating
a fast-rising demand for high-quality, sustained professional development,

*Portions of this chapter are adapted from Slavin, R. E., & Madden, N. A. (1999). *Disseminating Suc-
cess for All: Lessons for Policy and Practice*. Baltimore, MD: Johns Hopkins University, Center for Research
on the Education of Students Placed At Risk.

particularly the professional development needed for schools to adopt proven models of school change. Yet the national infrastructure for professional development of this kind is quite limited.

If reform is to produce results, major changes in the structure of professional development are needed. This chapter is intended to shed light on the question of how a national approach to professional development might enable professional development networks to bring proven school change models to scale by describing the lessons we have learned in disseminating Success for All (SFA), a comprehensive reform program for high-poverty elementary schools. In the course of disseminating SFA we have learned a great deal about the process of change, about factors that support and inhibit school-level reform, and about ways of enlisting others in support of our efforts. This chapter describes our experience with dissemination, the strategies we are pursuing, the relative success of various dissemination routes, and the implications of our experiences for public policies.

SUCCESS FOR ALL

As noted in chapter 1 of this volume, SFA (Madden, Slavin, Karweit, Dolan, & Wasik, 1993; Slavin, Madden, Dolan, & Wasik, 1996; Slavin, Madden, Karweit, Dolan, & Wasik, 1992; Slavin et al., 1992, 1994; Slavin & Madden, 1999b) is a program designed to comprehensively restructure elementary schools serving many children placed at risk of school failure. It emphasizes prevention, early intervention, use of innovative reading, writing and language arts curriculum, and extensive professional development to help schools start children with success and then build on that foundation throughout the elementary grades.

Research comparing SFA to control schools has consistently shown that SFA has substantial positive effects on student reading achievement throughout the elementary grades (Madden et al., 1993; Slavin et al., 1994b, 1996) as well as reducing special education placements and retentions and improving attendance (Slavin et al., 1992, 1996; Slavin & Madden, 1999, 2000). This research is summarized in chapter 2 of this volume.

More recently, primarily under funding from the New American Schools Development Corporation (NASDC), we have developed and evaluated programs in mathematics (MathWings) and in social studies and science (WorldLab). In general, schools implement SFA first, and then add MathWings, WorldLab, or both in subsequent years. Research also shows positive effects of MathWings (Madden, Slavin, & Simons, 1999) and WorldLab (Slavin & Madden, 1999a).

SFA was first piloted in one Baltimore elementary school in the 1987–1988 school year. In 1988–1989 it was expanded to a total of five schools in Baltimore and one in Philadelphia. Since then the number of schools has grown by 40% to 100% each year. In 1998–1999, SFA was being implemented in approximately 1550 schools in 670 districts in 48 states throughout the United States, and has been adapted for use in five other countries. Of these, approximately 150 were using MathWings, WorldLab, or both.

Table 9.1 (from chapter 1) shows the growth in numbers of schools implementing SFA from 1987 to the present. Figure 9.1 shows the same data for the years 1990–2000. Note that the annual percentage gain has never fallen below 38%, and every year the number of schools added is more than those added in the previous year. This is a very rapid rate of growth; for example, in 3 years (1995–1998), the total number of schools almost quadrupled, after sextupling in the 3 years before that. Over the past 2 years (1997–1999), the number more than doubled again. In 2000–2001, we are serving more than 1,800 schools, and about 1 million children. At this growth rate we have to continually focus on maintaining the quality of our implementations, as it becomes impossible for our central staff to know every school. This chapter discusses the successful as well as unsuccessful strategies we have pursued to enable us to scale up our operation without compromising on quality and effectiveness.

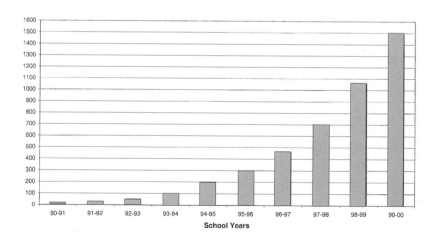

FIG. 9.1   Numbers of Success for All schools (1990–2000).

TABLE 9.1

Approximate Numbers of Success for All and Roots
& Wings Schools, 1987–1999

School Year	Schools	Gain	Percentage Gain
1987–1988	1		
1988–1989	6	5	
1989–1990	9	3	50
1990–1991	16	7	78
1991–1992	30	14	88
1992–1993	50	20	67
1993–1994	100	50	100
1994–1995	200	100	100
1995–1996	300	100	50
1996–1997	480	180	60
1997–1998	750	270	56
1998–1999	1090	390	52
1999–2000	1550	460	42

PROGRAM CHARACTERISTICS
AFFECTING DISSEMINATION

There are several unique characteristics of SFA that have an important
bearing on the strategies we use in disseminating the program. First, although SFA is always adapted to the needs and resources of each school using it, there are definite elements common to all. A fully functional SFA
school will always implement our kindergarten program and reading program in Grades 1 through 5 or 1 through 6, will have at least one certified
teacher tutor for first graders, and will have a full-time facilitator and a family support team. Other elements, such as preschool and full-day kindergarten, are optional, and schools vary in the number of tutors, the staff time

devoted to family support, and other features. Yet despite this variation, we believe that the integrity of the program must be maintained if schools are to produce the results we have found so consistently in our research. The whole school must make a free and informed choice to adopt SFA; we require a vote by secret ballot of at least 80%. But when schools make this choice they are choosing a particular model of reading instruction, a particular use of Title I and special-education resources, a particular within-school support structure, and so on. Unlike many alternative schoolwide change models, SFA is not reinvented from scratch for each school staff.

SFA requires substantial change in many aspects of curriculum and instruction. It takes time for teachers to learn and perfect new forms of instruction, and for facilitators, tutors, family support-team members, and principals to learn new roles. Therefore, the program requires a great deal of professional development done over an extended period of time. Although the initial training period is only 3 days for classroom teachers, many follow-up visits from SFA trainers take place each year. Schools budget for 25-person days of training in the first implementation year, 12 in the second, and 5 to 8 in each subsequent year.

SFA requires that schools invest in tutors, a facilitator, materials, and extensive professional development. Because of the focus of the program and its cost, the program is primarily used in high-poverty schools with substantial Title I resources. As of 1999–2000, the cost of the program for a school of 500 students averages $73,000 in the first year for materials and training, plus salaries for a facilitator, tutors, and other staff (usually reallocated from other functions). Until the Comprehensive School Reform Demonstration (CSRD) began in 1998 to give grants of at least $50,000 per year to help schools adopt proven, comprehensive reform designs, SFA schools rarely received funds beyond their usual Title I allocations. Only about 300 of the 1,800 schools have received CSRD funding. For the others, it might be said that the program has no incremental costs, but there are many schools that could not afford a credible version of the model (i.e., most non-Title I and low-funded Title I schools). Although the cost of the program does restrict its use, it also has an important benefit: it increases the likelihood that the school and district will take it seriously and work to see that their investment pays off.

The comprehensiveness, complexity, and cost of SFA have important consequences for dissemination. First, they mean that the program cannot be mandated en masse. Instead, districts usually start with a few schools and gradually add more. Second, they mean that the commitment to the program must be long term, and we must be prepared to be engaged with schools for many years, perhaps forever. Third, they mean that we must maintain a large, very highly skilled staff of trainers to work with schools. although we occasionally use teachers and facilitators from successful schools in our training programs, the program does not lend itself to an easy "trainer-of-trainers" strategy in which a small staff trains local trainers to work with schools.

DISSEMINATION STAFF

Until July 1998, the dissemination of SFA was primarily carried out by our staff at the Center for Research on the Education of Students Placed at Risk, Johns Hopkins University. Since that time, our dissemination has been moved to a separate not-for-profit organization, the Success for All Foundation, or SFAF. In fall 2000, our training staff consists of approximately 240 full-time trainers, plus 16 at the University of Memphis. Almost all of our trainers are teachers; most have been building facilitators or teachers in SFA schools. The only trainers who are not former teachers are those who focus on family support. Their backgrounds are usually in social work or counseling.

The trainers who work for SFAF are organized in 16 regions of the United States, each with a very experienced trainer as a regional manager. In addition, we have a small number of part-time trainers (some of whom have formerly worked for us) located in various parts of the country, and we will often ask an especially talented teacher or facilitator to help us with training and follow-up in their own area.

In addition to SFAF staff, there is a regional training program for SFA at the University of Memphis. This group, led by Steven Ross and Lana Smith, has had a long-standing involvement with SFA schools in Memphis and has conducted research on SFA in districts around the United States. The University of Memphis group has taken responsibility for implementing SFA in Tennessee, Arkansas and Mississippi, and serves a few schools in other states.

Formerly, WestEd, a federally funded educational laboratory, maintained a regional training program for SFA in most of California, Arizona, Utah, and Nevada. However, problems with this arrangement (see following) led to its cancellation in April 1998. Most of the SFA trainers working for WestEd moved to the SFAF, which now serves schools in the former WestEd region. In addition, a training contract with a for-profit company, Education Partners, ended in fall 2000.

DISSEMINATION STRATEGIES

Schools first become aware of Success for All in a variety of ways. Many articles have been written about the program in educational journals, and our

TABLE 9.2

Success for All Training Regions

Region	Headquarters	States Served
Mid-Atlantic	Baltimore	MD, PA, DC, NJ, DE
New York	New York City	NY
New England	Montreal	CT, RI, MA, ME, VT, NH
South	Montgomery, AL	AL, GA, NC, SC, VA
Florida-north	Orlando	FL (north)
Florida-south	Miami	FL (south)
Midwest	Charleston, WV	OH, IN, IL, WI, MI, MN, IA, KY, WV
University of Memphis	Memphis	TN, AR, MS, MO
Louisiana	Lafayette, LA	LA
Texas-east	Houston	TX (east)
Texas-south	San Antonio	TX (south and west)
High Plains	Lubbock, TX	TX (north), OK, KS, NE, SD, ND, WY, MT
Southwest	Phoenix	AZ, NV (south), UT, CO, NM
California-South	Los Angeles	CA (south), HI
California-North	Sacramento	CA (north), NV (north), AK, WA (Seattle)
Northwest	Seattle	OR, WA, ID

staff has made many presentations at conferences. We have an awareness video and materials, including a book describing the program and its outcomes. Educators may write for information, call members of our dissemination staff, or otherwise make contact with us. School or district staff may then invite our staff to make awareness presentations. These often take place as part of *effective methods fairs* in which large districts or states invite principals or school teams to learn about many promising models. We encourage schools to send delegations to visit other SFA schools in their region if at all possible. If there is interest in schools after these awareness presentations, school staff will send us a Preliminary Data Form, which enables us to calculate a price for training and materials. We will then negotiate a contract specifying what we and the school and the district promise to do. The contract makes our intentions and requirements clear. At some point a presentation will be made to the whole staff of each interested school. Following opportunities to examine materials, visit other schools, and discuss among themselves, school staffs vote by secret ballot. We require a positive vote of at least 80% of the professional staff. It is rare that we would go through the entire process and then have a vote of less than 80%; more often votes are closer to 100% positive. However, the exercise is essential in that it assures teachers that they had a free choice and that the program is supported by the great majority of their colleagues.

The integrity of this vote is so important to us that in some districts in which we suspect there may be pressure to implement SFA we have asked the local teacher's unions to monitor the voting. We have found that it is very difficult to work in schools in which the staff did not make an overwhelming, informed, and unfettered choice to work with us.

As soon as a school has decided to adopt the program, planning for implementation begins. A member of the SFAF staff or one of our regional training sites is appointed to serve as the school's lead contact.

A facilitator is then chosen, usually an experienced and respected teacher from within the school's own staff. The facilitator and the principal will attend a week-long training session in one of a few central locations in different parts of the United States held well in advance of training for the school staff. For example, we hold our main facilitator or principal "new sites" trainings in May, June, and July for schools planning their training for teachers in August. This gives the facilitators and principals time to work out issues of staffing, space, finances, ordering and storing materials, and so on. Facilitators may also visit other schools to see the program in action and to get a first-hand view of what facilitators are expected to do.

If a school is planning to begin SFA in September, training will generally take place over a 3-day period in August. Additional training is provided later for tutors and for family support staff. Some schools start at midyear, implementing portions of the program that can be started then, but holding off the first-grade reading program until the following September.

The initial training is typically done by the school's point trainer, other staff from SFAF or regional training organizations, and (occasionally) adjunct trainers who are facilitators or teachers in existing SFA schools. After initial training, follow-up visits will be conducted by these same staff. A first-year school will receive 12 to 16 person days of followup, usually in two-person, 2-day visits.

Our main objective during follow-up visits is to strengthen the skills of the building facilitators and principals. We cannot hope to adequately monitor and refine implementations from a great distance; instead, we must rely on the facilitator, who is the change agent within the school, as well as the principal and teachers. Our staff members jointly conduct an implementation review, visiting classes, interviewing teachers, family support members, tutors, and others, and looking together at the data on student performance, pacing, attendance, special education placements, and so on. Our trainers model ways of giving feedback to teachers, give the building facilitators advice on solving their problems, share perspectives on strengths and weaknesses of the program, and plan with the building facilitator and principal the goals for individual teachers and for general program implementation that the facilitator will follow up on. Trainers meet with teachers to provide additional training on such issues as writing, pacing, or classroom management. They respond to questions and discuss issues needing further attention. Later, trainers complete implementation check forms and write up site reports summarizing what they have seen, noting promises made, issues to be followed up on, and ratings of the quality of implementation of each program element.

In general, we are very satisfied with the dissemination model we are using. In regular implementation checks that are part of our follow-up visits, we find more than 90% of teachers to be doing an adequate job of implementing the programs, and many teachers are doing inspired teaching, using our materials and methods as a jumping-off point for innovative and exciting instruction. The relative prescriptiveness of the model and the training and follow-up that support it are sometimes perceived to be problematic before implementation begins, but are rarely a long-term problem, as teachers and other staff come to see the flexibility within the program and to see the outcomes for children. In fact, for teachers used to inadequate professional development without the material or human supports necessary to change their teaching on a day-to-day basis, the completeness of SFA, from materials to training to follow-up, is a major plus. The consistent positive findings in evaluations of SFA in its dissemination sites, and research on teachers' attitudes toward the program after one or more years of the program (see chap. 2, this volume), tell us that our model of dissemination is working.

However, although we are confident that the SFA program can be successfully adapted to local circumstances and replicated nationally using the model of dissemination we have evolved, the problem we face is how to provide such an intensive level of service on a broad scale. America has more than 50,000 Title I elementary schools. We are currently working in more than 1,550 schools, about 3%. Our network of schools has been expanding by about 40% to 50% each year, an enormous rate of growth. We have had to continually restructure ourselves to accommodate this growth without compromising on quality, and will need to continue to do so for the foreseeable future. We still have a long way to go.

OBEY-PORTER COMPREHENSIVE SCHOOL REFORM DEMONSTRATION (CSRD)

In 1997, the U.S. Congress allocated $150 million for a new program designed to assist schools in adopting proven, comprehensive reform designs. In 1999, this was increased to $175 million per year. These are programs that provide external assistance to schools to upgrade their curricula, parent involvement approaches, assessments, professional development approaches, and other features. SFA and Roots & Wings (R&W) were named in the legislation among 17 examples of such comprehensive designs. Schools can apply for 3-year grants of at least $50,000 per year to pay for the start-up costs of adopting comprehensive designs. Funds were also allocated for labs and state departments of education to help in the awareness and review process (see Slavin, 1998).

The CSRD program is beginning to have a profound impact on scaling up of SFA and R&W. Obviously, it provides funding for schools that might not have been able to afford adequate implementations. More importantly, perhaps, it raises the profile of programs like SFA and R&W at the policy level. State departments of education, laboratories, and districts are all engaged in disseminating information about comprehensive reform models, and this is having an impact on their own involvement in and knowledge about whole-school reform.

One difficulty inherent to CSRD, however, is that it is likely to greatly increase the demand for research-based reform models without increasing the supply. All existing programs will be struggling to add training capacity without reducing quality. Another potential difficulty with CSRD is the possibility that some schools will apply for funds because they want money, not because they are eager for reform. With this danger in mind, we have tried to ensure that our rigorous standards for schools to adopt SFA are followed in spirit as well as process. We are issuing certificates to schools that fully meet our standards, and are asking state departments to make sure that any application to implement Success for All or Roots & Wings encloses a certificate from us, which commits us to provide training and materials to the school if it is funded.

In CSRD grants made to date (spring 2000), about 300 out of 1,750 grants in 46 states have been made to schools to implement SFA and R&W. This is the largest number of grants to any program, more than to the next three programs combined. However, the surprise in the CSRD process is that grants are being made to support an enormous array of programs, many of which are neither well researched or even comprehensive. Collectively, the 17 programs listed in the legislation are receiving only about one half of the grants.

EXTENDING OUR REACH

As SFA has become a national program, we have had to confront the problem of providing adequate training and follow-up in many widely dispersed locations with very different needs, resources, and circumstances. Early on, we began searching for ways of engaging regionally based educators in training or support roles, to extend our training capacity, to reduce travel costs for schools, and to provide schools with trainers who are more familiar with the local scene. For a program as complex as SFA, with such extensive requirements for training and follow-up, it is not a simple matter to train trainers to work in their own areas. As we disseminate SFA we do not want to compromise on the quality or integrity of the model we have developed and researched. It is difficult to train educators who have not been teachers or facilitators in SFA schools, and the need for lengthy follow-up makes it difficult to have part-time trainers with other jobs play a major role in training. With these concerns in mind, however, we have pursued a variety of strategies for building a local and regional capacity for training, follow-up, and support. The following sections discuss our experiences with each.

REGIONAL TRAINING SITES

As noted earlier, we have a training site for SFA at the University of Memphis, and have experimented with other regional partners. The stories of how these sites were established and how other attempts to create regional training sites in other organizations have failed provide an interesting perspective on the possibilities and difficulties of regional training strategies.

Universities

One obvious candidate for regional training sites is universities. This is the route taken by several other national school reform networks, such as Reading Recovery (Pinnell, DeFord, & Lyons, 1988) and Accelerated Schools (Levin, 1987). However, SFA does not lend itself as easily to dissemination from universities. Reading Recovery is a tutoring program for at-risk first graders that provides its training as courses with graduate credit. Individual teachers can be trained as tutors without involving other school staff. It therefore fits easily in established structures. Accelerated Schools emphasizes an organizational development consulting approach that is also familiar to university faculty members (see McCarthy, 1991). In contrast, working with whole schools over extended time periods is an unusual activity for university faculty, who are typically too involved with courses, committees, and research to put much time into such activities. With the sole exception of the University of Memphis, no university has attempted to establish a regional training program for SFA.

Our successful training site at the University of Memphis exists because of some unusual circumstances. The University of Memphis has a Center for Research in Education Policy funded primarily by the State of Tennessee. Two researchers in that Center, Steven Ross and Lana Smith, developed a close relationship with the Memphis City Schools in the course of their research there. In 1989, they began working with one Memphis SFA school and assessing outcomes in that school. Later, we contracted with them to conduct independent evaluations of SFA in several additional districts. Initially, their main involvement with SFA was as researchers, not trainers. However, in 1992, a new superintendent in Memphis, Gerry House, became interested in SFA and asked their help in scaling it up. Since then, the University of Memphis center has begun work in additional districts in Tennessee, Georgia, Arkansas, Mississippi, Louisiana, and Missouri. They have built up their own training staff, and also coordinate with trainers who are from Memphis City Schools.

The success of the University of Memphis regional training site depends on several relatively unique characteristics. One is the existence of a research center at the university. Another is the unusual motivation and skill of the researchers, and their close relations both with SFA and with the Memphis City Schools. However, it is important to note that the University of Memphis training site came to being through a traditional university activity, research, and not training per se. In fact, the emphasis of this center is still as much on research as on training. Other attempts to recruit universities to house regional training programs have not worked out.

Education Partners

Education Partners (EP), a for-profit company, was the largest regional training program for SFA housed in a different organization. Headquartered in
San Francisco, EP served approximately 180 schools in the San Francisco Bay
Area, Oregon, Washington, Idaho, Colorado, and New Mexico. In 1996,
EP's President approached us about taking on a training role. At the time, EP
was very small, and had only been in operation for less than 2 years, contract-
ing to help reconstituted schools in San Francisco with professional development. EP proposed to carry out dissemination of SFA in a defined region
under a stringent set of performance standards, to be monitored by us, that required them to maintain a high quality of training and implementation at
each school they served. They agreed to pay Johns Hopkins University (JHU;
currently SFAF) a set fee on all revenues. We agreed to EP's proposal as an experiment, to see if a for-profit organization could do a better job than we could
as a not-for-profit. Later, when a contract with the Xerox Corporation to do
our printing and distribution fell apart in fall 1996, EP bid for and won a contract to take on this function as well.

Because EP started out so small, it was able to design itself solely for
the purpose of serving as a training program for SFA. With a few exceptions (e.g., a more proactive marketing plan), EP operated much the
same way as SFAF does. However, although there was an initial plan to
gradually expand EP's training territory, this did not occur. The main
problem was the for-profit nature of EP. Although any operating sur-
pluses in SFAF go into further development and research, those in EP go
to investors. The involvement of SFAF with a for-profit organization has
created some political and legal problems. For example, it led to concerns
at the Internal Revenue Service in terms of our not-for-profit status, and
concerns in teacher's unions and policy circles about our motives. Fric-
tion between SFAF and EP developed when EP made decisions that favored enhancing profits rather than serving children. As a result, the EP
training contract was taken to an arbitrator and, in fall 2000, was termi-
nated due to a failure to meet performance standards. Our experience
with EP does not support the idea of subcontracting to for-profit organizations for training services.

Educational Laboratories

The regional laboratories would appear to be ideal organizations to become
regional training sites for SFA. They are responsible for helping districts in
their regions learn about and implement effective programs. In fact, when
they were first established in the 1960s, labs were meant to complement the

work of national research centers, such as the one at Johns Hopkins in which SFA was developed and researched. As originally conceived, research centers were designed to do basic and applied research on important educational problems, whereas labs were supposed to interpret this research for their regions and help local schools apply the findings. Labs and centers are funded by the same agency and are still expected to work together.

In fact, lab-center collaboration is relatively uncommon, and it is almost unheard of for labs to actively disseminate programs developed and researched in research centers. Labs often develop (and disseminate) their own programs, and see little advantage in disseminating others' work. Also, labs must serve an enormous region, and it is difficult for them to provide direct services to individual schools.

Despite these problems, we attempted to engage labs in support of SFA dissemination. We spoke to lab directors and lab communication directors, and had various communications with individual labs. However, WestEd, in California, was the only lab to establish a regional training program for SFA. The North Central Lab (NCREL) was once helping us work with a few Chicago schools, but other labs have expressed little or no interest.

The arrangement with WestEd was initially successful, based in part on a history of prior collaboration between JHU and the individual who started the regional training program at WestEd. However, ultimately this arrangement did not work out. Part of the problem was in maintaining consistency between JHU and SFAF and WestEd; in many cases, WestEd reinterpreted SFA policies, failed to implement various program elements, or otherwise insisted on its own approaches. These and other problems led to a schism within the WestEd SFA staff, with more than half resigning or threatening to resign during the 1997–1998 school year. SFAF took back the region in April 1998.

Although our experiences with WestEd and with labs in general does not support the idea of having labs establish their own training programs, labs can be helpful in an awareness and brokering role. In particular, the Obey-Porter Comprehensive School Reform Demonstration, described earlier, provided $500,000 grants to each lab to help schools and districts in their regions learn about and adopt effective whole-school reform designs. The labs have been helping states set up awareness activities, such as effective methods fairs, to help schools and districts apply for funding to implement proven designs, including SFA and R&W.

State Departments of Education

One potential source of assistance in providing regionally based training and assistance to SFA schools is state departments of education. We have worked with a few state departments and have found them to be helpful in some ways but have not yet found a way to have state departments play a major role in dissemination of our program.

The state department with which we have had the greatest involvement is in New Jersey. There, starting in 1994, we worked with an Urban Education Initiative related to a statewide court-ordered plan to increase state funding to the 28 lowest wealth districts. The state-department staff involved with this initiative coordinated several meetings with high-poverty districts and intended to build its own training and support capacity for SFA. However, the political turmoil resulting in part from the tax increases necessitated by the funding equity decision caused a change of control in the legislature and then of the governorship, dooming the Urban Education Initiative. Still, our involvement with the New Jersey State Department resulted in our building a small network of schools that continued on its own with minimal involvement by the state. In 1998, the approval by the New Jersey Supreme Court of a plan to focus substantial new resources for these 28 districts on proven programs, with SFA prominently highlighted as the preferred model for elementary schools, has re-established a close collaboration with the New Jersey Department of Education, and an expansion in the number of SFA and R&W schools in the state.

Other state departments of education have highlighted SFA in state conferences and in other forums. The New York State Department is recommending SFA to schools identified as low achieving in state assessments, and is helping to fund the program in several New York City schools.

State departments of education have taken a central role in the Obey-Porter Comprehensive School Reform Demonstration. They are responsible for writing overall state plans, making schools and districts aware of options available to them, reviewing proposals, and making awards. In this process many state departments are becoming aware of the capacity problem among existing research-based programs, and are beginning to think about ways to support quality adoptions and thereby attract national programs to their states and increase their ability to work with large numbers of schools.

In general, state departments of education have been important in providing appropriate policy environments, awareness, and (in NJ, OH, IN, NV, and NY), money for implementing schools, but have not taken a serious direct role in extending or supporting SFA implementations.

School Districts

School districts are logical sources of training and follow-up for SFA and other reform models. Many school districts with several schools implementing SFA designate a district coordinator for the program. The district coordinator is intended to serve as a liaison between our staff, the schools, and the central administration. In some districts this person is expected to learn the program and provide direct support to teachers, facilitators, and other staff, much like that which our staff gives to schools in follow-up visits.

Our experience with district coordinators is that they can be very useful in their liaison function, but are rarely effective in training or follow-up with schools. The need for a liaison is great, especially in large districts. District coordinators can and do help make sure that schools get the resources they need and that district policies are interpreted for the SFA schools. For example, if the district adopts a new reading curriculum, the liaison can help figure out whether SFA schools should simply be exempted from it, or whether some attempt should be made to adapt the SFA curriculum to the new guidelines. The district coordinator can advocate for the program within the central office and see that it remains on the district's broader agenda. He or she can provide a single point of contact for our program staff on all issues that go beyond individual schools, from arranging for ordering, duplication, and delivery of materials, to helping with assessments, to keeping our staff aware of changes in district policies.

As important as the liaison role is, our experiences with district coordinators have been mixed. In some districts, district coordinators have been people who already have many other responsibilities, and SFA is added to their list with nothing else being removed. Further, there is often an institutional imperative to contain, isolate, and marginalize innovations, even ones valued by the administration and that are clearly, demonstrably effective. Assigning a program to a relatively low-ranking central-office official can be one way to ensure that a project remains at the periphery of the district's operations (even if it was no one's intention that this take place). We have found that it is important to maintain close relationships with someone in the district who has line authority (e.g., the superintendent, assistant superintendent for instruction, or Title I director) and not to let the project be seen as "belonging" to a lower-level district coordinator.

We have only occasionally found district coordinators to be helpful in training or implementation monitoring. Most often, district coordinators do not have the time to devote many whole days to detailed, classroom-level follow-up. More importantly, most district coordinators have no experience in SFA schools, so after a short time every teacher and administrator in the schools knows more about the program than they do. The district coordinators who have been most useful in training and follow-up have been former principals or facilitators in SFA schools. As time goes on we expect to see district coordinators recruited from within SFA schools able to take on more of the training and follow-up role for SFA than they have previously. This is working moderately well in Memphis and Houston, two of our largest implementations, where the districts have designated staff with responsibility for training and follow-up.

Regionally Based Project Staff

As the SFA network has expanded and matured, another means of establishing regional training sites has become dominant. This is the establishment of regional training programs staffed by trainers who are full-time employees of SFAF but remain in their home areas. This arrangement solves several problems. First, we often find staff in SFA schools who are outstanding educators, excellent trainers, willing to leave the security of their school district jobs, are eager to travel and work with schools all over the country, but are not willing or able to move to Baltimore. In our early years we did require most new trainers to relocate to Baltimore, but found that a requirement that such unusually able and exceptional people also must be willing to move to Baltimore put a severe constraint on our hiring qualified staff. Having regionally based full-time staff allows us to hire the very best experienced trainers more or less regardless of where they happen to be located.

Second, hiring trainers to serve a region gives us far more control and assurance of fidelity to our program's goals than does engaging regional training sites in universities or other existing agencies, which may have their own agendas and constraints. Otherwise, regionally based SFAF trainers have the same advantages as institutionally based regional training sites. They reduce travel costs to local districts and increase the probability that our training staff will know about and can adapt to local circumstances and needs.

On the other hand, regionally based SFAF trainers also have several drawbacks. One is that they are often isolated, working from their own homes without the informal collegial supports that are so important to our Baltimore staff. Operating far from our center, these trainers cannot routinely attend meetings or keep up easily with the latest information or developments. To deal with this, we hold regular frequent meetings within regions plus national staff retreats at least three times a year, as well as meetings around other functions, to keep everyone on the same wavelength. These meetings have major costs, but are essential in a widely distributed organization. As noted earlier, we have put in place a system of regional managers to help with training, mentoring, and supervision of new and junior trainers in their areas in five regions, plus the University of Memphis. Although regionally based trainers can decrease costs for the districts they serve, they increase costs for us, such as unreimbursed travel costs to bring these trainers to Baltimore for meetings, telephone costs for coordination, costs of setting up home offices, and costs of supervision.

Despite the problems of coordination and the additional costs involved, our system of regional training centers staffed by full-time SFAF trainers works very well. In fact, this is the only dissemination model we expect to expand in the coming years.

For SFA, our Baltimore training center has become just one of 16 regional offices, serving the Mid-Atlantic region. It is interesting to note, however, that in our much smaller and newer training programs for MathWings and WorldLab (social studies and science), we have also started off relying on Baltimore-based trainers until training in these areas becomes more routine and well-specified.

Networking

Building a national network of SFA schools is one of the most important things we're trying to do (Cooper, Slavin, & Madden, 1998). An isolated school out on the frontier of innovation can sometimes hang on for a few years, but systemic and lasting change is far more likely when schools work together as part of a network in which school staff share a common vision and a common language, share ideas and technical assistance, and create an emotional connection and support system. This is the main reason we have annual conferences for experienced sites. At the annual conference we provide valuable information on new developments and new ideas (most of which we have gotten directly from the schools we work with). We are also trying to build connections between the experienced schools, so that they can share ideas on issues of common interest and build significant relations with other schools pursuing similar objectives. We are also trying to create an esprit de corps, a pride in what we are all trying to do together, an understanding and acceptance of the struggle needed to achieve the goal of success for every child. We have "t-shirt days" and team-building activities that can be as important as the formal sessions. The breaks, when staff from different schools get to know each other and exchange information and telephone numbers, may be even more important.

In addition to the national conferences, there are many other things we try to do to build an effective support network. Our newsletter, *Success Story*, is one example. Our training sessions and the manuals and materials we produce invariably use contributions from experienced SFA schools and reflect them back to all schools. In particular, our family support and facilitator's manuals are primarily composed of ideas we have gotten from extraordinary SFA schools, and we keep revising these and other materials as we learn more from the schools. For example, school staff often modify various materials, forms, and assessments for their own use. We pay attention to these modifications and if they seem broadly applicable, we use them to revise our materials. Furthermore, in our conversations with schools we are constantly putting schools in touch with other schools to help them with specific issues, such as bilingual education, year-round schedules, use of Title I funds in non schoolwide circumstances, use of special education funds to support tutoring, and so on.

Many local support networks for SFA arise in informal ways, in which individual principals or facilitators happen to be friends or get to know one another at SFAF conferences or other activities related to SFA. Mentoring relationships between experienced and new schools often grow into local support networks. In other cases, local support networks have been established by school districts or (in the case of NJ) by the state department of education.

Local Meetings.   One of the most common activities of local support networks for SFA is regular meetings among key staff. Most often it is facilitators or facilitators and principals together who meet about once a month to discuss common problems and explore ways to help each other. Sometimes principals meet separately from time to time to discuss issues of particular concern to them. Principals, facilitators, and family support team members can learn a great deal from others who are facing similar problems in similar environments under similar circumstances. Furthermore, regular meetings among the leaders of SFA schools provide routine opportunities for these staff to build positive relationships and to establish opportunities for other types of mutual assistance.

Some local support networks schedule some sort of demonstration at the host school for the visiting staff from other schools. For example, the host school may have developed a new computer system to help with regrouping, a new thematic unit for preschool or kindergarten, or a family involvement or parent volunteer program they want to show off. The demonstration might take place before or after the meeting.

Local Conferences.   One of the problems with our national SFA conferences is that because most school staff must travel great distances to attend, few schools send more than one or two people, usually the facilitator, the principal, or both. Because of funding limitations, some schools cannot send anyone. Yet a similar purpose is sometimes served by holding local conferences. These can be scheduled on designated staff-development days so that all staff can attend. The activities are like those of the national conference, with various inservices, updates, and other sessions, and with opportunities for schools to show off their accomplishments in a variety of ways. SFAF staff participate, but center stage is reserved for the schools themselves. This provides a basis for local networking among the whole staffs of the schools that has remained long after the conference.

Sharing Resources.   There are many ways in which SFA schools make effective use of limited resources by working together in a local support network. For example, schools often schedule combined training sessions. This does not work if numbers get too large, but if, for example, there is a training session just for kindergarten teachers or just for tutors, then it makes sense for this training to be offered to all members of a local support network.

Schools involved in local support networks also collaborate on development of new materials. This happens occasionally when a district adopts a basal or literature series for which supportive materials do not exist. The district or several individual schools often designate a development team of teachers from several schools to create these materials (using our format and standards) and then share them with all schools. We often contract to pay some of the costs of this development if we can then share the new materials with all districts using the same books.

ORGANIZATION AND CAPITAL

Scaling up a successful school reform model is not only a question of building a strong training corps capable of working nationally. It also involves creating an organization capable of supporting trainers, developing materials and strategies, carrying out research and awareness activities, and so on. This, in turn, requires capital. Any reform organization needs to spend large amounts of money each year on recruiting and training new trainers, developing and printing materials, and other activities, many months before school districts pay their bills. This means that a line of credit is needed indefinitely, over and above whatever funding was necessary to initially develop and evaluate the program.

These issues, both creating an efficient organization and securing operating capital, have consumed enormous amounts of our energies in recent years. For 10 years, SFA existed as part of JHU. When the program was small, this worked very well. JHU took care of most routine business functions, such as payroll, benefits, insurance, and some legal services. It allowed us to run a deficit each spring as long as we had accounts receivable to cover the deficit when schools paid us in the fall.

However, by the summer of 1997 it became apparent that this arrangement could no longer work. On our side, the university's salary scales, policies, and practices were constant impediments to growth. We could not hire trainers in the Northeast, for example, because JHU salary scales were much lower than those of Northeastern school districts. Similarly, we had difficulty hiring business-related staff, such as accountants, human-resources staff, and a finance director because the University's rates for such staff were half of what commercial businesses were paying. On the University's side, the size and complexity of our operation were very difficult and time consuming to manage, and the University was understandably uncomfortable advancing us ever-larger amounts of capital each spring.

As a result, we decided to separate from the University. We reached agreement with University officials by February 1998 and completed the separation by July 1, 1998, establishing the SFAF as a not-for-profit entity to be responsible for the development and dissemination of SFA and Roots & Wings.

One of the key issues we had to resolve early on was whether to remain as a not-for-profit organization. This was a difficult decision. On one hand, it was clear that as a for-profit we would have no problem raising capital; many venture capital firms and individuals courted us heavily. However, there were several factors that led us to strongly favor staying in the not-for-profit world if we could. One was a desire to maintain an institutional ethos that focused on what is best for children, not what is best for profits or investors. Our staff is deeply committed to children and to school reform, and we did not want to undermine this spirit in any way. Another factor related to the public perception of our efforts. Watching the hostile reception in many quarters to the Edison Project and other for-profit education reform groups, we wanted to be sure that our program was seen as having unmixed motivations. The American Federation of Teachers and, to a lesser extent, the National Education Association, have strongly supported us (and opposed Edison). We did not want to endanger support of that kind. Finally, as a practical matter, we wanted to be certain that any operating profits would go back into development, research, and quality control, not to investors or taxes.

The decision to remain as a not-for-profit organization did have serious costs, however. We found that banks were unwilling to make loans to us unless we had substantial assets. We were able to secure approximately $5 million in grants and loans from two family foundations, the MacArthur and Ford Foundations, and New American Schools; on the basis of these assets, we obtained a line of credit from a commercial bank. Even with this we remain seriously undercapitalized for an organization of our size and rate of growth. For example, we have an annual printing bill of about $20 million, which we must pay many months before school districts begin to pay us. If we had investors rather than loans, these problems would not have existed. On balance, we are sure we made the right decision, and, in the long run, we will be much stronger as a not-for-profit organization.

In addition to capital needs, we have had to recruit a large corps of people to duplicate all of the functions the University had previously fulfilled: finance, accounting, payroll, benefits, insurance, legal services, information technology, space, and so on. All of these new people had to be recruited and trained at the same time that we were increasing our number of schools by about 50% and our total institutional budget by almost double. As these people have settled in, it has become apparent that we can do a much better job outside of the University, creating an organization completely tailored to our needs.

LESSONS LEARNED

Our experience with the national dissemination of SFA has led us to several conclusions. These are as follows:

- Successful dissemination of a program as comprehensive and complex as SFA requires a combination of two types of assistance to schools. One is a core of talented, dedicated trainers operating from the project's home or regional training sites closely coordinated with the project headquarters. The second is a local and national network of schools willing and able to provide technical and emotional support to schools entering the network.
- Although other institutions can be helpful in dissemination, we are finding greater success in employing staff from outstanding SFA schools to be full- or part-time trainers. Regional laboratories, other universities, and state departments of education have been helpful in our dissemination efforts, but with the exception of the University of Memphis they have not taken major responsibility for disseminating SFA in their regions. District coordinators are very helpful as liaisons between our project, SFA schools, and their central offices, but have been less helpful in training or follow-up. Regionally based trainers on our payroll and staff in Success for All schools who are willing to do some training and follow-up for us are usually much more effective.
- Quality control is a constant concern. Whatever dissemination strategy we use, constantly checking on the quality of training, implementation, and outcomes is essential. Without it, all programs fade into nothingness.

- To maintain over a long period of time, schools implementing innovations must be part of a national network of like-minded schools. To survive the inevitable changes of superintendents, principals, teachers, and district policies, school staffs need to feel that there is a valued and important group beyond the confines of their district that cares about and supports what they are doing.

SFA is only one of many national models of school reform, and it has unique characteristics that may make some dissemination strategies effective and others difficult or ineffective. Other types of programs may find very different strategies to be more effective. However, to the extent that other programs emphasize a strong research base, a well-specified set of materials and procedures, and a comprehensive approach to reform, we believe that our experiences will be a useful guide and will inform policies regarding technical assistance and reform at the local, state, and federal levels.

POLICY IMPLICATIONS

Our experiences with the dissemination of SFA have given us some degree of insight into the ways that systemic issues, such as federal, state, and local policies, can promote or inhibit school-by-school reform, and have given us some ideas about how these policies might change to support what we and other school change networks are trying to do.

Substantial positive change in student learning can only come about on a broad scale when major changes take place in the daily interactions of teachers and students. Ideally, we would have a variety of curricula, instructional methods, professional development methods, and school organizational forms for each subject and grade level, each of which has been rigorously researched and evaluated in comparison to traditional practices and found to be effective on valid measures of student achievement. School staffs would be made aware of these effective alternatives and would have the time and resources to learn about them, visit schools using them, see videotapes on them, and ultimately make an informed choice among them. Their exploration of alternatives might be assisted by local brokers who are knowledgeable about effective programs, organizational development, and the change process, and are aware of local needs, circumstances, and resources (see Slavin, 1997, 1998).

School staffs would control significant resources for materials and professional development and would be able to invest them in the exploration process and in well-developed models supported by national training staffs and local support networks. These national programs would themselves be primarily supported by revenues from schools but would also have seed money for developing materials and awareness and training materials, establishing national networks and regional training sites, and building qualified staffs of trainers and support personnel. Federal and state policies would support the process of school-by-school change by developing and promulgating standards, assessments, and accountability mechanisms likely to encourage school staffs to explore alternative models for change and to invest in professional development. They would push existing resources (e.g., Title I, Title VI, and Goals 2000 funds) to the school level, with a clearly stated expectation that these funds are intended for whole-school reform, not for maintaining current operations or patching around the edges. Some portion of school change funds would be provided on a competitive basis to schools, based on their willingness to engage in whole-school reform and allocate their own resources (especially Title I) to this purpose. Furthermore, funds would be allocated to outstanding exemplars of school reform methods to compensate them for the costs of serving as demonstration sites, mentoring other schools in their local networks, and participating in local training and follow-up.

The remainder of this chapter discusses the current state of policy support for school-by-school changes and the policy reforms needed to provide this support on a broad scale.

INCREASE SUPPORT FOR RESEARCH AND DEVELOPMENT OF SCHOOL CHANGE MODELS

One of the most important deficiencies in the current structure of professional development is a shortage of whole-school reform programs proven in rigorous research to be markedly more effective than traditional instruction, and thus ready for national dissemination (see Slavin & Fashola, 1998). Besides SFA, only a few, such as the Comer project (see Becker & Hedges, 1994) and Direct Instruction (Adams & Engelmann, 1997) have conducted and reported comparisons with traditional methods. Even at the classroom level, there are only a few proven, well-evaluated methods capable of national dissemination, such as Reading Recovery (Pinnell et al., 1994) and cooperative learning (Slavin, 1995). There is progress on the development of new school change models; the New American Schools (NAS) funded seven design teams to develop such models. However, there is no current plan to formally evaluate the outcomes of these new designs in comparison to traditional methods.

It is interesting to note that until recently, the federal involvement in the development, evaluation, and dissemination of these models has been minimal. Private foundation and corporate funding has almost entirely been responsible for the development and dissemination of the Comer, Levin, and

Sizer projects. SFA has benefitted from federal funding (its development and evaluation have been part of the work of the Center for Research on the Education of Students Placed At Risk at JHU), but it could not have been successfully developed and evaluated without funding from private foundations, especially the Carnegie and Pew Foundations and NAS.

There is a need for federal investment in the development of schoolwide change models, in evaluation of these models by their developers, and in third-party evaluations that compare the effects of the models to the effects of traditional methods (see Slavin, 1997, for more on this). The U.S. Department of Education has recently begun to do this, with a set of contracts for development and evaluation of new programs for middle and high schools, a level at which there are few proven models. Only when we have many successful models with clear and widely accepted evidence of effectiveness will we be able to confidently offer schools an array of choices, each of which may be quite different in philosophy or main elements but each of which is known to be effective under well-specified and replicable conditions of implementation.

HELP PROVEN PROFESSIONAL DEVELOPMENT NETWORKS BUILD CAPACITY

The most important limitation on the broad dissemination of SFA is our own capacity to provide high-quality professional development services to a very large number of schools. Our model requires a great deal of training and follow-up, and any equally ambitious restructuring program that intends to change the daily instructional practices of all teachers would require equally intense training. We can only add so many schools each year without overtaxing our staff's considerable energies, hiring more trainers than we can train and mentor, or seeing the quality of professional development decline. As a result, we must decline to work with further schools whenever our training calendars are full.

Our professional development organization is self-funding; our trainers' salaries are supported by fees we charge schools for their time. However, rapid scale-up has costs. While we are training new trainers, we must pay their salaries, fly them to observe schools or training sessions, and so on. Costs for establishing trainers in sites other than the project's home site may be particularly great, as these trainers must travel frequently to the home site. There is no source of funding for these costs. By the time a trainer is fully operative and bringing in enough revenue to cover his or her salary, we may have spent more than $50,000. As noted earlier, an even larger problem of scale-up is obtaining a line of credit to cover printing and other cyclical costs.

There is a need to provide training organizations like ours with funds to scale-up their operations. Ultimately such organizations must be self-funding, but they need capitalization as they begin their work and as they engage in significant expansion of their national capacity. As noted earlier, private foundations have largely fulfilled this capitalization function for some projects, including SFA, but if training organizations are to remain in the not-for-profit sector and to operate at significant scale, there must be much larger sources of capital for this purpose from government or donors. Recently, the U.S. Department of Education let one-year contracts for existing reform organizations, including SFAF, to build up their training and technology capacity.

PROVIDE RESOURCES TO SCHOOLS EARMARKED FOR ADOPTION OF EFFECTIVE PROGRAMS

Serious reform at the school level takes serious funding at the school level. School staffs must have control of resources they can spend only on professional development, especially on adoption of demonstrably effective programs. For example, the Commission on Title I (1992), led by David Hornbeck, proposed a 20% set-aside of Title I funds for professional development. However, this did not prevail in Congress.

School staffs should control professional development funds so that they can choose the development that they feel will meet their needs. When they freely select a given program or service provider, they will feel a commitment to that choice, in contrast to the more common case in which teachers resist inservice presentations that they feel do not respond to their needs. A school should be able to purchase services from any provider, including universities, regional laboratories, federal, state, or local technical assistance centers, professional development networks (such as the National Writing Project), or even their own district's staff development office. Funds for this purpose may be awarded on a competitive basis.

The Obey-Porter Comprehensive School Reform Demonstration is making an excellent start in this area, at least as far as whole-school, comprehensive designs are concerned. As noted earlier, this initiative is providing modest funding on a competitive basis both to help schools adopt research-based programs and to give them an incentive to use their existing resources (especially Title I) on programs likely to make a difference in all aspects of school functioning and in student achievement (see Slavin, 1998).

PROVIDE AWARENESS AND BROKERING SERVICES
TO SCHOOLS SO THEY CAN CHOOSE PROFESSIONAL
DEVELOPMENT SERVICES WISELY

Individual school staffs are poorly placed to select promising or effective programs, as they may not be aware of what is available or how to go about obtaining the programs and materials they need.

Providing awareness (and some brokering) of promising programs is one area in which the federal government has played a significant role. The National Diffusion Network (NDN) provided small Developer/Demonstrator grants to developers of programs that met an evaluation standard. NDN state facilitators organized awareness conferences and helped schools adopt these "validated" programs. However, the evaluation standards were low, and NDN funding was never adequate to provide much more than a clearinghouse, informational function (although, even with its limitations, NDN efforts led to thousands of successful adoptions of research-based programs in every state). In 1996, funding for the NDN was eliminated.

There is a need for far more ambitious outreach to school and district staffs to help them assess their needs and make them aware of a range of alternative programs and services available to them. Schools might invest their own professional development resources in such brokering services, or might pool resources with other schools to bring in awareness presentations on a variety of available programs and practices. State or federal support might be important in helping establish brokering agencies or individuals, but in a system in which professional development resources are focused at the school level, agencies or individuals providing any professional development services to schools would ultimately have to support themselves on fees from schools. Existing agencies, such as the regional laboratories and the new regional comprehensive assistance centers, could also play an important role in helping schools make wise choices of professional development services and programs. A process of this kind has been set in motion by the Obey-Porter Comprehensive School Reform Demonstration, which provides funds to labs and state departments to increase awareness of proven, comprehensive models.

PROVIDE FUNDS TO SUCCESSFUL EXEMPLARS
OF PROVEN PROGRAMS TO SERVE
AS DEMONSTRATION/TRAINING SITES

One thing we have learned in the dissemination of SFA is how important it is to have schools successfully implementing the program whose staffs are willing to receive visitors and assist neighboring schools in the process of adopting the program. Many of our outstanding schools have put hundreds or thousands of person-hours into helping other schools start and maintain the program.

However, all this help comes at a price. Many schools can provide only minimal assistance to other schools without overly taxing their own staff resources. Some principals are concerned that if they let their best staff members work to help other schools, they will be hired away. More often, school staffs find that although their efforts to help other schools bring them recognition and satisfaction, they must put a limit on this activity.

It is unfair and unrealistic to expect that outstanding exemplars of proven programs will work indefinitely as demonstration and training sites without any outside compensation. There is a need to provide resources to these schools for the real costs of serving as demonstration sites (such as hiring substitutes when staff are elsewhere helping other schools) and to help them see aiding other schools as a part of their responsibilities. A model for this is professional development schools associated with schools of education.

Schools willing to serve as demonstration/training sites might receive funds amounting to half of their facilitators' salary (about $25,000). In return, they would be expected to be open to a specified number of formal visits (e.g., one visit per month) and to provide some number of person days of training and follow-up to other schools (e.g., 40 person days per year). This would create a situation in which schools would be motivated to serve as demonstration/training sites, and would receive special recognition (as well as funds) for agreeing to serve in this role.

CONCLUSION

Our experience in the national dissemination of SFA is instructive in many ways. We have discovered that there are far more schools eager to make thoroughgoing changes in their instructional programs than we or other national training networks can possibly serve. Policy changes, such as those contained in the reauthorized Title I, the Obey-Porter Comprehensive School Reform Demonstration, and state and local systemic reforms, are further motivating schools to seek high-quality, intensive, and extensive professional development services to fundamentally transform themselves. The key limitation in making this change take place is the limited national capacity to provide schools with well-researched models backed by networks of trainers, demonstration schools, materials, and other requirements.

The focus of this chapter is on the ways we have tried to expand the capacity of our SFA program to serve a rapidly expanding network of schools across the United States, and on the policy changes that would be needed to support our network and others in building our nation's capacity for quality professional development. In brief, we have found that our network of schools and our own dedicated staff are the bedrock of a national dissemination strategy and that building on the strengths of this network is the most promising approach to scale-up. Federal, state, and other support to help establish and maintain professional development networks like ours, along with providing money to schools earmarked for professional development, are most likely to create conditions in which schools throughout the United States will focus their energy on exploring alternatives, seeking professional development appropriate to their needs, and then engaging in a long-term, thoughtful process of change that results in measurably improved achievement for all children.

REFERENCES

Adams, G., & Engelmann, S. (1997). *Research on Direct Instruction: 25 years beyond DISTAR*. Seattle, WA: Educational Achievement Systems.

Becker, B. J., & Hedges, L. V. (1992). A review of the literature of effectiveness of Comer's school development program. Unpublished manuscript, Michigan State University.

Commission on Title I (1992). *Making schools work for children in poverty*. Washington, DC: Council of Chief State School Officers.

Cooper, R., Slavin, R. E., & Madden, N. A. (1998). Success for All: Improving the quality of implementation of whole-school change through the use of a national reform network. *Education and Urban Society, 30*(3), 385–408.

Levin, H. M. (1987). Accelerated schools for disadvantaged students. *Educational Leadership, 44*(6), 19–21.

Madden, N. A., Slavin, R. E., Karweit, N. L., Dolan, L. J., & Wasik, B. A. (1993). Success for All: Longitudinal effects of a restructuring program for inner-city elementary schools. *American Educational Research Journal, 30*, 123–148.

Madden, N. A., Slavin, & Simons, K. (1999). *Effects of MathWings on student mathematics performance*. Baltimore, MD: Johns Hopkins University, Center for Research on the Education of Students Placed At Risk.

McCarthy, J. (1991, April). *Accelerated —The Satellite Center Project*. Paper presented at the annual meeting of the American Educational Research Association, Chicago, IL.

Pinnell, G. S., DeFord, D. E., & Lyons, C.A. (1988). *Reading Recovery: Early intervention for at-risk first graders*. Arlington, VA; Educational Research Service.

Slavin, R. E. (1995). *Cooperative learning: Theory, research, and practice* (2nd ed.). Boston: Allyn & Bacon.

Slavin, R. E. (1997). Design competitions: A proposal for a new federal role in educational research and development. *Educational Researcher, 26*(1), 22–28.

Slavin, R. E. (1998). Far and wide: Developing and disseminating research-based programs. *American Educator, 22*(3), 8–11, 45.

Slavin, R. E., & Fashola, O. S. (1998). *Show me the evidence: Proven and promising programs for America's schools*. Thousand Oaks, CA: Corwin.

Slavin, R. E., & Madden, N. A. (1999a). *Disseminating Success for All: Lessons for policy and practice*. Baltimore, MD: Johns Hopkins University.

Slavin, R. E., & Madden, N. A. (1999a). *Success for All/Roots & Wings: 1999 summary of research on achievement outcomes*. Baltimore: Johns Hopkins University.

Slavin, R. E., & Madden, N. A. (1999b). Roots & Wings: Effects of whole-school reform on student achievement. *Journal of Education for Students Placed At Risk, 5*(1& 2), 109–136.

Slavin, R. E., Madden, N. A., Dolan, L. J., & Wasik, B. A. (1996). *Every child, every school: Success for All.* Newbury Park, CA: Corwin.

Slavin, R. E., Madden, N. A., Dolan, L. J., Wasik, B. A., Ross, S. M., & Smith, L. J. (1994). "Whenever and wherever we choose … ": The replication of Success for All. *Phi Delta Kappan, 75*(8), 639–647.

Slavin, R. E., Madden, N. A., Dolan, L. J., Wasik, B. A., Ross, S. M., & Smith, L. J. (1994b, April). *Success for All: Longitudinal effects of systemic school-by-school reform in seven districts.* Paper presented at the annual meeting of the American Educational Research Association, New Orleans, MO.

Slavin, R. E., Madden, N. A., Karweit, N. L., Dolan, L., & Wasik, B. A. (1992). *Success for All: A relentless approach to prevention and early intervention in elementary schools.* Arlington, VA: Educational Research Service.

Author Index

A

Abrami, P. C., 96, 103, 108, *109*
Adams, G., 220, *225*
Adams, M. J., 8, 15, 113, *144*
Alberg, M., 42, *47*
Ali-Said, M., 163, *176*
Anderson, M., 76, 77
Andrade de Herrera, V., 181, *193*
Andrews, S., 113, 138, 139, *144*
Aslin, L., 108, *109*
August, D., 37, *46*

B

Baird, H., 153, *176*
Barber, L., 94, *109*
Barr, R., 120, 140, 141, *146*
Barth, R. S., 187, *193*
Becker, B. J., 220, *225*
Ben-Ari, R., 150, *176*
Ben-Shushan, N., 152, *175*
Berman, P., 45, 46, 55, 76, 77
Blachman, B. A., 127, 137, *147*
Board of Studies (Australia), 115, *144*
Bodilly, S. J., 95, *109*
Bowey, J. A., 141, *144, 146*
Boykin, W., 184, *193*
Bradley, L., 137, *144*
Bryant, B. R., 99, *110*
Bryant, P. E., 137, *144*
Bryk, A. S., 40, *46*
Burns, M. S., 111, *147*
Byrne, B., 127, 136, 137, *144*

C

Cain, K., 112, 113, 142, *144*
Calderón, M. E., 9, *15*, 38, 46, 149, 150, 153, 154, 158, *175, 176*, 187, *193*
Campbell, D., 101, 102, *109*
Carriedo, R., 94, *109*
Casey, J. P., 30, 33, 40, 43, *47, 48*, 49, 58, 59, 60, 77, 78, 95, *110*, 141, *146*
Castle, J. M., 107, *109*
Catterson, J. H., 55, 77, 99, *109*
Center, Y., 113, 121, 122, 123, 137, 142, *144, 145*
Chall, J. S., 118, *145*
Chambers, B., 96, 103, 108, *109*
Chapman, J. W., 111, 141, *145, 147*
Chen, R. S., 112, 138, 141, *145, 147*
Clay, M. M., 116, 120, *145*
Cohen, J., 72, 77
Coleman, M. A., 11, *15*
Commission on Title I, 222, *225*
Conference Board of Canada, 94, *109*
Cook T., 101, 102, *109*
Cooper, R., 28, 46, 214, *225*
CTB/McGraw-Hill, 55, 77

D

Davis, B., 182, *193*
DeFord, D. E., 40, 46, 208, 220, *225*
Denckla, M. B., 112, 138, 141, *147*
Denton, W., 94, *109*
Dianda, M., 24, 47, 54, 78, 95, 99, 105, *110*
Dolan, L. J., 7, 11, *15*, 24, 32, 43, *47, 48*, 52, 54, 78, 82, 83, 91, 92, 95, 99, 100, 105,

108, *109, 110,* 113, 141, *147,* 149,
   177, 179, *193, 198, 226*
Dunn, L. M., 59, *77,* 99, *109,* 116, *145*
Durrell, D. D., 55, *77,* 99, *109*

E

Eden, D., 152, *175*
Ehri, L. C., 137, 138, 139, *145*
Engelmann, S., 220, *225*

F

Farnish, A. M., 8, 9, *15, 158, 176*
Farrell, D., 112, *146*
Fashola, O. S., 108, *110,* 220, *226*
Feitelson, D., 166, *175*
Fielding-Barnsley, R., 127, 136, 137, *144*
Flaherty, J., 37, 39, *46*
Fletcher, J. M., 112, *145*
Foorman, B. R., 112, *145*
Francis, D. J., 112, *145*
Freeman, L. B., 113, 121, 122, 123, 137, 142,
   144, 145
Freiberg, H. J., 30, *46*
Frith, U., 137, *145*
Frymier, J., 94, *109*
Fullan, M., 81, *92*

G

Gambrell, L. B., 142, *145*
Gansneder, B., 94, *109*
Gariépy, W., 94, *109*
Gough, P. B., 112, 113, 135, 141, 143, *146*
Griffin, P., 111, *147*

H

Hakuta, K., 37, *46*
Hansen, J., 141, *146*
Hanson, R. A., 112, *146*
Hardy, J., 94, *109*
Harris, A., 83, 84, 90, *92*
Hartas, D., 83, 84, 90, *92*
Haxby, B., 11, *15*
Hedges, L. V., 220, *225*
Herman, R., 17, 45, *46,* 54, *77*
Hertz-Lazarowitz, R., 38, *46,* 149, 150, 152, 153,
   154, 155, 156, 158, 159, 160, 162,
   163, 164, 168, 172, 174, *175, 176,*
   177
Hoover, W. A., 112, 113, 135, 141, *146*
Hopfenberg, W. S., 41, *46*

Hopkins, D., 83, 84, 90, *92*
Horn, S. P., 50, 63, 69, *78*
Hrimech, M., 94, *109*
Huang, S., 30, *46*
Huitema, B., 101, *109*
Hunter, P., 26, 30, *46,* 61, 75, *77,* 95, 105, *109*

I

Iversen, J. A., 140, *146*

J

Jagger, A. M., 120, *147*
Jawitz, P. B., 142, *145*
Johnson, B., 58, *78*
Johnson-Lewis, S., 94, *109*
Jorm, A. F., 139, *146*

K

Karweit, N. L., xi, *xiv,* 6, 7, 10, 11, *15,* 43, 48,
   100, 105, *109, 110,* 113, 141, *147,*
   198, *225, 226*
Kelly, P. R., 120, *146*
Kemp, K., 113, *146*
Kerr, B. M., 113, *146*
Ketelsen, J. L., 30, *46*
Klein, A. F., 120, *146*

L

Lasaga-Flister, M., 11, *15*
Lazarowitz, R., 150, 153, *176*
Leinhardt, G., 51, *77*
Lerner, M., 156, 159, 160, 168, *176*
Levin, H. M., 41, *46,* 208, *225*
Lewis, T., 27, 28, *47,* 49, 61, 62, 67, 75, *77,* 78
Livermon, B. J., 7, *15*
Livingston, M. A., 9, *15,* 37, 39, *46*
Loera, A., 180, *193*
Lohr, L. L., 51, *78*
Lyons, C. A., 40, *46,* 208, 220, *225*

M

Madden, N. A., xi, *xiv,* 6, 7, 8, 9, 10, 11, 14, *15,*
   24, 28, 32, 33, 35, 37, 39, 43, 45, *46,*
   47, 48, 52, 54, 78, 82, 83, 91, 92, 95,
   99, 100, 105, 108, *109, 110,* 113,
   141, 143, *147,* 149, 158, *176, 177,*
   179, 193, 198, 214, *225, 226*
Martin, F., 113, *146*
Mason, J. M., 113, *146*

Massue, F., 96, 103, *109*
McAdoo, M., 30, *46*
McCarthy, J., 208, *225*
McDill, E. L., 51, *77*
McLaughlin, M. W., 45, 46, 55, 76, *77*
McNelis, M., 42, 47, 51, *78*
Mehta, P., 112, *145*
Morrison, S., 96, 103, 108, *109*

N

National Academy of Sciences, 37, *46*
Natriello, G., 51, *77*
New American Schools, 95, *109*
Nicholson, T., 107, *109*
Nunnery, J., 26, 27, 28, 30, 39, 40, 44, 46, 47, 49,
    51, 61, 62, 75, 77, 78, 95, 105, *109*

O

Oakhill, J. V., 112, 113, 142, *146*
O'Toole, J., 192, *193*
Outhred, L., 142, *145*

P

Paivio, A., 142, *146*
Pallay, A., 51, *77*
Patel, S., 112, 113, *146*
Peterson, C. L., 112, 113, 141, *146*
Pinnell, G. S., 40, 46, 120, *146*, 208, 220, *225*
Plourde, L., 116, *146*
Pogrow, S., 72, 73, 74, *77*
Pratt, A., 112, 138, 141, *147*
Pratt, C., 113, *146*
Prochnow, J. E., 111, 141, *145*, *147*
Purnell, S., 95, *109*

R

Rakow, J., 44, *47*
Rashotte, C. A., 141, *147*
Reichhardt, R., 95, *109*
Riach, J., 107, *109*
Rich, L., 51, *78*
Rich, Y., 150, *176*
Robertson, G., 113, 121, 122, 123, 142, *145*
Robertson, N., 94, *109*
Ross, S. M., 18, 24, 26, 27, 28, 29, 30, 32, 33, 39,
    40, 41, 42, 43, 44, 46, 47, 48, 49, 51,
    54, 55, 58, 59, 60, 61, 62, 63, 67, 68,
    73, 74, 75, 77, 78, 95, 99, 105, 108,
    109, 110, 141, 146, 198, *226*
Ryan, H. A., 111, *147*

S

Sanders, W. L., 28, 29, 30, 41, 47, 50, 63, 68,
    69, 74, 75, *78*
Saxon, A. M., 69, *78*
Scanlon, D. M., 112, 138, 141, *146*, *147*
Scarratt, D. R., 138, 139, *144*
Schaedel, B., 150, 153, 156, 158, 159, 160, 163,
    164, 168, 172, *176*, *177*
Schafschneider, C., 112, *145*
Schuyler, G., 95, *109*
Secretaría de Educación Pública (Mexico), 183,
    184, *193*
Seltzer, M., 40, *46*
Shachar, H., 150, *177*
Shanahan, M., 120, 140, 141, *146*
Sharan, S., 150, *177*
Sharan, Y., 150, *177*
Share, D. L., 112, 137, 138, 139, *146*
Shimron, J., 166, *177*
Simons, K., 14, 15, 198, *225*
Singe, P., 192, *193*
Sipay, E. R., 112, 138, 141, *147*
Slavin, R. E., xi, *xiv*, 6, 7, 8, 9, 10, 11, 13, 14,
    15, 24, 26, 28, 30, 32, 33, 35, 37, 38,
    39, 40, 42, 43, 45, 46, 47, 48, 49, 52,
    54, 61, 75, 77, 78, 82, 83, 84, 90, 91,
    92, 95, 99, 100, 105, 108, 109, *110*,
    113, 141, 143, *146*, *147*, 149, 153,
    158, *175*, *176*, *177*, 179, *193*, 198,
    214, 220, 221, 223, *225*, *226*
Small, S. G., 112, 138, 141, *147*
Smith, J. O., 116, *145*
Smith, L. J., 26, 27, 28, 30, 32, 33, 39, 40, 42,
    43, 44, 46, 47, 48, 49, 51, 54, 55, 58,
    59, 60, 61, 62, 67, 73, 75, 77, 78, 95,
    99, 105, 108, 109, 110, 141, *146*,
    198, *226*
Smith-Burke, M. T., 120, *147*
Snow, C. E., 111, *147*
Stanovich, K. E., 112, 113, 135, 137, 138, 139,
    141, *146*, *147*
Statistics Canada, 94, *110*
Stein, T. A., 30, *46*
Sterbin, A., 44, 47, 62, 67, *77*
Stevens, R., 8, 9, 10, *15*, 158, *176*
Stringfield, S. C., 30, 41, 47, 54, 63, 68, 74, *78*
Stubbs, J., 26, 30, 46, 61, 75, 77, 95, 105, *109*
Sumara, D. J., 182, *193*

T

Tangel, D. M., 127, 137, *147*
Théoret, M., 94, *109*
Tinajero, J. V., 148, 150, 153, 158, *175, 176*
Torgesen, J. K., 141, *147*
Tov-Lee, E., 168, *176*
Treiman, R., 118, *147*
Tunmer, W. E., 111, 112, 140, 141, 143, *145, 146, 147*

V

Vellutino, F. R., 112, 138, 141, *145, 146, 147*

W

Waddington, N. J., 138, *147*
Wagner, R. K., 141, *147*
Walsh, E. J., 60, *78*
Wang, L. W., 30, 41, *47*

Wang, W., 18, 48, 63, 68, 74, *78*
Wasik, B. A., 10, *15*, 24, 32, 43, *47, 48*, 52, 54, 78, 82, 83, 91, *92*, 95, 99, 100, 105, 108, *109, 110*, 113, 141, *147*, 149, *177*, 179, *193*, 198, 226
Webb, C., 153, *176*
Wiederholt, J. L., 99, *110*
Wilce, L. S., 137, *145*
Woodcock, R. W., 55, *78*, 99, *110*
Wordsworth, J., 83, 84, 90, *92*
Wright, S. P., 28, 29, 30, 41, *47*, 60, 63, 68, 74, 75, *78*

Y

Young, P., 40, *46*
Youngman, M., 83, 84, 90, *92*
Yuill, N. M., 112, *146*

Z

Zelniker, T., 150, 158, *176*

Subject Index

A

Abbottston Elementary school (Baltimore), xii
Accelerated Schools, 41–42, 44, 208
Acre, Israel
ALASH in, 149–151, 158–165
  community research and evaluation model,
      156–157, 172–175
  cooperative learning and, 153–156
  history of, 151
  school system of, 151–152
  SFA in, 149–151
    evaluation studies, 167–172
    implementation, 165–167
Administrative support
  Memphis SFA schools and, 75–76
  Mexican SFA program and, 188
Administrators, professional development and,
    188
Advisory committees, 13, 166
ALASH, 149–151
  community research and evaluation model,
      156–157, 172
  cooperative learning and, 153–156
  evaluation methodology, 158–159
  evaluation results, 159–165
Alas para Leer program, 9
American Federation of Teachers, 217
American Institute for Research, 17, 45, 54
Amichai, Yehudi, 168
Arabic
  ALASH program and, 158, 159, 162–163,
      165
  in Israeli schools, 151
  SFA program evaluations, 167–168

Arab schools
  in Acre, 151–152
  ALASH evaluations in, 158–165
Arab students
  ALASH program evaluations
    in Arabic, 158, 159, 162–163, 165
    in Hebrew, 158, 159, 160–162, 163–165
  in Israeli schools, 151
  SFA program evaluations, 167–168
Arizona, 40–41
Asian students, 38–39
Assessments
  of reading, 10
  SWELL program and, 118, 120
Atlas, 41
Attendance, Mexican schools and, 185, 186,
    189
Audrey Cohen College, 41, 71
Australia, *see also* Schoolwide Early Language
    and Literacy
  early reading programs in, 114–116

B

Baltimore, xii, 6–7, 32, 43
Becoming Literate (SWELL program), 117–118
Berrúm, Trini, 189
Bilingual Cooperative Integrated Reading and
    Composition (BCIRC), 38, 149,
    153, 154
Bilingual programs, 7, 9, 37–38, *see also* Éxito
    Para Todos
Boots Company, 88
Burt Word Reading Test, 124

C

Caldwell, ID, 40, 41
California, 37–38, 39
California Achievement Test, 55
Cambodian-speaking students, 38–39
Canada, school dropout and literacy problems, 94
Canada, Success For All in
    funding issues, 108
    implementation, 95–96, 100–101, 107–108
    quasiexperimental study
        analysis, 101–103
        dependent measures, 99–100
        discussion, 105–108
        limitations of, 106–107
        participants, 97–99
        procedures, 100–101
        results, 103–105
    reading achievement evaluations, 93, 103–106
Carnegie Foundation, 221
Center for Research in Educational Policy (University of Memphis), 62, 208
Center for Research on the Education of Students Placed at Risk (CRESPAR), 17, 167, 202
Certificates, 207
Ciudad Juárez
    Éxito Para Todos in, 180–193
    schools in, 180
Classroom Listening and Speaking (CLAS), 116
Classrooms, cooperative learning model, 153
Clover Park, WA, 41–42
Cohen-Asaf, Shlomit, 163
Cohorts, 25
Comer project, 220, 221
Community
    cooperative learning and, 153–156
    SFA-UK and, 88
Community research and evaluation, 156–157, 172–175
Comprehension instruction, 118, 119
Comprehensive School Reform Demonstration (CSRD), xiii, 54, 76, 201, 210–211, 222–223
Comprehensive Test of Basic Skills (CTBS), 32, 55
Computer-supported tutoring programs, 108
Concordia University, 101
Co-nect, 41, 44, 71
Consistency Management/Cooperative Discipline, 30
Cooperation, investigation, literacy and community (CILC) model, 154–155
Cooperative Integrated Reading and Composition (CIRC), xi

Cooperative learning, 220
    in Israel, 149–150, 153–156
    student behavior and, 86
    teachers and, 88
Corporate funding, 221
CSRD, see Comprehensive School Reform Demonstration
Cumulative percent of norm, 63–67
Curiosity Corner, xiii

D

Decentralization, Mexican schools and, 181
Demonstration/training schools, 224
Department for Education and Employment (U.K.), 81, 83
Developmental spelling tests, 121, 124, 127, 129
Direct Instruction, 54, 220
Dissemination (of SFA), 224–225
    capacity building and, 221–222
    certificate program, 207
    consequences for organization and capital, 216–218
    CSRD program and, 206–207
    dissemination staff, 202, 204
    lessons learned from, 218–219
    program characteristics affecting, 200–202
    regional training programs, 202–204
    regional training sites, 208–216
    strategies in, 204–206
District coordinators, 212, 213
Durrell Analysis of Reading Difficulty, 24, 99
Durrell Oral Reading Inventory, 99, 103, 104
Durrell Oral Reading Scale, 24, 28, 55, 73, 93, 99–100

E

Early Learning program, 86
Early literacy instruction, see also Schoolwide Early Language and Literacy; Success For All
    in Australia, 114–116
    importance of, 5, 6
    word recognition and listening comprehension in, 112–113
Edison Project, 217
Education
    defining success in, 4
    student failure and, 3–4
Educational laboratories, 210–211
Education Partners, 202, 209–210
Education reform, see also School reform
    in the United Kingdom, 81–82, 91–92
Effective methods fairs, 204

Effective Programs for Students at Risk (Slavin,
      Karweit, Madden), xi–xii, 6
Effect sizes, 25
      changes over years of implementation, 36–37
      relation to implementation quality, 26–28
El Paso, TX, 187–188
Embry, Robert, 6
Emergent Literacy (SWELL program), 116–117
Emergent Writing (SWELL program), 116–117
English language learners
      SFA and, 37–39
      SWELL program and, 118
Evaluations
      Israeli ALASH studies, 158–165
      SWELL program
            discussion, 135–144
            methodology, 121–123
            results, 124–135
Evaluations (of SFA), 95
      Canadian quasiexperimental study
            analysis, 101–103
            dependent measures, 99–100
            discussion, 105–108
            limitations of, 106–107
            participants, 97–99
            procedures, 100–101
            results, 103–105
      of changes in effect sizes through time, 36–37
      comparisons to matched control groups,
            24–26
      comparisons to other programs, 41–42
      comparisons to Reading Recovery, 39–41, 95
      of effects on district-administered
            standardized tests, 28–36
      for English language learners, 37–39
      history of, 18
      of implementation effects, 26–28
      Israeli studies, 167–172
      in Memphis schools
            of extended-day tutoring, 62
            of grades K-3, 55, 57–60, 61, 62–63
            of implementation quality, 61, 67
            overview of, 55, 72
            summary of findings, 56(table), 57(table)
            of teacher effectiveness and mobility,
                  68–71
            of teacher reactions, 60–61
            TVAAS studies, 28–30, 63–67
      Mexican study, 189–192
      overview of, 18, 44–46
      in SFA-UK, 83–84
      of teachers' attitudes, 44
Exception words, 117
Éxito Para Todos, 37–38, *see also* Mexico, Éxito
      Para Todos in
Expeditionary Learning, 41, 44, 71
Expressive language development, 116

Expressive Word Attack Skills (EWAS) Test,
      127, 129
Extended-day tutoring programs, 62

F

Family Support Teams, 11–12, 13
      Israeli SFA schools and, 166
      Mexican SFA program and, 180, 186, 189
Fischer Family Trust, 83
Flint, MI, 32–33
Florida Elementary School (Memphis), 50, 52,
      55–58
Ford Foundation, 218
Fort Wayne, IN, 33, 43
Framework for Teaching (U.K.), 82

G

Getting Along Together programs, 12
"Gift, The" (Amichai), 168–169
Graduation Really Achieves Dreams (GRAD)
      project, 30, 31
Gray Oral Reading Test, 24, 93, 99–100

H

Haifa University, 157
Hawthorne effects, 95, 97, 104, 106
Hebrew
      ALASH program and, 158, 159, 160–162,
            163–165
      in Israeli schools, 151
      SFA program evaluations, 167–172
Hettleman, Kalman, xii, 6
Hispanic English language learners, 39
Hornbeck, David, 222
"Hour Between Green and Purple, An" (Meir),
      161
House, Gerry, 54, 75–76, 208
Houston, TX, 26–27, 30–31, 38
Houston Independent School District, 31

I

Idaho, 40, 41
Implementation (of SFA)
      in Canadian schools, 95–96, 100–101,
            107–108
      effects on SFA bilingual programs, 38
      effects on SFA success, 26–28
      impact of teacher training on, 63
      in Israeli schools, 165–167
      in Mexican schools, 181–193
      process of, 204–205
      Roots & Wings and, 53, 54, 61

SFA-UK and, 83, 89–91
significance of, 82–83
student achievement and, 26–28, 61, 67, 75, 90–91
Improving Schools program (U.K.), 81
Interactive-compensatory reading theory, 113
International Association for the Study of Cooperation in Education (IASCE), 150
Investigation Task Forces (Israel), 154–155
Irregular words, 117
Israel
  absence of national or district evaluation in, 173
  cooperative learning in, 149–150
  Melting Pot ideology, 150
Israel, Success for All in, 149–151
  community research and evaluation model, 156–157, 172–175
  cooperative learning and, 153–156
  evaluation studies, 167–172
  implementation issues, 165–167
ISTEP, 33
"I Want a Friend" (Shenhav), 163

J

Jewish schools
  in Acre, 151–152
  ALASH evaluations in, 158–162, 164, 165
Jewish students
  ALASH program and, 158, 159, 160–162, 165
  in Israeli schools, 151
  SFA program evaluations, 167–172
Johns Hopkins University, xi, xiii, 17, 167, 202, 217
Joplin Plan, 10

K

Kindergarten
  SFA programs for, 11
  SFA-UK and, 86
  Success For All-Canada and, 100

L

Lackland Elementary School, TX, 35
LaRose Elementary School (Memphis), 52
Lee Conmigo, 7, 9
Levin project, 221
Limited English Proficient (LEP) students, 38–39
Listening comprehension
  in early literacy, 112–113

SWELL program and, 117, 118, 119, 142, 143
Listening Together (SWELL program), 119
Literacy
  in Canada, 94
  current concerns with, 111–112
  in the United Kingdom, 82
Literacy acquisition, 112
Literacy instruction, *see* Early literacy instruction; Schoolwide Early Language and Literacy; Success For All
Literacy Task Force (U.K.), 82
Literature books, Mexican SFA program and, 183–184
Little Rock, AR, 44
Livermon, Barbara, xii
Local conferences, 216
Local meetings, 215–216
Local support networks, 215–216

M

MacArthur Foundation, 218
Maryland, 33–35, *see also* Baltimore
Maryland School Performance Assessment Program (MSPAP), 33
Mathematics curriculum, *see* MathWings
MathWings, xii, 14, 198, 214
Matrix sampling, 33
Meir, Mira, 161
Melting Pot ideology, 150
Memphis City Schools, 49, *see also* Memphis SFA schools
  administrative support for SFA, 75–76
  conditions and practices prior to SFA, 50–52
  introduction and expansion of SFA, 52–54
  national and local events affecting, 54–55
  size of, 50
Memphis SFA schools, 49–50
  administrative support for, 75–76
  establishment and growth of, 52–54
  implementation quality and, 27–28, 61, 67, 75
  longitudinal evaluations
    of extended-day tutoring, 62
    of grades K-3, 55, 57–60, 61, 62–63
    of implementation quality, 61, 67
    overview of, 55, 72
    summary of findings, 56(table), 57(table)
    of teacher effectiveness and mobility, 68–71
    of teacher reactions, 60–61
    TVAAS studies, 28–30, 63–67

national and local events affecting, 54–55
reasons for success, 75–77
student achievement, 72–74
teacher effects, 74–75
Title I support, 76
University of Memphis partnership, 53, 76, 208, 209
Memphis Volunteer Center, 62
Mexican-American English language learners, 39
Mexico
  educational context in, 181–182
  limited resources for schools and teachers, 184–185
  need for SFA in, 179–181
Mexico, Éxito Para Todos in
  background of, 179–181
  future of, 193
  implementation challenges
    administrative support, 188
    current situation, 192–193
    literature books, 183–184
    parental involvement and support, 188–189
    schedules, interruptions, and time on task, 185–186
    school resources and teacher pay, 184–185
    staff development, 186–188
    student evaluation, 189–192
  implementation history, 182–183
Michigan Educational Assessment Program (MEAP), 32
Modern Red Schoolhouse, 44
Montreal, 94, see also Canada, Success For All in
Montreal Island School Council, 94
Move-It Math, 30
Multisite replicated experiments, 24

N

Narrative event structure training, 142
National Diffusion Network (NDN), 223
National Education Association, 217–218
National Literacy Strategy (U.K.), 82, 89, 91
National Tests (U.K.), 84–86
National text (Mexico), 181–182, 183
Networking, 214–216
  local conferences, 215
  local meetings, 215–216
  resource sharing, 215
Neverstreaming concept, 42–43
New American Schools (NAS), xii, 53, 54, 95, 218, 221
New American Schools Development Corporation (NASDC), xii, 7, 198

"New Friend, A" (Cohen-Asaf), 163
New Jersey State Department of Education, 211
New South Wales, Australia, 113, 121, see also Schoolwide Early Language and Literacy
New York State Department of Education, 211
North Central Lab, 210
Nottingham, U.K., 82, see also Success For All-United Kingdom

O

Obey-Porter Comprehensive School Reform Demonstration, see Comprehensive School Reform Demonstration
Office for Standards in Education (U.K.), 89
Ontario, 96

P

Parent Learning Communities, 187
Parents
  Family Support Teams, 11–12
  involvement in SFA-UK, 88–89
  Mexican SFA program and, 188–189, 190, 192
Passage Comprehension test, 24, 55, 93, 103, 104, 105
Peabody Language Development Kits, 8
Peabody Language Development Program, 116
Peabody Picture Vocabulary Test (PPVT), 24, 41, 59, 61
Peabody Picture Vocabulary Test-Revised (PPVT-R), 99
Pew Foundation, 221
Philadelphia, 37, 38–39
Phonemic awareness, 112
  SWELL program and, 117, 136–137
Phonics instruction, 107
Phonological recoding, 112
  SWELL program and, 116, 117, 136–137, 138–139
Pinderhughes, Alice, 6
Poem composing, 168–172
Prekindergarten/Preschool, 11, 100
Pretesting, in Canadian SFA evaluation, 101
Prevention, importance of, 5, 6
"Prince and His Sense of Humor, The," 162
Print, learning about, 116
Private foundations, 221
Professional development, see also Staff development
  providing resources for, 222–223
  school reform and, 198
  SFA program and, 201

Professional development services
building capacity of, 221–222
providing awareness and brokering services, 223
Program facilitators, 12
impact of, 63
Israeli SFA schools and, 166
Mexican SFA program and, 182
selection and training of, 204–205
significance to SFA-UK, 90
Project GRAD, 30, 31
Pseudoword decoding, 138
Pseudoword reading tests, 121, 124, 127, 129, 132
Pull-out programs, 51

Q

Quebec, 94, 96, *see also* Canada, Success for All in
Quebec Ministry of Education, 108

R

Raising Readers program, 12
RAND Institute on Education and Training, 95
Reading, word recognition and, 135–136
Reading achievement, *see also* Student achievement
in Memphis SFA schools, 72–74
SWELL program and, 135–144
Reading assessments, 10
Reading comprehension, SWELL program and, 141–142, 143
Reading Corners (Mexico), 183
Reading evaluations, *see* Evaluations
Reading groups, in Memphis schools, 51
Reading programs, in SFA, 8–10
Reading Recovery, 18, 220
compared to SFA, 39–41, 95
overview of, 120–121
regional training sites, 208
special education and, 43
SWELL program and, 114, 118, 121, 140–141, 143
evaluation studies, 122–123, 129
Reading Roots, xii, 8–9, 165
Reading Time (SWELL program), 119–120
Reading Together (SWELL program), 119
Reading tutors, 10–11
Reading Wings, 9, 165
Receptive language development, 116
Regional training programs, 202–204
Regional training sites
educational laboratories, 210–211

Education Partners, 209–210
regionally based staff, 213–214
school districts, 212–213
state departments of education, 211–212
universities, 208–209
Regrouping
English SFA schools and, 89–90
Israeli SFA schools and, 165–166
Remedial instruction, criticisms of, 4–5, 51
Resource sharing, 216
Rincones de Lectura, 183
Roots & Wings
commitment to child success in, 14–15
CSRD program and, 206–207
evaluations of, 28–30, 33–35
in Memphis schools
evaluations of, 59, 61, 62–67
implementation, 53, 54, 61
student achievement in, 73–74
teacher effectiveness and mobility, 68–71
origins of, xii, 7
overview of, 13–14
Rosario Fernández Foundation, 180–181, 182, 188
Ross, Steven, xii, 202, 208

S

San Antonio, TX, 35, 44
San Antonio Independent School District, 44
Sanders, William, 28, 50, 63
Scheduling, Mexican SFA program and, 185–186
School attendance, in Mexico, 185, 186
School districts, as sources of training and follow-up for SFA, 212–213
School dropout rates, in Canada, 94
School inspections, 89
School reform
future challenges, 197–198
goals of, 4
policy insights, 219–220
policy recommendations, 220–224
professional development and, 198
SFA and, 45–46
School restructuring, 94–95
Schools
assisting demonstration/training sites, 224
cooperative learning and, 154
definitions of success in, 4
provision of funds earmarked for professional development, 222–223
secret ballot voting, 204
SFA program characteristics and, 200–202

SFA program costs and, 201
  student failure and, 3–4
  support networking and, 214–216
Schoolwide Early Language and Literacy
    (SWELL)
  English language learners and, 118
  evaluation studies
    discussion, 135–144
    methodology, 121–123
    results, 124–135
  Reading Recovery and, 114, 118, 121,
    140–141, 143
  SFA and, 143
  stages of, 114, 116–121
    becoming literate, 117–118
    emergent literacy, 116–117
    toward literacy competence, 118–120
    underlying theory of, 113
Science curriculum, see WorldLab
SFA, see Success For All
Shared stories, 117
Shenhav, Hagar, 163
Sizer project, 221
Small group teaching, 150
Smith, Lana, xii, 202, 208
Social studies curriculum, see WorldLab
Southwest Regional Laboratory (SWRL), xiii
Spanish bilingual programs, see Bilingual
    programs
Special education
  Reading Recovery and, 43
  SFA and, 13, 42–43
Spelling, SWELL program and, 117–118, 137, 139
Staff development, see also Professional
    development; Teacher training
  implementation quality and, 63
  Mexican SFA program and, 186–188
Standardized tests, effects of SFA on, 28–35, 55,
    57, 58, 59–60, 62, 73
State departments of education, 211–212
Stories, shared, 117
Story book composing, 167–168
Story Telling and Retelling (STaR)
  Israeli SFA schools and, 166
  in kindergarten and preschool, 11
  overview of, 8
  SWELL program and, 116
Student achievement, see also Reading
    achievement
  implementation quality and, 26–28, 61, 67,
    75, 90–91
  in Memphis SFA schools, 72–74, 75
Student achievement evaluations, see Evalua-
    tions
Student behavior, impact of SFA on, 86
Student failure

importance of prevention and early
    intervention, 5, 6
  overview of, 3–4
  remedial learning and, 4–5
  society's attitudes toward, 5–6
Student motivation, 86
Students-at-risk
  Canadian SFA study and, 97, 98, 101,
    105–106
  failure in school, 4
  importance of prevention and early
    intervention for, 5, 6
  remedial learning and, 4–5
  SWELL program and, 135–136, 138–139,
    140–141, 142, 143, 144
Success for All (SFA), see also Dissemination;
    Evaluations (of SFA)
  commitment to child success, 6, 14–15
  components of, 7–15
  costs of, 201
  effectiveness of, 44–46
  for English language learners, 37–39
  funding sources, 221
  goals and principles of, 5, 95
  growth of, 7, 8(figure), 199, 200(table),
    206–207
  history of, xi–xiv, 6–7
  overview of, 198–199
  program characteristics, 200–202
  research and, 17
  school reform and, 45–46
  significance of implementation, 82–83
  special education and, 42–43
  support networking and, 214–216
  underlying assumptions, 6
Success for All Foundation (SFAF), xiii, 53, 90,
    202, 204
  Education Partners and, 209–210
  establishment as a not-for-profit
    organization, 217–218
  WestEd and, 210
Success for All Middle School, xiii
Success for All-United Kingdom (SFA-UK)
  community involvement, 88
  future of, 91–92
  impact on National Test results, 84–87
  impact on reading levels, 83–84
  impact on teachers, 87–88
  implementation issues, 83, 89–91
  kindergarten program, 86
  parental involvement, 88–89
  regrouping and, 89–90
  student behavior and, 86
  student motivation and, 86
Success Story (newsletter), 215
Support networking, 214–216

SWELL, *see* Schoolwide Early Language and Literacy

T

Teacher effectiveness
  in Memphis SFA schools, 68–70
  in SFA-UK, 87–88
Teacher mobility, 70–71
Teachers
  attitudes toward SFA, 44
  in Canada, issues and concerns with SFA, 96, 107
  cooperative learning and, 88
  in Memphis SFA schools, 57, 60, 68–71, 74–75
  in Mexico, 184, 185, 186–188, 189
  roles in SFA, 12–13
  in SFA-UK, 87–88
Teachers' Learning Communities, 187–188
Teacher training, *see also* Professional development; Staff development
  impact on implementation, 63
  in SFA, 12–13, 205
Team Accelerated Instruction (TAI), xi
Tennessee Comprehensive Achievement Test, 41
Tennessee Comprehensive Assessment Program (TCAP), 29, 30, 55, 57, 58, 59, 60, 62
Tennessee Value-Added Assessment System (TVAAS), 28–30, 41, 63–67, 68–71
Texas, 30–31
  binational Teachers' Learning Communities, 187–188
Texas Assessment of Academic Success (TAAS), 30, 31, 35
Title I, xiii
  Memphis SFA schools and, 76
  professional development and, 222
  SFA program costs and, 201
Toward Literacy Competence (SWELL program), 118–120
Trainers, regionally based, 213–214
Treasure Hunts, 183, 184
Tutoring programs
  computer-supported, 108
  criticisms of, 51
  evaluations of, 62

Tutors
  in reading, 10–11
  voluntary, 88
TVAAS, *see* Tennessee Value-Added Assessment System
TVAAS Teacher Effect (TTE), 68–71

U

United Kingdom, *see also* Success For All-United Kingdom
  education reform and, 81–82, 91–92
  literacy in, 82
U.S. Department of Education, 221, 222
Universities, as regional training sites, 208–209
University of Memphis, 53, 76, 202, 208–209

V

Visual imagery instruction, 142
Voluntary tutors, 88

W

Washington, 41–42
WestEd laboratory, 18, 202, 204, 210
White Paper Excellence in Schools, 81–82
Whole language instruction, 107
Whole-school reform programs, 220–221
"Wise Farmer and His Sons, The," 160, 161
Woodcock Reading Mastery Test, 24, 28, 93
Woodcock Reading Mastery Test-Revised, 99, 103, 104, 105
Word Attack Skills Test, 24, 55, 93, 99, 103, 104, 105, 124
Word Identification Test, 24, 55, 93, 99, 103, 104, 105
Word recognition
  in early literacy, 112–113
  reading for meaning and, 135–136
WorldLab, xii, 14, 198, 214
Writing
  poem composing, 168–172
  storybook composing, 167–168
  in SWELL instruction, 116, 117